IMAGES
of America

WORCESTER COUNTY'S POLISH COMMUNITY

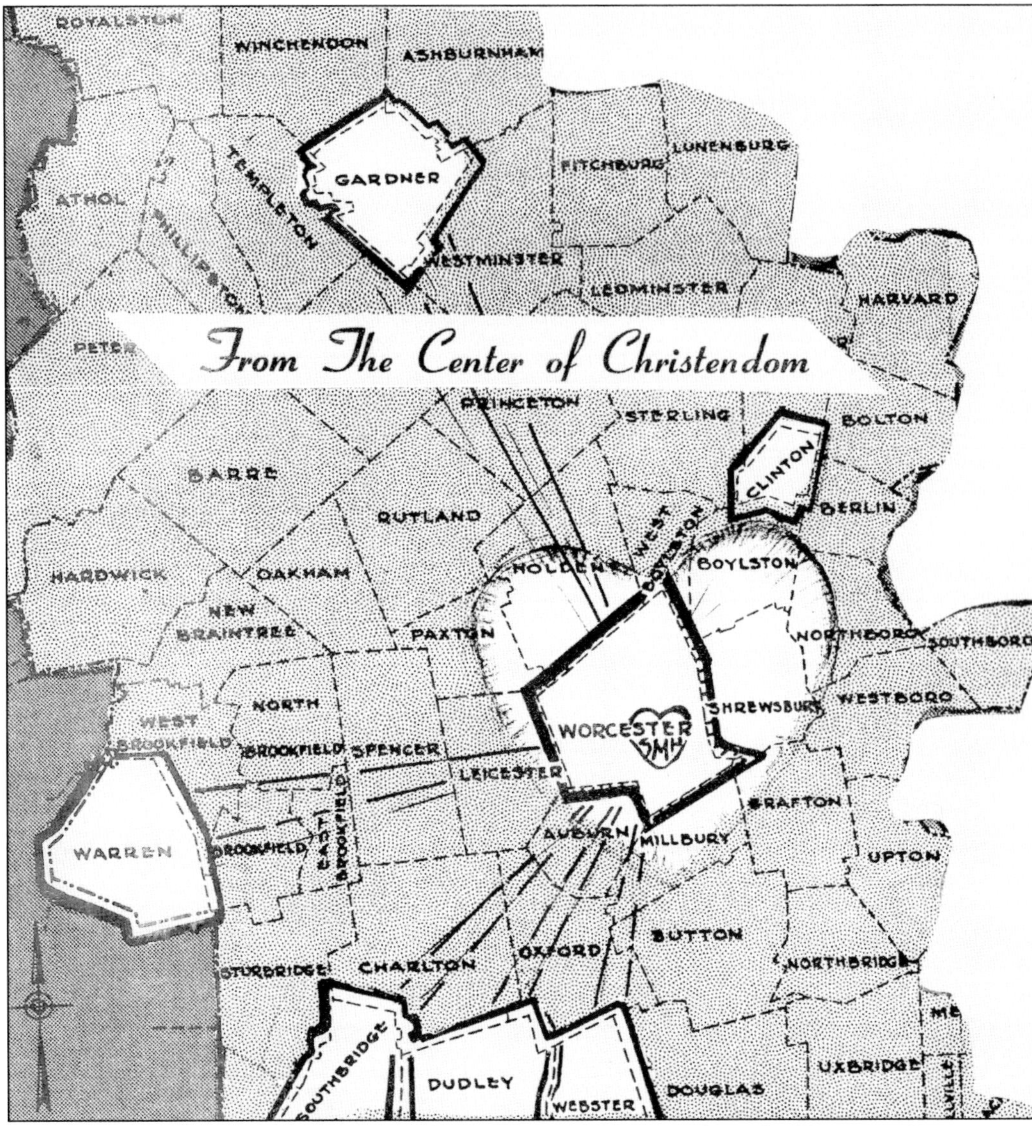

This map of the Worcester Diocese, whose territory corresponds with Worcester County, was created for a 1958 publication of Our Lady of Czestochowa Parish, Worcester. Highlighted are the seven communities with Polish parishes: Clinton, Dudley, Gardner, Southbridge, Webster, West Warren, and Worcester. The heart encircling "SMH" within Worcester represents St. Mary's High School. The only coeducational Polish high school in New England, St. Mary's attracts students from throughout central Massachusetts.

On the cover: Please see page 113. (Courtesy of Rita Novak.)

IMAGES
of America

WORCESTER COUNTY'S POLISH COMMUNITY

Barbara Proko and
Janice Baniukiewicz Stickles
with Our Lady of Czestochowa
Guild of Catholic Women

ARCADIA
PUBLISHING

ISBN 978-0-7385-5454-9

Published by Arcadia Publishing
Charleston SC, Chicago IL, Portsmouth NH, San Francisco CA

Printed in the United States of America

Library of Congress Catalog Card Number: 2007923782

For all general information contact Arcadia Publishing at:
Telephone 843-853-2070
Fax 843-853-0044
E-mail sales@arcadiapublishing.com
For customer service and orders:
Toll-Free 1-888-313-2665

Visit us on the Internet at www.arcadiapublishing.com

In memory of Adolph John Prokopowicz (1938–2000), my cousin, friend, and mentor in Polish genealogy. He researched tirelessly, taught patiently, and shared enthusiastically.

—Barbara Proko

To my best friends, Maureen Abramoski and Joan Demorest, for many good years of their unconditional friendship and sense of humor.

—Janice Baniukiewicz Stickles

Authors' note: The typeface used in this book does not allow representation of the diacritics of the Polish alphabet.

CONTENTS

ACKNOWLEDGMENTS

The concept for this project was conceived by fellow genealogist Daniel Kaczynski of Gardner, who suggested that we follow up *The Polish Community of Worcester* (Arcadia, 2003) with a book exploring the Polish experience countywide. Along with the photograph donors named below, many participants have helped make this idea a reality by contributing invaluable assistance and resources: our Polish parishes, their pastors, and staffs; Polish American organizations; the Connecticut Polish American Archives at Central Connecticut State University; public libraries, coffee shops, and bookstores; and local media, particularly the *Catholic Free Press* and Eugene Stodulski at WCUW-FM. We are grateful to the *Worcester Telegram and Gazette* for permission to use Al Banx cartoons and to Seagrave Studio for photograph use.

For generously sharing their treasured photographs and memorabilia, we are deeply indebted to Antoinette Andriski, Donald Babinski, Stella Bailey, Katherine Banach, Cecelia Baniukiewicz, Joseph Baniukiewicz, Robert Baniukiewicz, Mary Benedict, John and Genevieve Bartosiewicz, Patricia Biron, Mary Bochniak, Theresa Canavan-Loe, Edwin Chadwick, Shirley Chaisson, Hedwig Chesna, Kathleen Coggins, Veronica Cosetta, Lorraine Courtemanche, Sylvia Cummings, Glenn Czabaj, Anthony Czernicki, Patty Davis, Mary Dalton, Philip Duszlak, Mary Engelhardt, William Giguere, Eleanor Gilmartin, John Grzyb, Sally Harris, Anthony Hmura, Daniel Kaczynski, Henry Karolkiewicz, Hedi Kay, Mary Ann Kirklauskas, Joseph Kowal, Edward Krupinski, Dorothy Kuczka, Joseph Kuras, Arlene Kusek, Christine Kwasny, Kristina Laber, Linda Langevin, Patricia Lasky, Edward Lepkowski, Albin Linga, Jane Lucas, Janice Makowski, Marc Michalski, Barbara Marczewski, Chester Morrison, Susan Mosczynski, Halina Murphy, Evelyn Nieszczezewski, Rita Novak, Cecilia Olearcek, Theresa Osowski, Lorraine Ostrokolowicz, Caroline Ouellette, Theodore Pikora, Albert Pulawski, Irene Radziewicz, Romuald Radziewicz, Stasia Rawinski, Phyllis Recko, Wanda Renes, Mary Repik, Stephen Sablack, Paul and Diane Salek, Joseph Sendrowski, Anna Sielawa, Phyllis Smyth, Stanley Sobiech, Genevieve Sobiek, Pauline Sroczynski, Janet Stoica, Arline Stratford, Nancy Swiacki, Robert Szklarz, Joanne Szlyk, Chester and Gloria Szydlik, Susan Teixeira, Stanley Tozeski, Marilyn Travinski, Anthony Wagner, John Wojcik, Walter Wojnar, Regina Wolanin, Richard Wolosz, Barbara Wyatt, Judith Wypych, Raymond and Gertrude Zaleski, and Paul Zdanowicz.

Finally, we thank Arcadia Publishing, whose commitment to preserving local history makes this book possible.

INTRODUCTION

Poland's complex history makes it difficult to consider its 19th- and early-20th-century emigrants as a single group. Between 1793 and 1918, Poland did not exist as an intact, sovereign nation. Its lands were partitioned and governed by three abutting empires: Prussian (German), Russian, and Austro-Hungarian. Although ethnic Poles may have never lost sight of their identity, the world viewed them as citizens of these empires. When they emigrated for economic, political, or other reasons, their documents defined them as Prussian, Russian, or Austrian Poles. This classification carried over into the United States where census and other records noted immigrants' countries of origin. It carries over into this photographic history as well. Unlike other parts of Massachusetts, and perhaps New England as a whole, Worcester County has a unique history as home to substantial numbers of Roman Catholic immigrants from all three sectors of partitioned Poland.

Polish settlement in Worcester County began rather inauspiciously in the late 1860s with a few immigrants from the Prussian partition. By the 1890s, their continuing influx gave the abutting communities of Webster and Dudley the only significant population of German Poles in Massachusetts. That decade also marked the beginning of a much greater immigration from the Russian and Austrian partitions, the latter familiarly known as Galicia. Where these Roman Catholic Poles settled in greatest concentrations, they founded parishes that enabled them to practice their faith in their native language.

New England's first Polish parish, St. Joseph's, was established in 1887 in Webster, near the Connecticut state line. The German Poles of St. Joseph's reached out to help the newer Russian- and Austrian-empire immigrants establish Our Lady of Czestochowa Parish (1903) in Worcester 15 miles north and St. Joseph's Parish (1908) in Gardner over 50 miles north, near the New Hampshire border. St. Joseph's also founded missions in Southbridge and Dudley. In 1913, at the eastern and western ends of Worcester County, St. Mary's Parish (later renamed Our Lady of Jasna Gora) was founded in Clinton and St. Stanislaus in West Warren. St. Hedwig's was formed in Southbridge in 1916 and became a parish in 1918. The Dudley mission, dedicated to St. Andrew Bobola, had its own church in 1954 and became an independent parish in 1963. Although numerous ethnic churches nationwide have closed in recent decades, the seven Polish parishes of the diocese of Worcester endure.

The parishes formed the bedrock of Worcester County's Polish community. Much more than places of worship, as important as their faith is to Polish Roman Catholics, the parishes were the focal point of the immigrants' lives. The first organizations they typically formed were societies that raised funds for church construction. The churches, once built, gave rise to devotional groups. Pastors were instrumental in helping the immigrants organize local chapters of national organizations such as the Polish National Alliance, Polish Roman Catholic Union, and Polish Falcons, along with local societies to meet social, political (that is, citizenship), educational, and athletic needs. The Webster, Worcester, and Clinton parishes founded schools that incorporated Polish Catholic ideals and heritage into their curriculums.

However, not all communities with Polish populations were in themselves large enough to warrant a Polish parish. In these smaller towns, Polish halls and Pilsudski clubs became central gathering places. From parish to "Polish Home" to a farmer's back 40, the immigrants and their Polish American children and grandchildren found places to congregate all over Worcester County. Society meetings, wedding receptions, team sports, dances, parades, processions, and Polish picnics fostered a sense of community among people whose roots were as widespread as Poznan, Lomza, Krakow, Plock, Wilno, and Tarnow. Business and professional connections strengthened the ties; marriages formalized them.

Worcester County today embraces the original immigrants' descendants, some well into their fifth or sixth generation as Polish Americans, along with the families of displaced persons who came in the wake of World War II, others who left communist-controlled Poland in the 1960s, and still others who more recently left a free Poland. Each wave of immigrants, each generation has infused its own unique life experiences into the collective Polish consciousness of central Massachusetts. According to the 2000 U.S. census, more than 51,000 Worcester County residents identify themselves as being of Polish ancestry. Poles rank fifth among the dozens of ethnic groups in central Massachusetts. Of the 68 languages spoken in the homes of Worcester County, Polish is the fifth most common, following English, Spanish, French, and Portuguese. But where those Polish homes are today is not necessarily where they were a century ago, when they were tightly clustered around the ethnic parishes.

The census sheds light on these demographic shifts. With 10,482 total, the city of Worcester claims the third-highest number of Poles in Massachusetts; Webster ranks eighth with 3,744. Percentages offer a different perspective. In West Warren, 27.7 percent of the population has Polish roots; Dudley, 25.3 percent; Webster, 22.8 percent; Gilbertville, 20.8 percent; and Warren, 17.3 percent. With 10-12 percent are Fiskdale, New Braintree, North Oxford, Charlton, and Oxford; with 8-10 percent, Barre, Oakham, West Brookfield, Paxton, Sutton, and Brookfield.

Immigrants a century ago found their best economic opportunities within walking distance of mills and factories where wages were low but jobs were abundant. The sprawling brick complexes that still survive in Worcester County have largely been retrofitted to accommodate cutting-edge biotechnology and health services, finance and retail sectors, and arts and culture. Today's Polish Americans are living the lives their ancestors could only dream of, with good educations and good incomes. Their lives afford them many choices—and maintaining their heritage is one of them.

Although many, many thousands of Poles and Polish Americans have lived in Worcester County over the past 135 years, local history books have virtually overlooked them, and few of their stories have been told. Polish life here has been documented almost exclusively by the Polish parishes' and organizations' jubilee books (*pamietniki*) marking 25th, 50th, and 100th anniversaries. Local newspapers have provided coverage as well. Pamietniki and newspapers are the major sources that inform this book. We attempt to offer a representative, if not a comprehensive, picture in which the spirit of the times and the character of the people ring true.

In "First Poles in America" (Our Lady of Czestochowa Parish, 1958), an essay on Worcester Diocese's Polish parishes observed: "Our quest for data, maps, and photographs made us aware that a history of great and compelling interest lay hidden within the pages of the chronicles of these parishes. Their history is a legacy of the religious, social, and cultural achievements. . . . This heritage is an overwhelmingly rich one and those who bequeathed it to us have a claim to a remembrance in these pages."

Our quest leaves us equally appreciative of the heritage of Worcester County's Polonia. "Those who bequeathed it to us" indeed deserve remembrance, and much more of their story remains to be told.

One

ROOTS

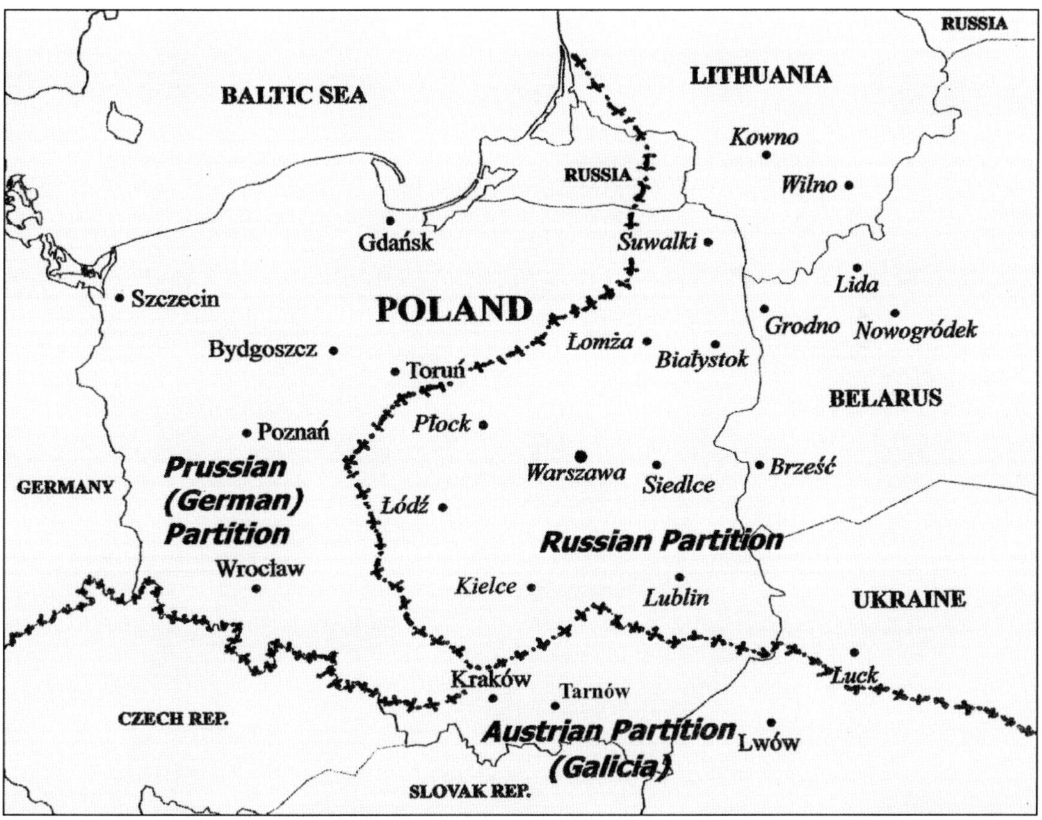

A contemporary map of Poland and neighboring countries is overlain with dashed lines approximating the historic boundaries of the Prussian (German), Russian, and Austro-Hungarian Empires. From 1793 to 1918, Poland was partitioned, with the Prussian Empire claiming its western section; the Russian Empire, the eastern; and the Austro-Hungarian Empire, the southern.

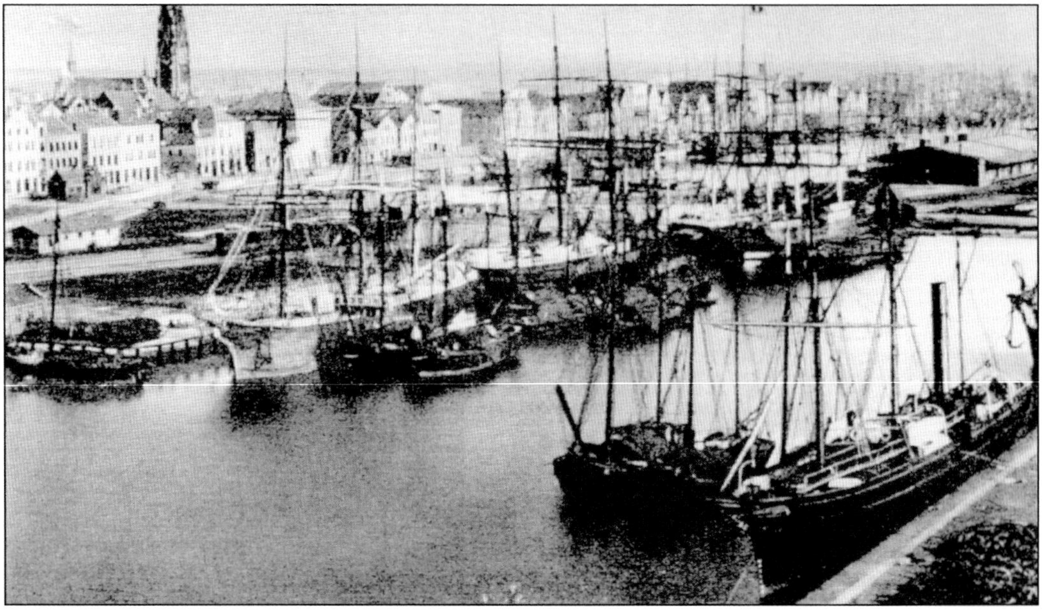

The port of Bremen, Germany, shown here in 1866, was the busiest point of departure for emigrants leaving northern, central, and eastern Europe from the mid-19th through the early 20th century. Hamburg, Germany, was second busiest; by building facilities to accommodate emigrants, Hamburg eventually surpassed Bremen in departure numbers. Polish emigrants also sailed out of Rotterdam, Antwerp, and Libau (Liepaja). Trains and other means of overland travel brought inland Poles to the port cities.

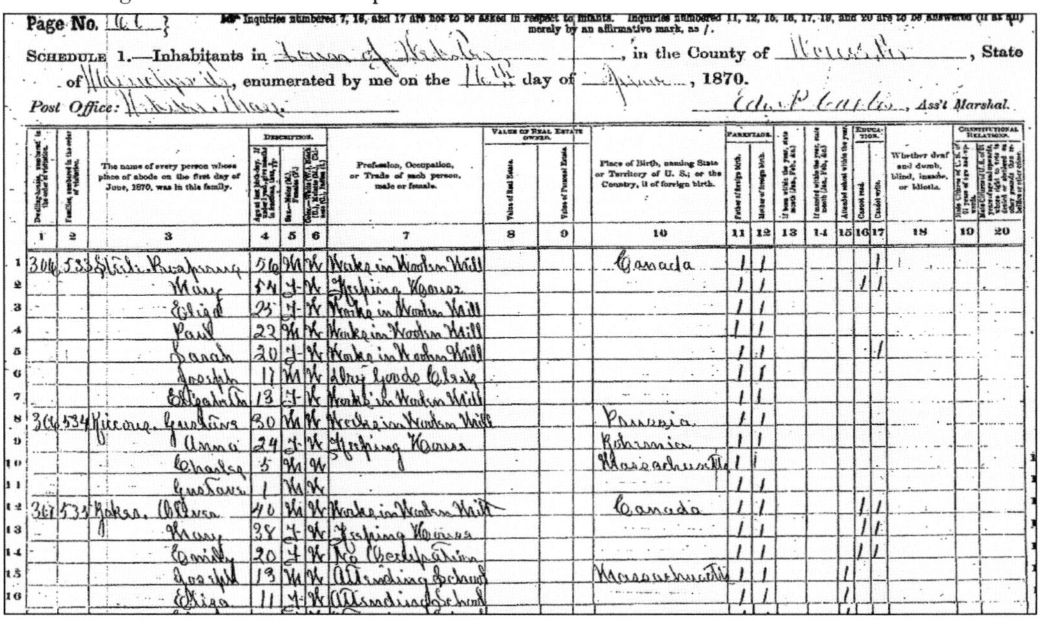

Page No.

SCHEDULE 1.—Inhabitants in ______, in the County of ______, State of ______, enumerated by me on the ______ day of ______, 1870.

Post Office: ______ Ass't Marshal.

Misspelled surnames in U.S. records are a constant challenge to Polish Americans tracing their family roots. The 1870 U.S. census identifies the Kreft family as Polish residents in Webster but records the name as "Croft" and misspells some first names as well. The household comprised John and Caroline Kreft and eight children, along with Joseph Reglinski (listed as "Radinski"). Reglinski married the Krefts' daughter Frances.

Adalbert (George) Kapulka's life mirrored those of countless Polish immigrants who came to the United States with one destination in mind but ultimately settled elsewhere. Born in Galicia in 1878, Kapulka headed to Pennsylvania, where he married Anna Barna in 1904 and began a family. Around 1917, the Kapulkas moved to Worcester. Economic factors, personal relationships, and basic preferences such as city versus country all played a part in such relocation.

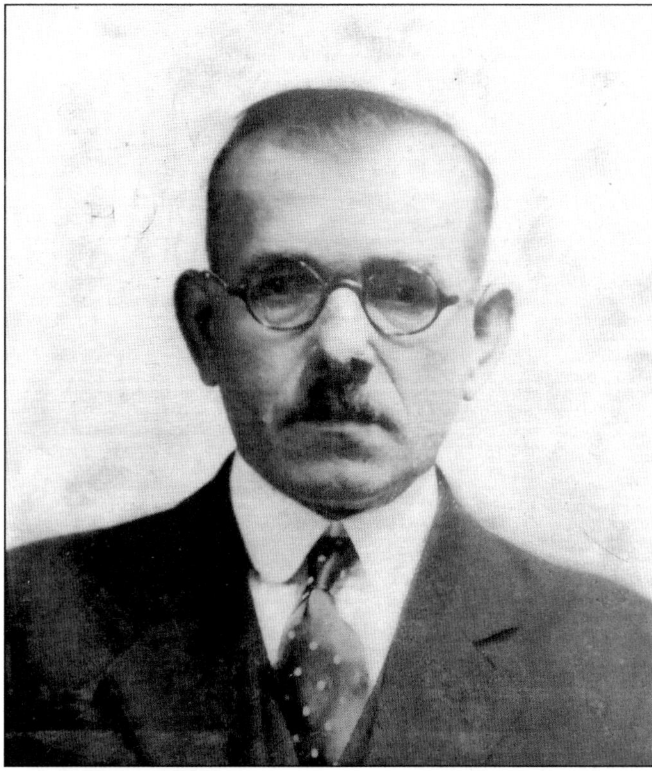

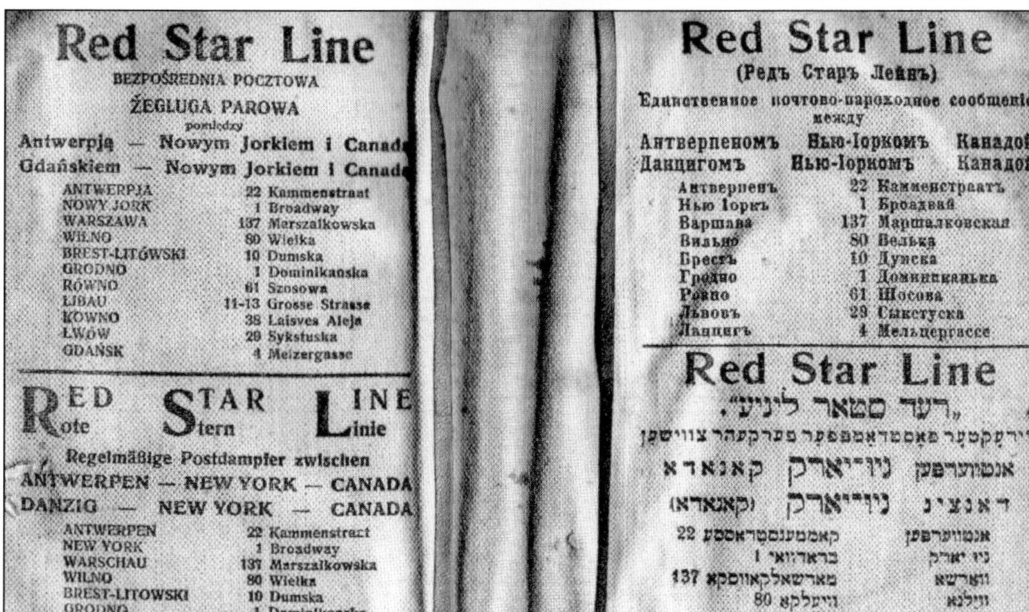

A canvas ticket pouch such as this one produced for the Red Star Line was handy for holding an emigrant's steamship ticket, passport, and other papers. The inside pockets are imprinted with the addresses of Red Star ticket agents in major cities: Antwerp, New York, Warsaw, Wilno, Brest-Litowski, Grodno, Rowno, Libau, Kowno, Lwow, and Gdansk. The information is provided in Polish, German, Russian, and Hebrew.

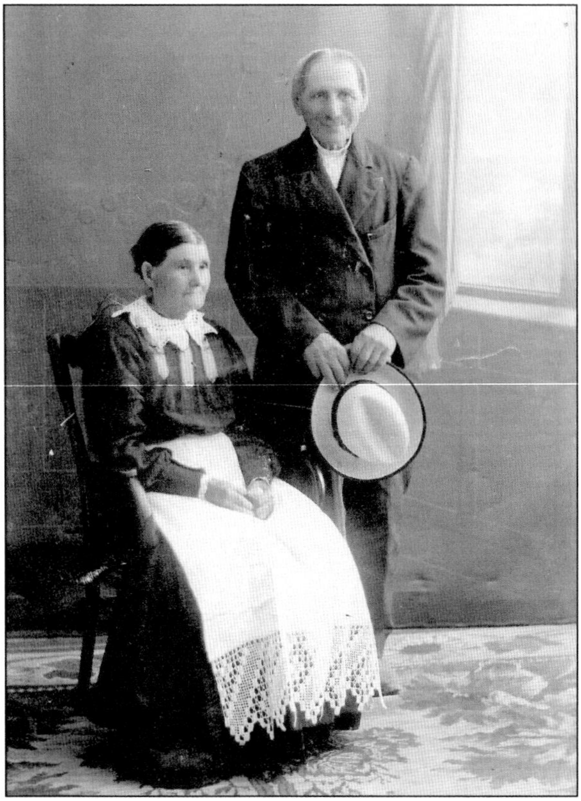

This portrait of Maria Magdelena Kardas (born in 1842) and her husband, Maciej Pajdos (born in 1840 in Boleslaw), was made at Atelier Marya, a studio in Tarnow, Galicia (Austrian Poland). The couple was married in 1866. Younger family members made their way to Massachusetts. Michal Pajdos arrived from Boleslaw in 1898; his sister Marja followed a year later. They both found mill jobs and boarded in Gilbertville.

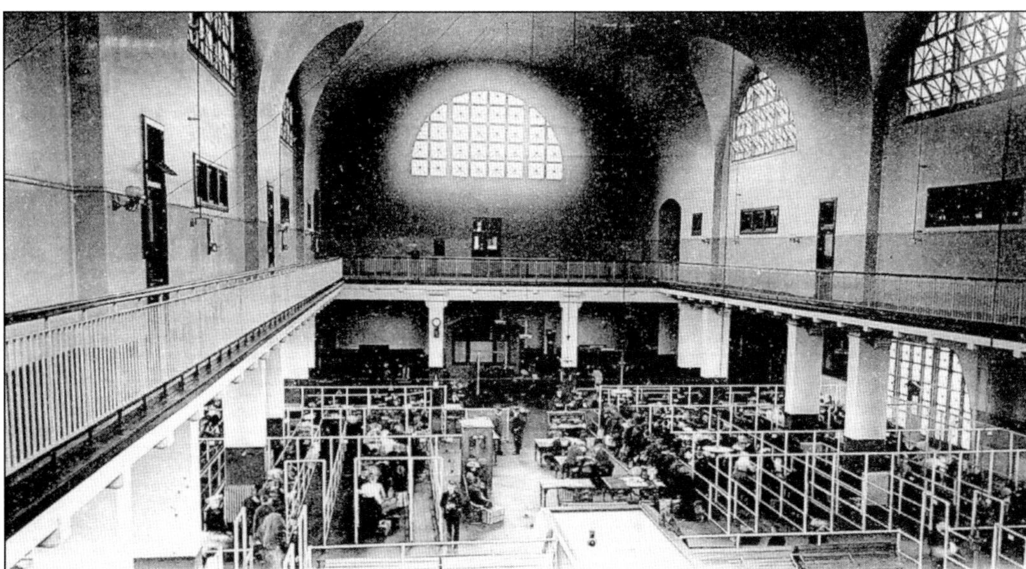

Ellis Island in New York harbor was the primary immigrant-receiving station in U.S. history. In operation between 1892 and 1924, it processed an estimated 12 million immigrants who became permanent American residents. The registry room, shown here, was where immigrants underwent the main examination that determined their fate: entry to the United States or deportation back to their homeland. Boston, Philadelphia, and Baltimore were other busy ports.

Jakie pytania stawiają oni pasażerom?	What questions do they ask the passengers?	Huot kueszczns du dej ask dy pesendżers?
Pytania urzędników imigracyjnych.	The immigration officers questions.	Dy ymygrejszn ofysers kueszczns.
Zaraz pan usłyszy.	In a minute you will hear them.	Yn ej mynyt ju uyl hijr dem.
Pańskie imię i nazwisko?	Your christian name and surname?	Jor kryszczn nejm end sernejm?
Wiek?	Your age?	Jor ejdż?
Pan żonaty, czy wolny?	Are you married or single?	Ar ju meryd o syngl?
Wolny.	Single.	Syngl.
Żonaty.	Married.	Meryd.
Pani mężatka?	Are ju married?	Ar ju meryd?
Pani niezamężna?	Are you not married?	Ar ju not meryd

Umiem czytać, pisać.	I can read and write.	Aj ken rijd end rajt.
Wasza narodowość?	Your nationality?	Jor naszjonalyty?
Wasze ostatnie miejsce zamieszkania?	Where did you live last?	Huer dyd ju lyw last?
Dokąd pan jedzie?	Where are you going?	Huer ar ju going?
Kto płacił za waszą jazdę?	Who paid for your trip?	Hu pejd for jor tryp?
Czy macie 50 dolarów?	Have you fifty dollars?	Hew ju fyfty dolars?
Ile dolarów macie?	How many dollars have you got?	Hau meny dolars hew ju got?
Czy jedziecie do krewnego?	Are you going to relations?	Ar ju going tu relejszns?
Jak on się nazywa?	What is his name?	Huot yz hyz nejm?
Gdzie krewny wasz mieszka?	Where does your relation live?	Huer daz jor relejszn lyw?

Rozmowki Polsko-Angielskie dla Uzytku Emigrantow (Polish-English Conversations for Emigrants' Use), published in Warsaw, was a phrase book designed to help Poles negotiate the various stages of immigration and settlement in English-speaking countries. Complete with English pronunciation, it presents typical dialogue that an immigrant would have encountered at Ellis Island and other ports, such as "Who paid for your trip?" and "Are you going to relations?"

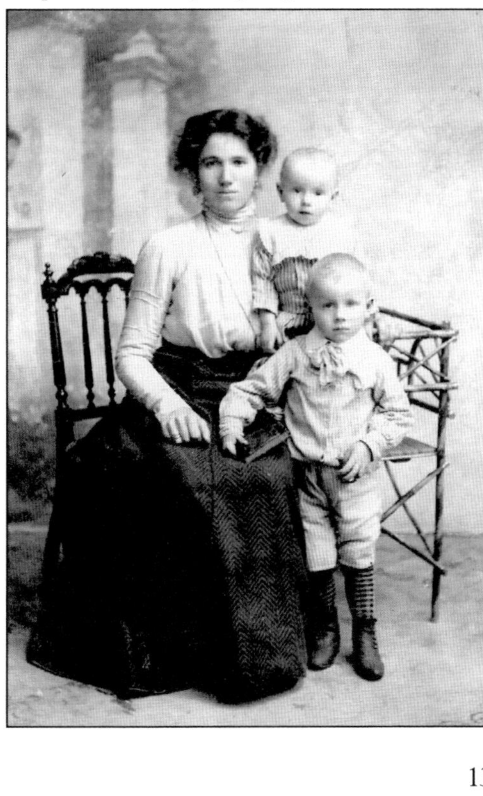

Jozefa Czajkowska Lesnieska and her sons Franciszek (born in 1909) and Jozef (born in 1906) pose for a studio portrait in Lomza. It may have been made for Jan Lesnieski to carry with him when he left for America in March 1910. Jozefa and the boys joined him in July 1912. Jozefa died in the 1918 influenza epidemic; Jan remarried. The John Lesneski family lived on Limerick Street in Gardner's "Patch" neighborhood.

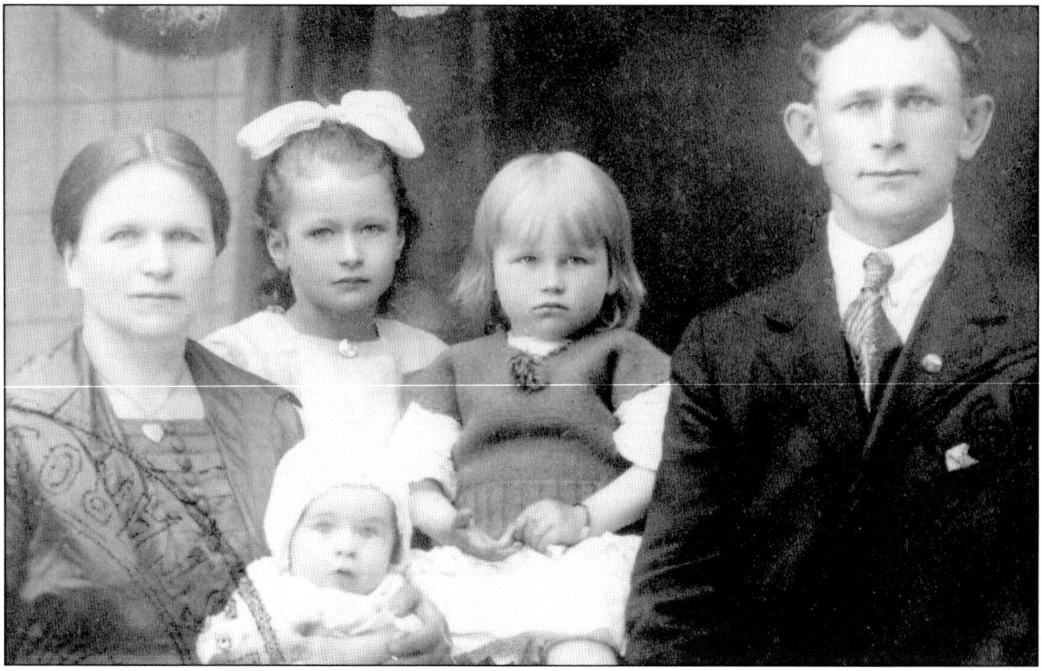

Immigration was not always a permanent one-way move. The Pietrzak family used this passport photograph in 1923 for their final departure from Poland. From left to right are Czeslawa, holding son Joseph on her lap, daughters Helen and Blanche, and Joseph Pietrzak. The couple originally emigrated from Lomza in 1910. Missing their families, they returned to Poland in 1921. However, they stayed only two years before returning to Worcester.

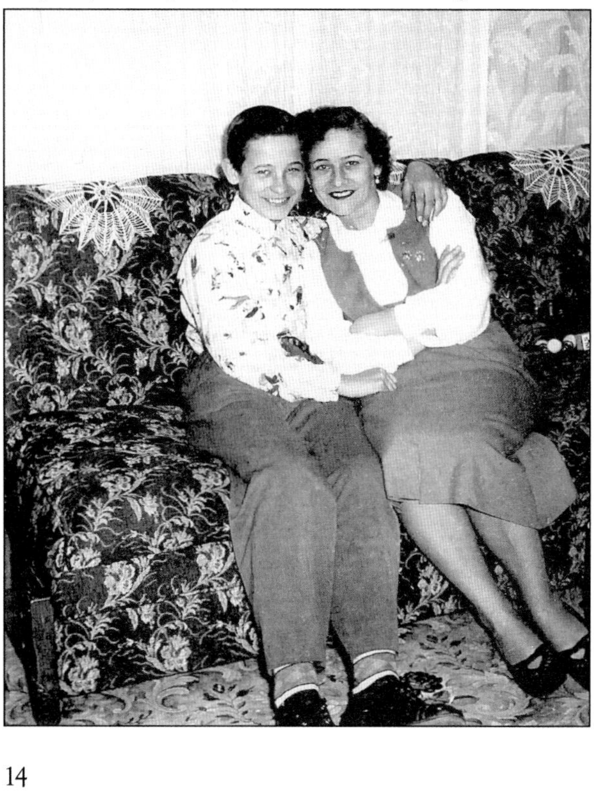

Thomas Mark Sieminski and his mother share a happy moment in Clinton after their arrival in the United States in January 1948. Born in Massachusetts, Isabella Irene Lepkowski grew up in Poland, where she married Apolinary Sieminski and gave birth to Mark. Apolinary, a Polish Army officer, was killed in the Katyn massacre of 1940. Irene and Mark began a new chapter in their lives when they connected with family in America.

Albin Linga and Victoria Babicz relax against a Buick parked at a picnic in 1949, about a year before their marriage. Born in Worcester but raised in Kiwance, north of Lida, Linga escaped forced conscription in the Russian army during World War II only because his birth certificate proved U.S. citizenship. Gaining readmittance to the United States after the war was problematic; he was finally successful in December 1946.

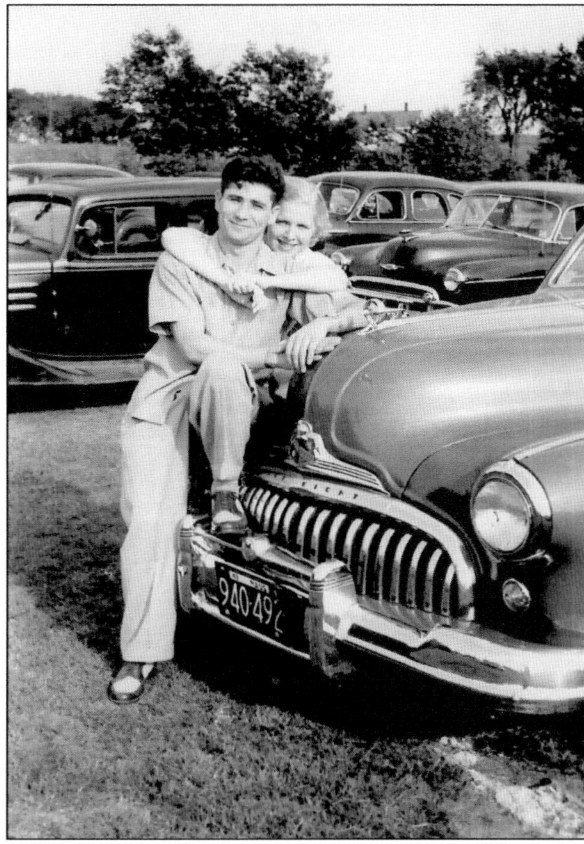

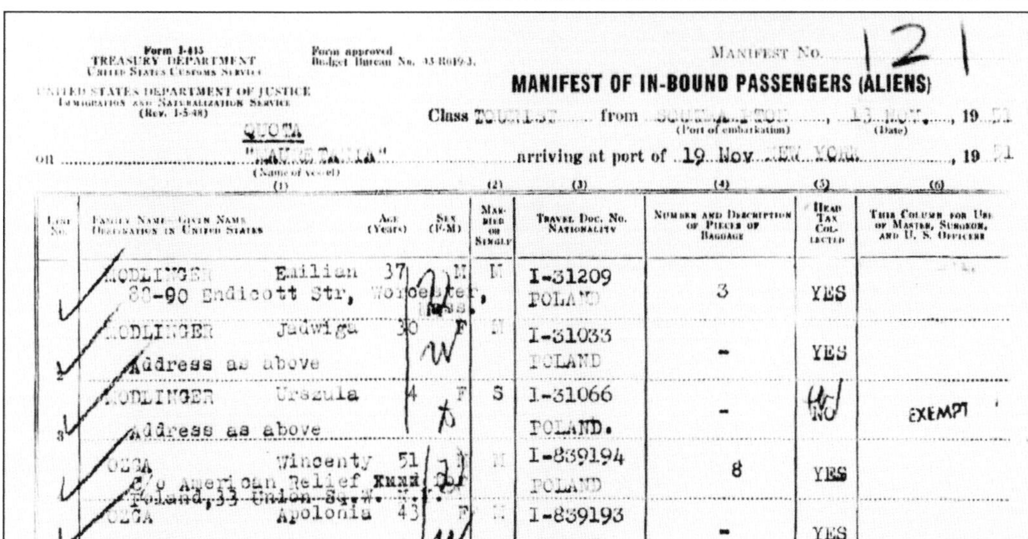

Form I-415
TREASURY DEPARTMENT
United States Customs Service
UNITED STATES DEPARTMENT OF JUSTICE
Immigration and Naturalization Service
(Rev. 1-5-48)

Form approved
Budget Bureau No. 43-R619.3.

MANIFEST No. 121

MANIFEST OF IN-BOUND PASSENGERS (ALIENS)

QUOTA

Class TOURIST from SOUTHAMPTON, 13 NOV., 1951 (Port of embarkation) (Date)

on "MAURETANIA" (Name of vessel) arriving at port of 19 Nov NEW YORK, 1951

Line No.	(1) Family Name—Given Name, Destination in United States	Age (Years)	Sex (F-M)	(2) Married or Single	(3) Travel Doc. No. Nationality	(4) Number and Description of Pieces of Baggage	(5) Head Tax Collected	(6) This Column for Use of Master, Surgeon, and U. S. Officers
1	MODLINGER Emilian, 88-90 Endicott Str, Worcester, Mass.	37	M	M	I-31209 POLAND	3	YES	
2	MODLINGER Jadwiga, Address as above	30	F	M	I-31033 POLAND	-	YES	
3	MODLINGER Urszula, Address as above	4	F	S	I-31066 POLAND.	-	NO	EXEMPT
4	OZGA Wincenty, c/o American Relief for Poland, 33 Union Sq. W. N.Y.	51	M	M	I-839194 POLAND	8	YES	
5	OZGA Apolonia, Address as above	43	F	M	I-839193 POLAND	-	YES	

This manifest for the SS *Mauretania* names Polish nationals and others left stateless by the aftermath of World War II; they arrived in New York in November 1951 as displaced persons. Heading this page is a family destined for 88–90 Endicott Street, Worcester: Emilian Modlinger, 37; his wife, Jadwiga, 30; and daughter, Urszula, 4. Through the Displaced Persons Act of 1948, several hundred Poles found new homes in Worcester County.

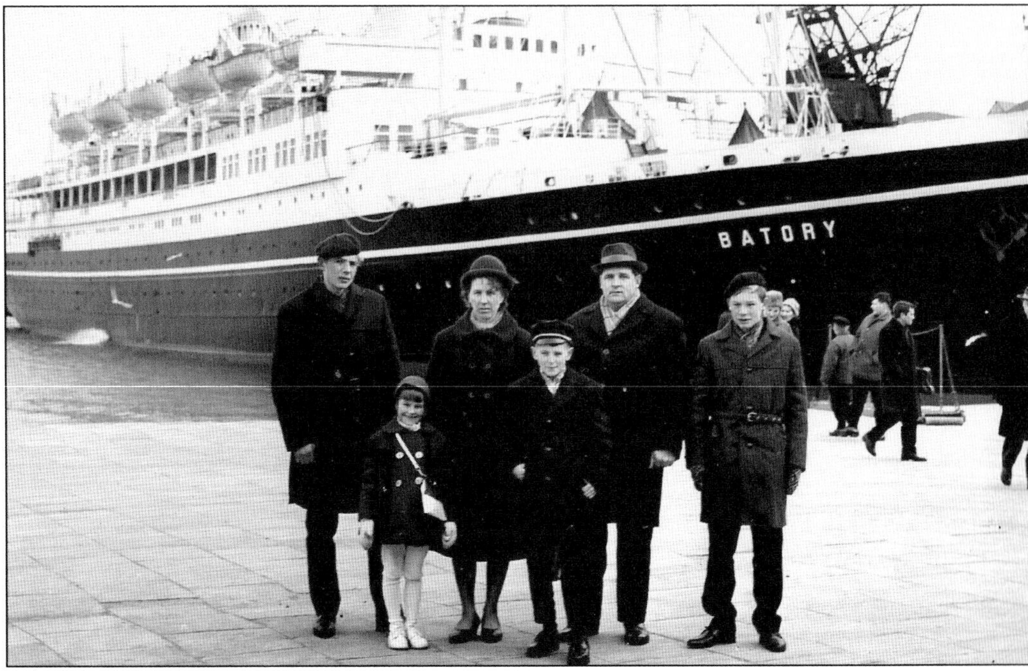

The Sobiech family, originally from the Ostroleka area in northeastern Poland, stands before the SS *Batory*, which they sailed from Gdynia to Quebec in March 1966. From left to right are (first row) daughter Janina and son Jan; (second row) son Kazimierz, mother Wladyslawa, father Boleslaw, and son Stanislaw. The family settled on Coral Street in Worcester, and the father and sons found work at John J. Adams Die Corporation.

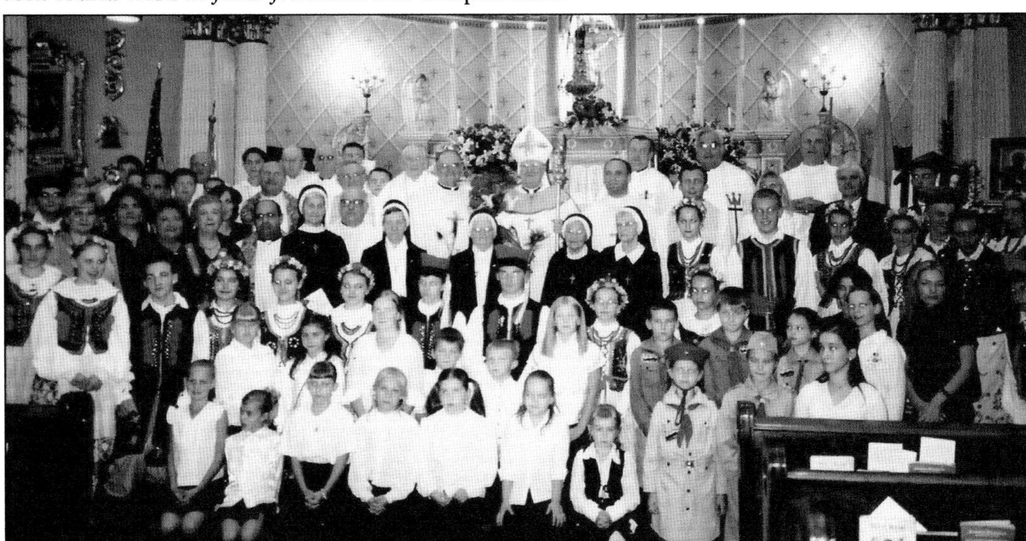

Our Lady of Czestochowa Parish, Worcester, celebrated its centennial in October 2003. The parishioners who gathered for this commemorative photograph represent every wave of Polish immigration to the city, from descendants of late-19th-century immigrants to postwar refugees and émigrés from Soviet-controlled Poland, to the current influx of new young families. The latter have established a Saturday school, Scout troops, a dance ensemble, and other organizations that foster Polish culture.

Two

PARISHES

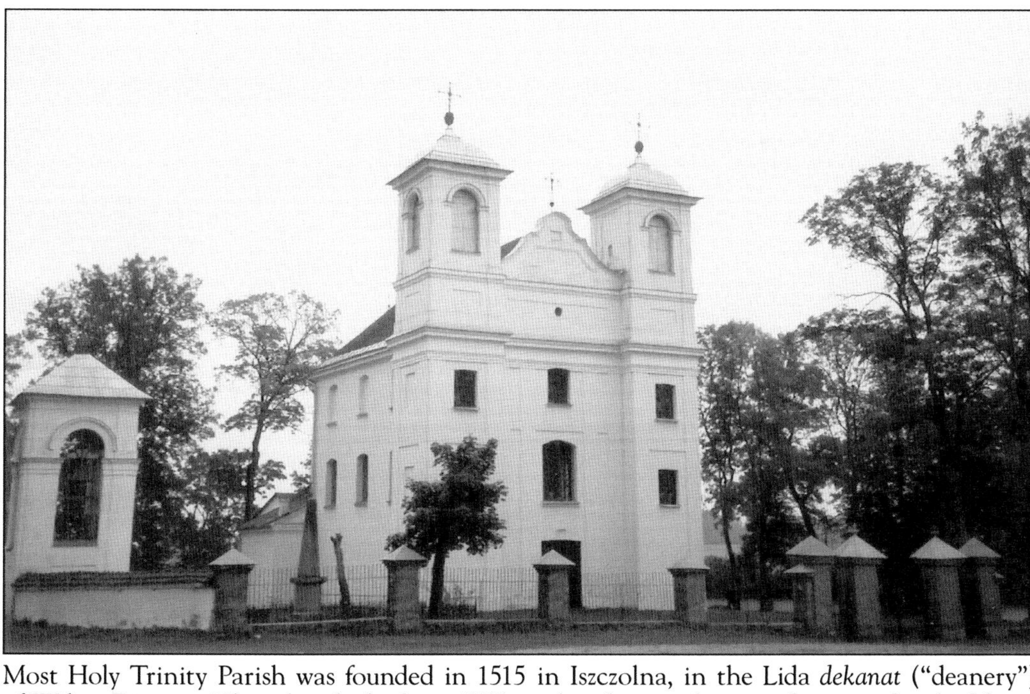

Most Holy Trinity Parish was founded in 1515 in Iszczolna, in the Lida *dekanat* ("deanery") of Wilno Diocese. This church, built in 1758, replaced an earlier wooden one that had been destroyed by fire. For Poles accustomed to centuries of continuity in their places of worship, the need to create parishes in the United States was often a new experience. Iszczolna parish remains active in western Belarus today.

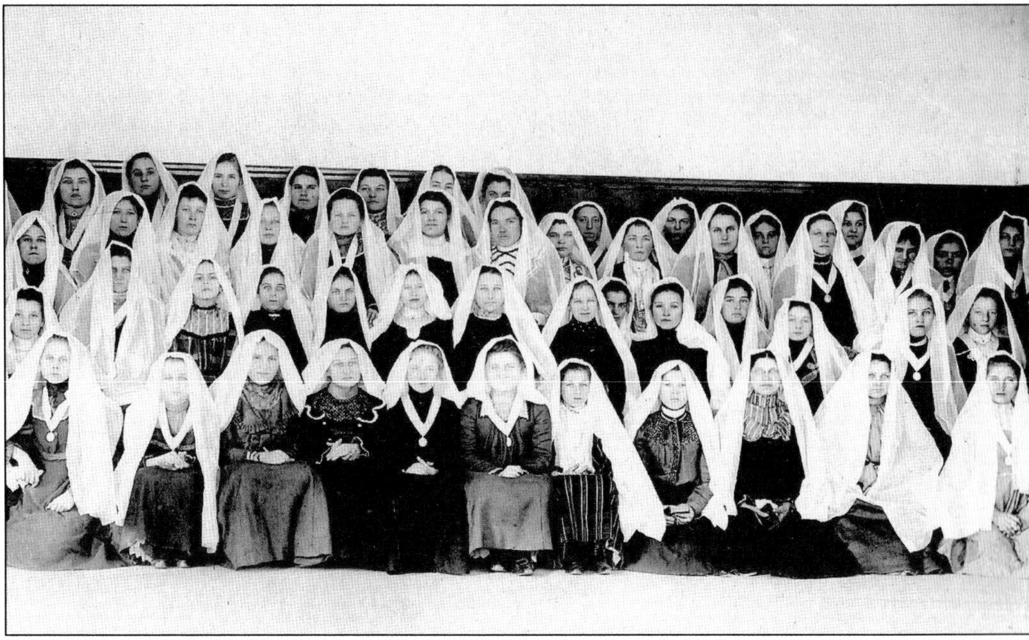

An early organization at St. Joseph's Parish was the Society of the Children of Mary (Towarzystwo Dzieci Marji). White veils typically signify membership in a sodality. Identified in the first row, fourth from right, is Annie Patrowicz. This image is the right half of a photograph made around 1897 and cut decades ago.

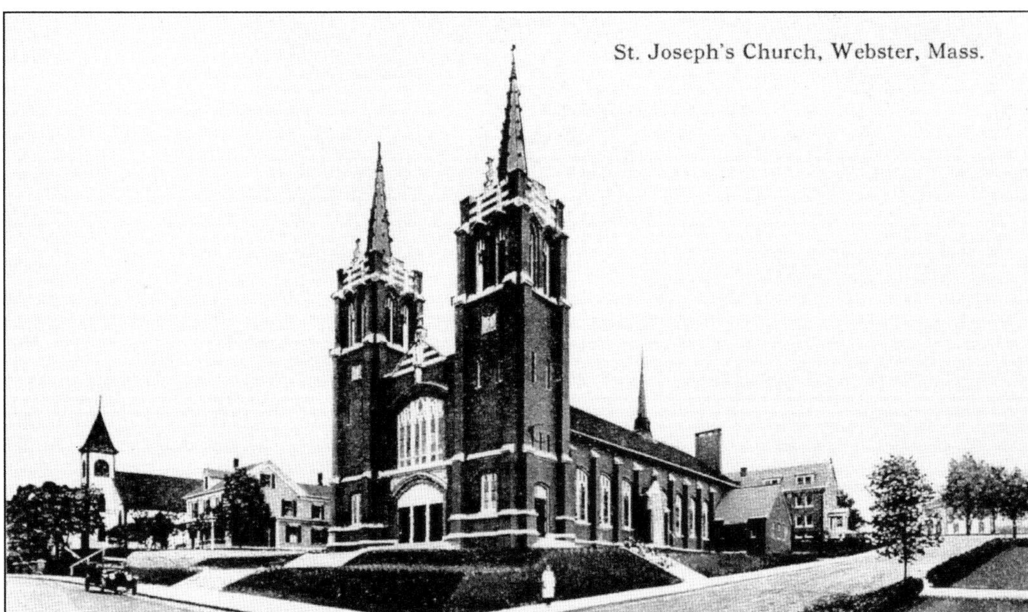

This 1921 postcard shows most of St. Joseph's Parish complex in Webster. From left to right on Whitcomb Street are the original wood church, rectory, and large brick church completed in 1914. To the rear is the Felician Sisters' convent, built in 1910 on the Maynard Street side of the property. The original school is obscured from view. The current St. Joseph School (1924) stands on the original church site.

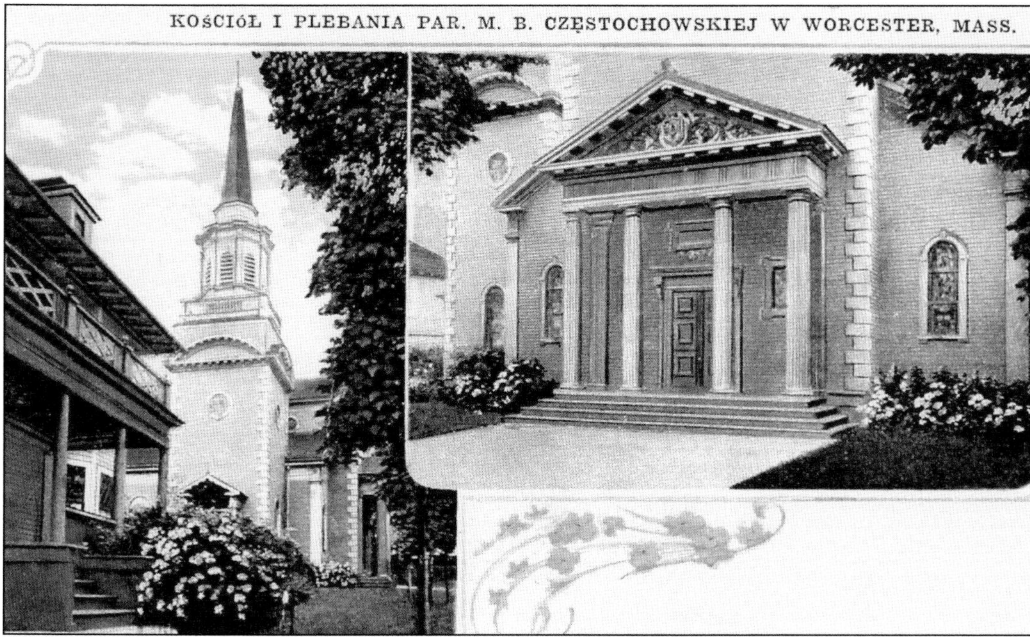

Printed soon after Our Lady of Czestochowa Church was completed on Richland Street, Worcester, in 1906, this postcard displays two views: at left, the rectory and east side of the church; at right, the front entrance. The Ward Street side of the property featured a shrine to the Blessed Virgin. Behind the church and rectory was a schoolhouse where catechism classes were held before St. Mary's School opened in 1915.

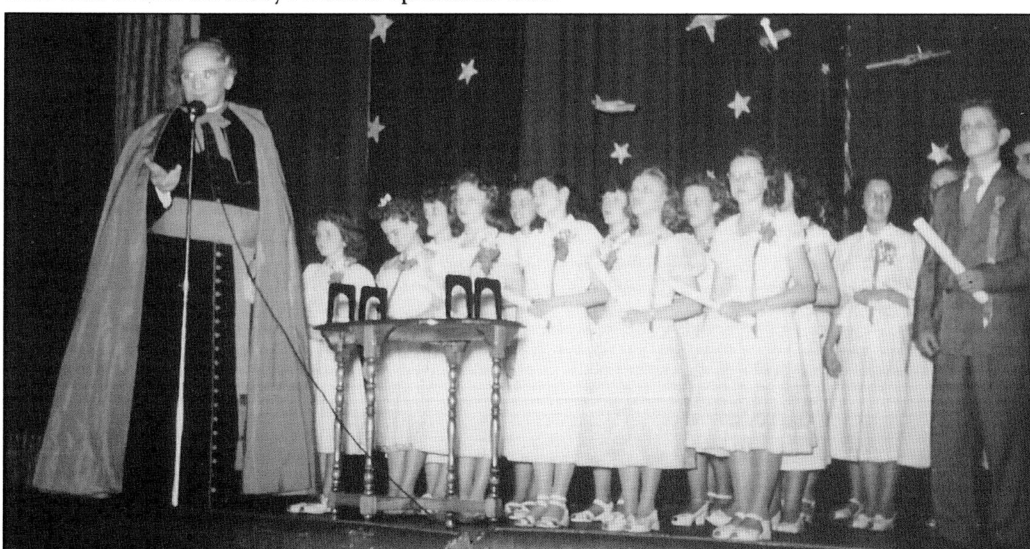

Msgr. Boleslaw Bojanowski, an outspoken advocate for Polish Catholic education, speaks at St. Mary's graduation ceremonies in 1948. A political émigré born in Plock province of Russian Poland, Bojanowski came to Our Lady of Czestochowa Parish, Worcester, in 1913 and was elevated to monsignor in 1934. In his 40 years as pastor, he spearheaded the development of the parish's kindergarten-through-12th-grade schools and numerous religious, social, cultural, political, and athletic organizations.

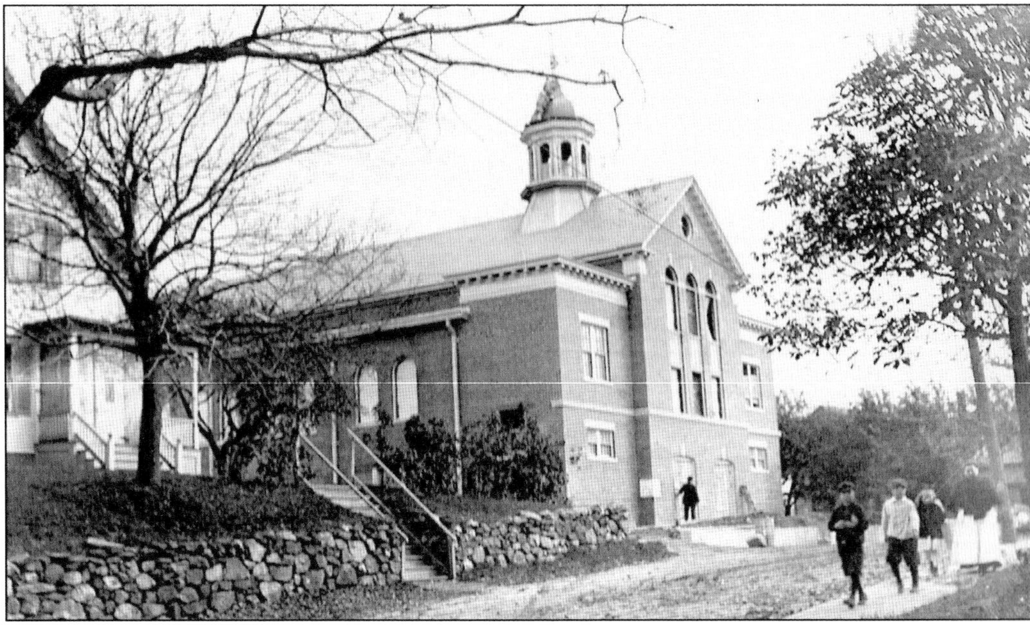

A priest, possibly Rev. Stanislaus Chlapowski, stands near the door of St. Joseph's Church on Pleasant Street, Gardner, in this candid 1915 photograph. The church, seating 825, was dedicated in March 1913. The rectory is at left. The parish was established in December 1908. It is a namesake of St. Joseph's in Webster, in recognition of the latter's position as the oldest Polish parish in New England.

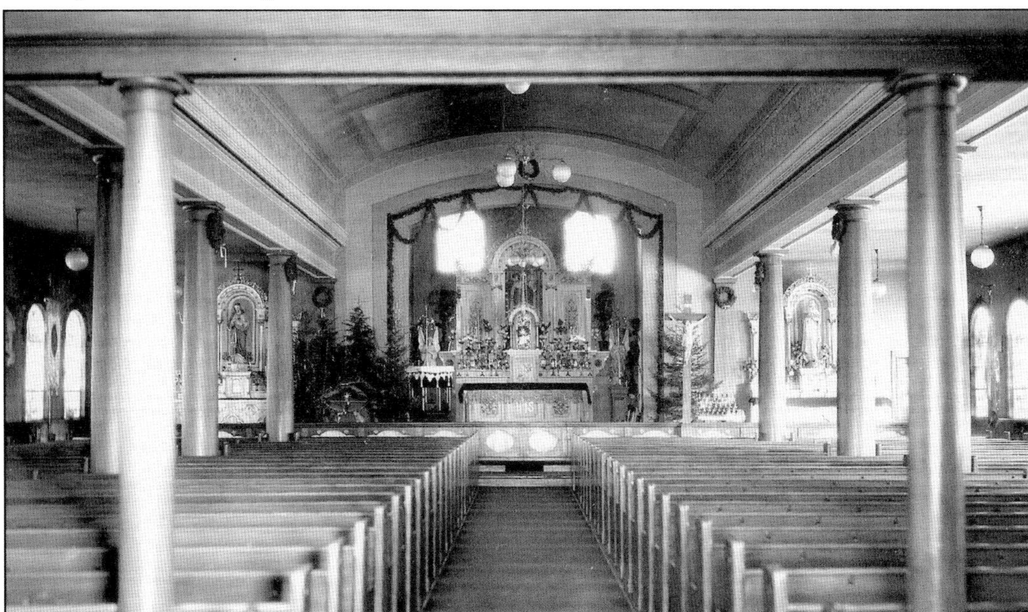

Fir trees and a crèche add a Christmas touch to the interior of St. Joseph's Church, Gardner, in 1928. Renovations made in 1956 symbolized its unity with the other Polish parishes of Worcester Diocese. On the ceiling, a gold Roman cross featured a medallion of St. Joseph at its center, surrounded by medallion paintings of Our Lady of Czestochowa, St. Hedwig, St. Stanislaus, and St. Andrew Bobola.

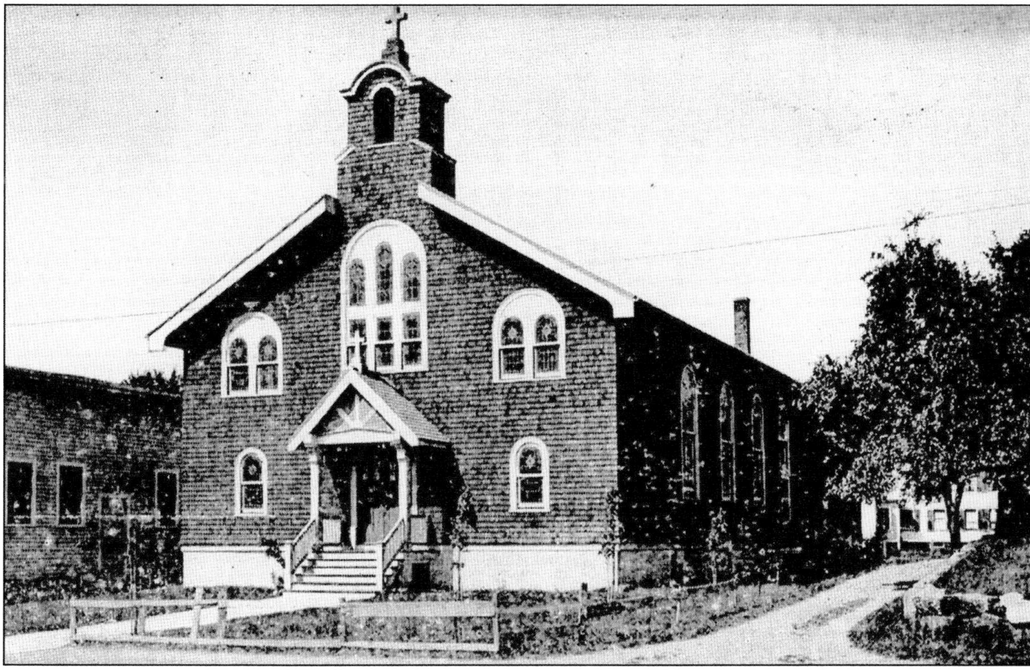

St. Stanislaus Parish was established in West Warren in 1913, and its church opened on Christmas 1917. Its Galician immigrant founders were largely from the Dabrowa Tarnowska and Szczucin areas. Many worked for local cotton textile manufacturers such as the Thorndike Company. Ten pastors served St. Stanislaus in its first 50 years. In the 1950s, Rev. Charles Chwalek, a hands-on pastor, led the construction of a new parish social center.

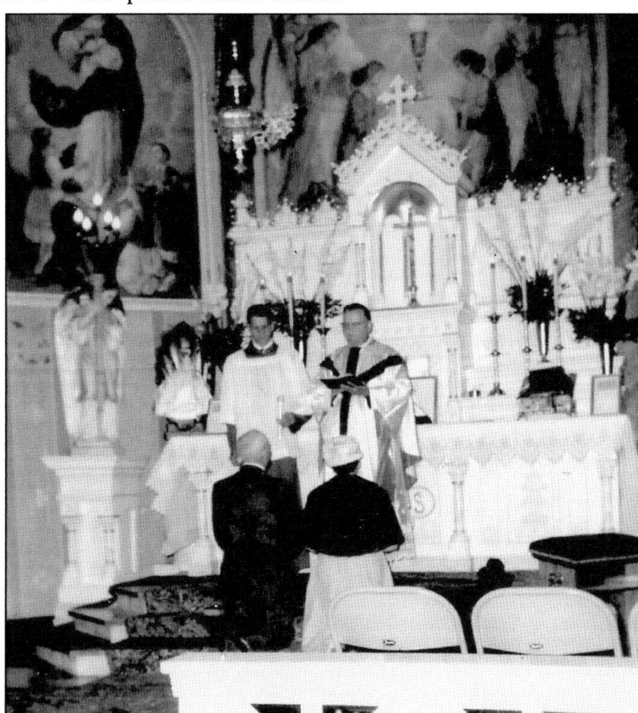

Pastor Casimir Swiacki (right) blesses his parents, Francis and Helen Kosakowska Swiacki, at their 50th wedding anniversary service at St. Stanislaus Church, West Warren, in 1961. The couple's grandson Robert Kochanowski serves as altar boy. St. Stanislaus was designed by Bruno Wozny of Springfield, who advertised himself as the only Polish architect in Massachusetts. Reverend Chwalek, pastor from 1952 to 1956, designed and carved the church's side altars.

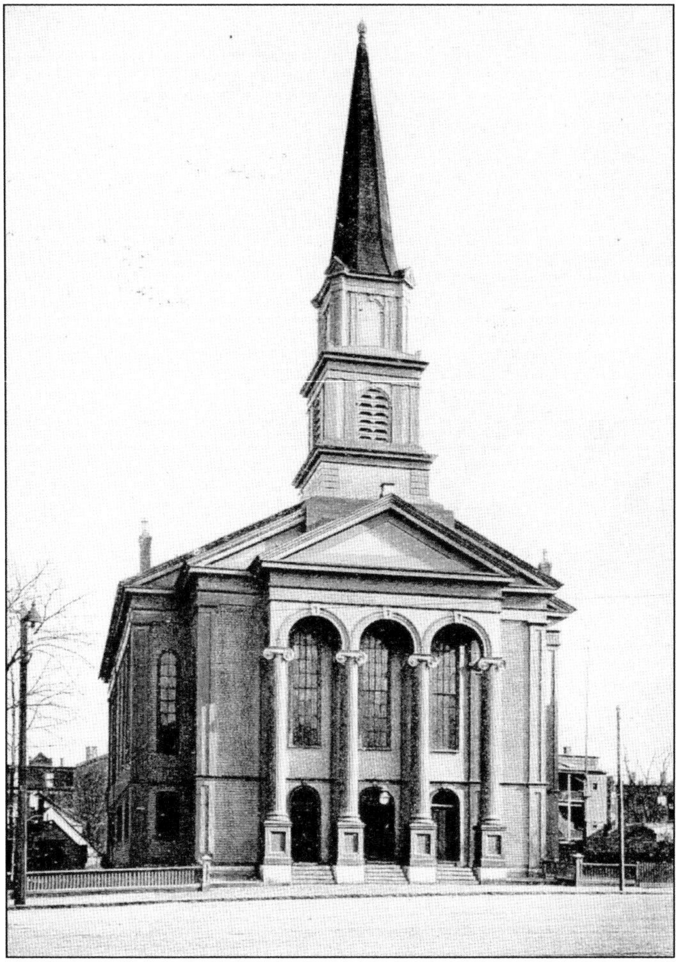

In the early years of Polish settlement in Worcester County, before the immigrants were strong enough in numbers and resources to propose their own parishes, they worshiped at existing Catholic parishes—typically Irish or French Canadian. In Worcester, the early Notre Dame Church on Park Street, pictured here, was one option; St. John's and Sacred Heart were others. In Webster, it was St. Louis Church, and in Clinton, St. John's.

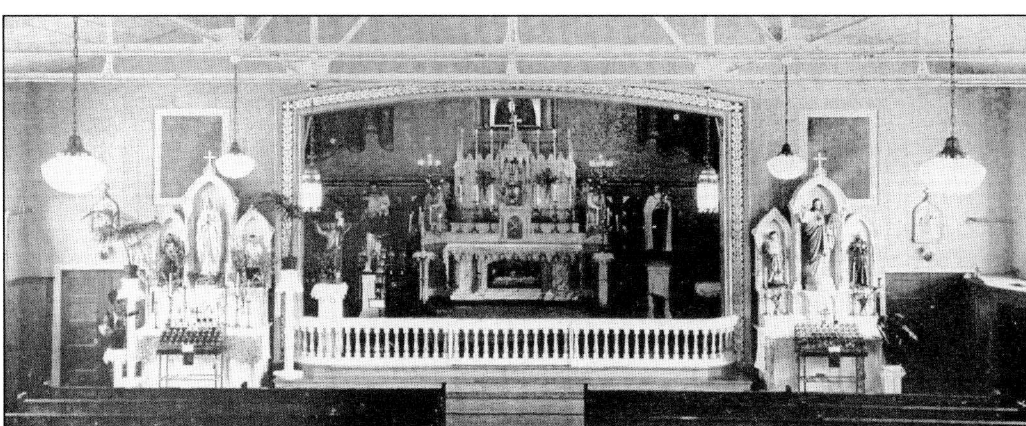

The interior of St. Mary's Chapel, Clinton, in 1939, reflects renovations to the altars, statues, windows, and church vessels overseen by Rev. John Oszajca, the pastor. An oil painting of Our Lady of Czestochowa was imported from Poland and installed as well. A belfry was added to the exterior to house the church bell.

St. Hedwig's Parish, Southbridge, had its origins as a mission organized in 1916 by St. Joseph's in Webster. It was declared a parish in 1918, with Rev. Martin Hanyz as pastor; he served his congregation for 53 years. To help raise funds for church construction, Southbridge residents traveled to more developed Polish communities in Webster and Worcester, literally asking for dimes and quarters. The 450-seat church was dedicated in September 1920.

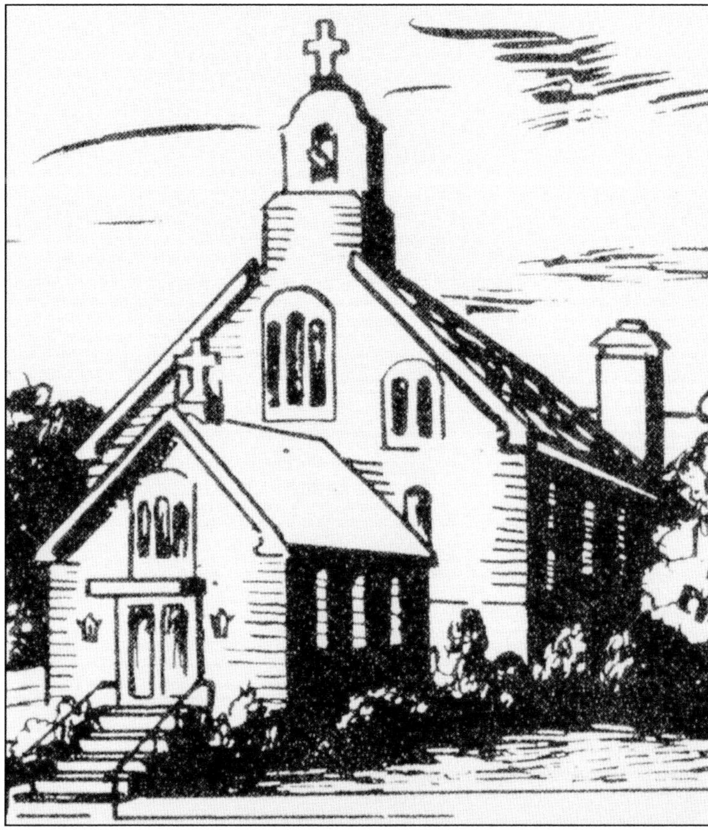

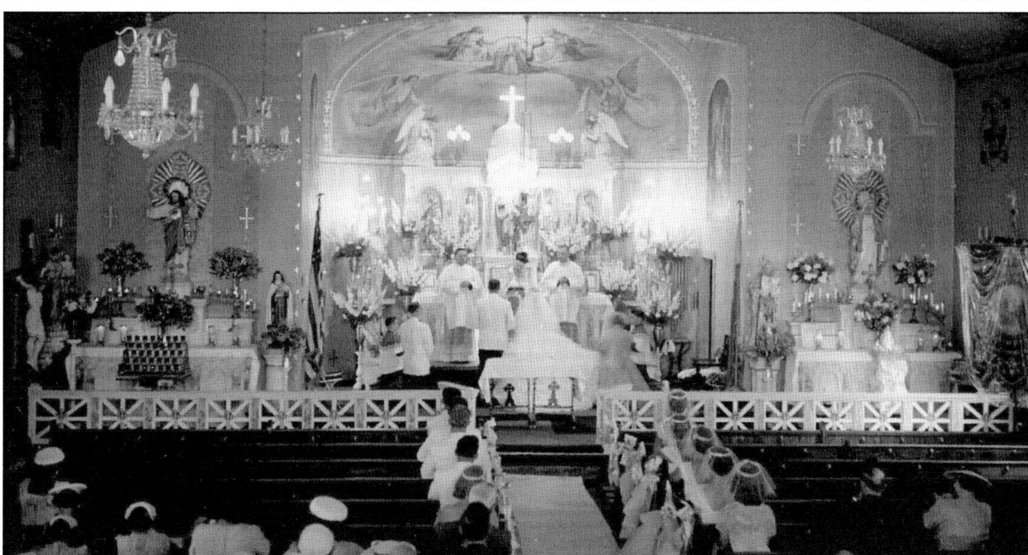

A view from the choir loft shows a wedding in progress at St. Hedwig's Church in August 1957. The ceremony featured Masses celebrated concurrently at the church's three altars. Rev. Martin Hanyz, the pastor, married Gloria Lehonczak and Chester Szydlik. Observing at this point in the ceremony are Reverends John Szamocki (left) and Casimir Swiacki, the latter a native son of the parish.

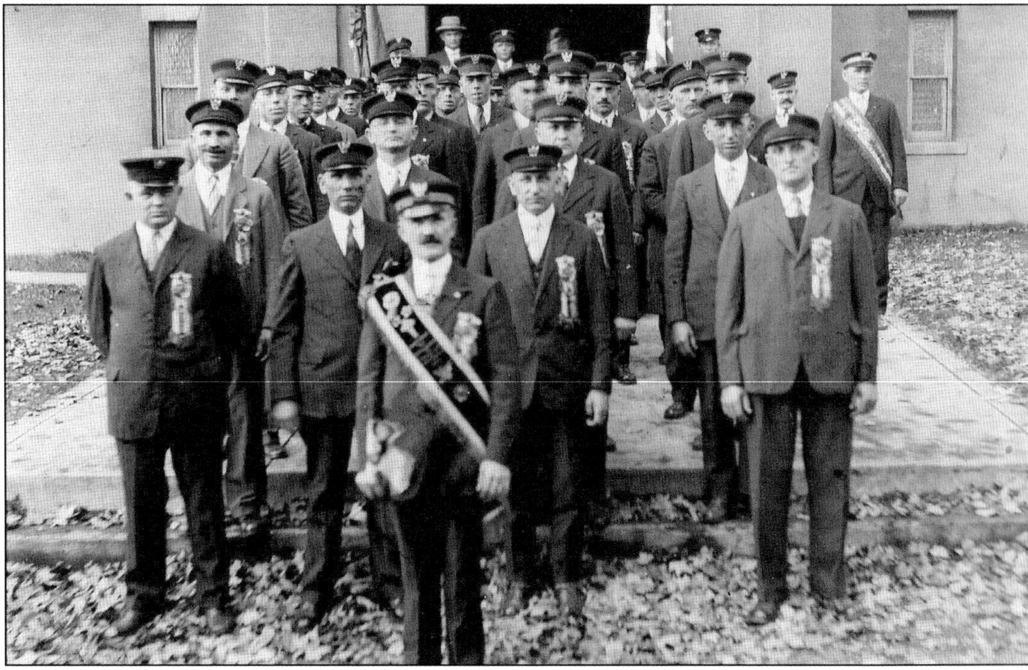

St. Stanislaus Society, organized in 1912 with Walter Kania as president, initiated action for formation of a Polish parish in Southbridge by securing Rev. Anthony Cyran of Webster to offer Sunday Masses in the town and by raising $3,000 toward church construction. The members stand before the church soon after its completion in 1920. Identified in the sixth row, far right, is a mustached Walter Pulawski.

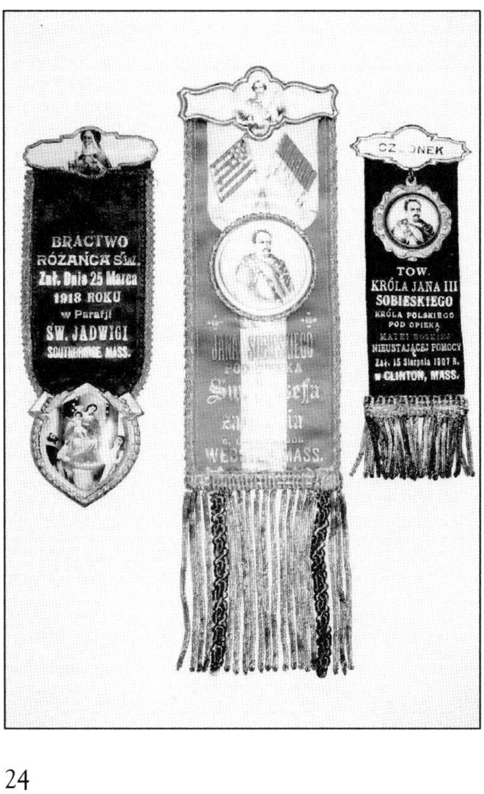

Inscribed in Polish, these ribbons represent three early parish societies, from left to right, the Holy Rosary Society of St. Hedwig's Parish, Southbridge, and the King John Sobieski societies of St. Joseph's, Webster, and St. Mary's (later Our Lady of Jasna Gora), Clinton. Societies such as these often filled several functions, ranging from spiritual and social to practical and financial.

St. Andrew Bobola in Dudley is believed to be the first church in the United States and in the western hemisphere dedicated to this 17th-century Polish martyr. The 500-seat redbrick church opened in 1954 in response to the growth of the area's Polish population. Begun as a mission, St. Andrew Bobola Parish was decreed independent in 1963.

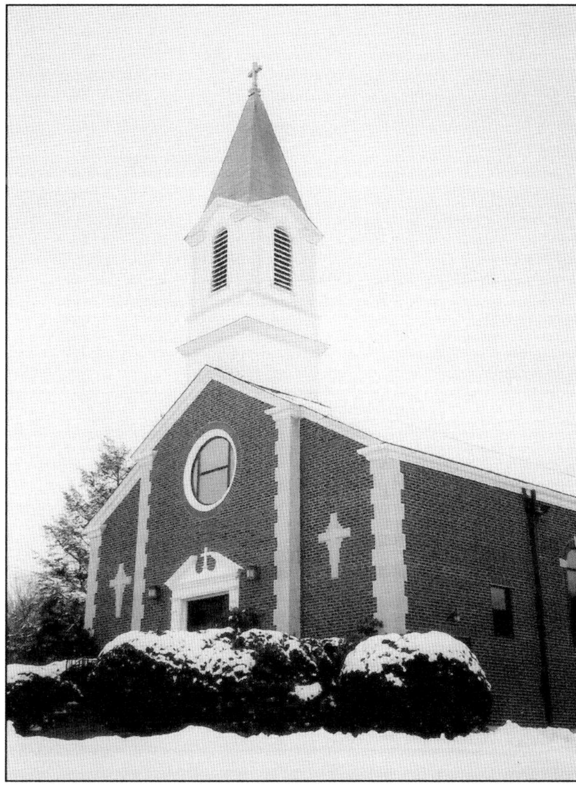

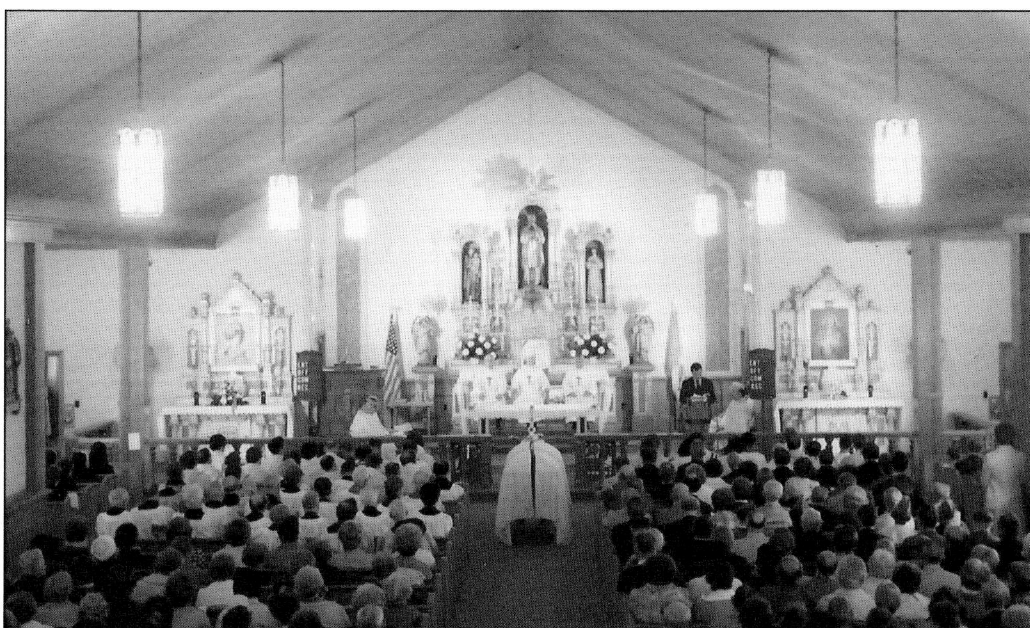

The interior of St. Andrew Bobola Church features hand-carved oak main and side altars that were imported from Italy. Its distinctive decor includes statues of three Polish saints—Andrew Bobola, Stanislaus Kostka, and Blessed Bronislawa—and urns containing soil from the historic Polish sites of Legnica, Wawel, Czestochowa (Jasna Gora), and Szczepanow, and ashes from Auschwitz.

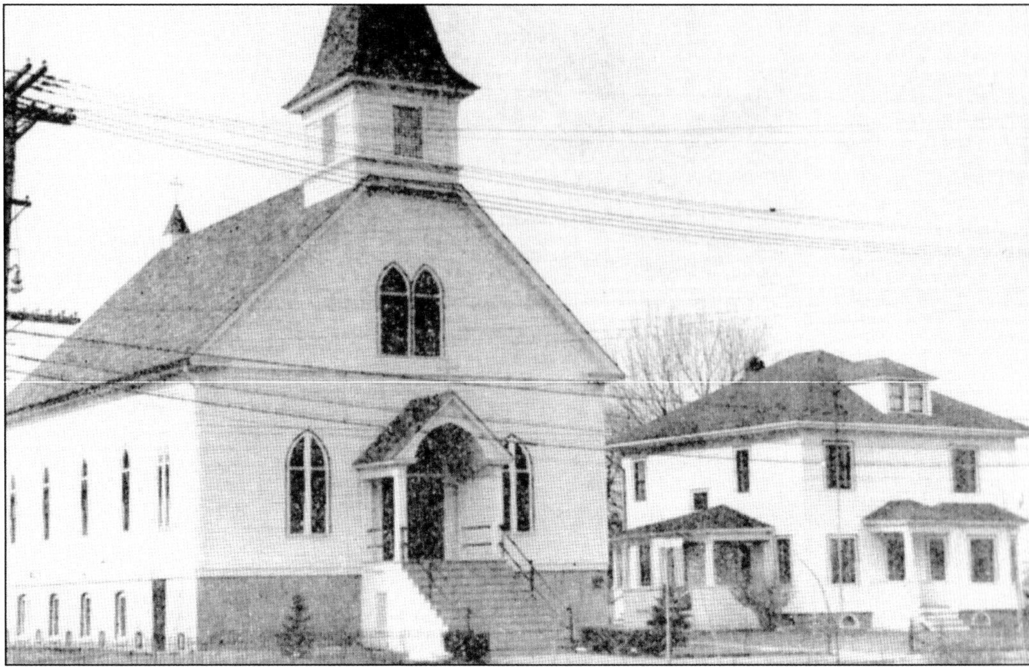

Holy Trinity Parish of the Polish National Catholic Church (PNCC) was founded in Webster in 1913; its church and rectory are pictured in 1957. Holy Trinity is the only PNCC parish extant in Worcester County. One other, Good Shepherd in Worcester, was founded in 1946 but lost its church to downtown urban renewal in the mid-1960s. The PNCC has also had a membership base in Southbridge and Gilbertville.

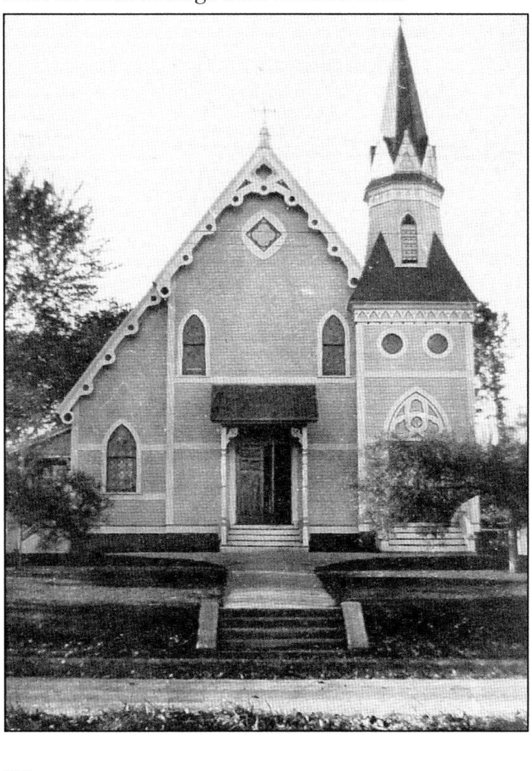

St. James Church, South Grafton, was built in 1884 on land donated by the Canal Cotton (later Fisher) Manufacturing Company and established as a parish in 1887. Galician immigrants joined the predominantly French Canadian parish because the closest Polish church was in Worcester, 10 miles away. Polish priests visited St. James occasionally to hear confessions, giving the immigrants an opportunity to practice their religion in their native tongue.

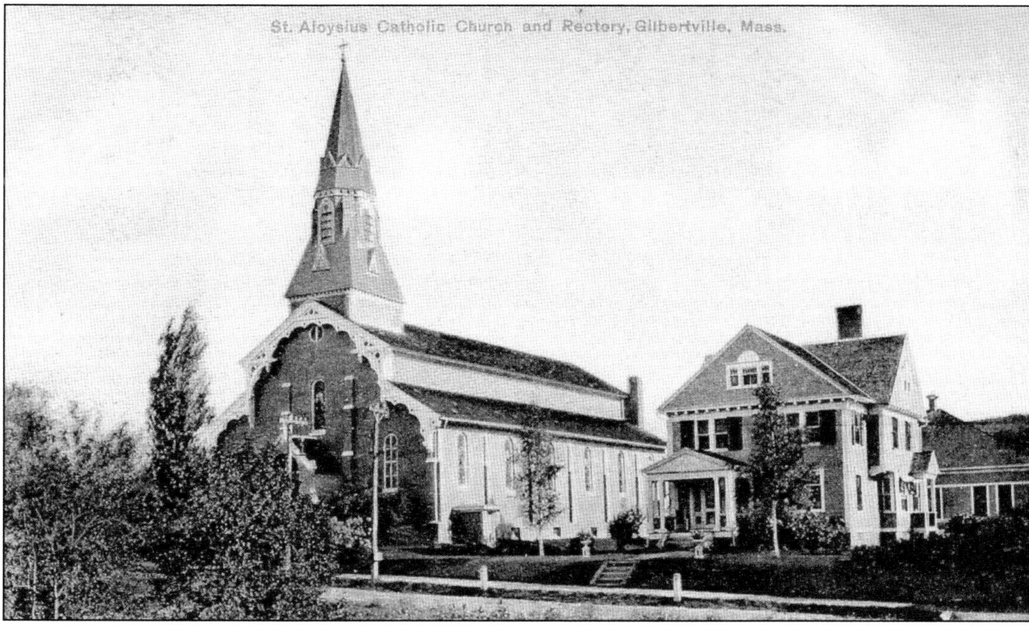

After two decades as a Ware parish mission, St. Aloysius in Gilbertville was established as a parish in 1894. The church, built in 1872 and shown here in 1911, has been served by several Polish priests. Its early members were primarily immigrants who worked at the George H. Gilbert Manufacturing Company. A parish census taken in 1895 identified 619 Irish members, 535 French, and 100 Polish.

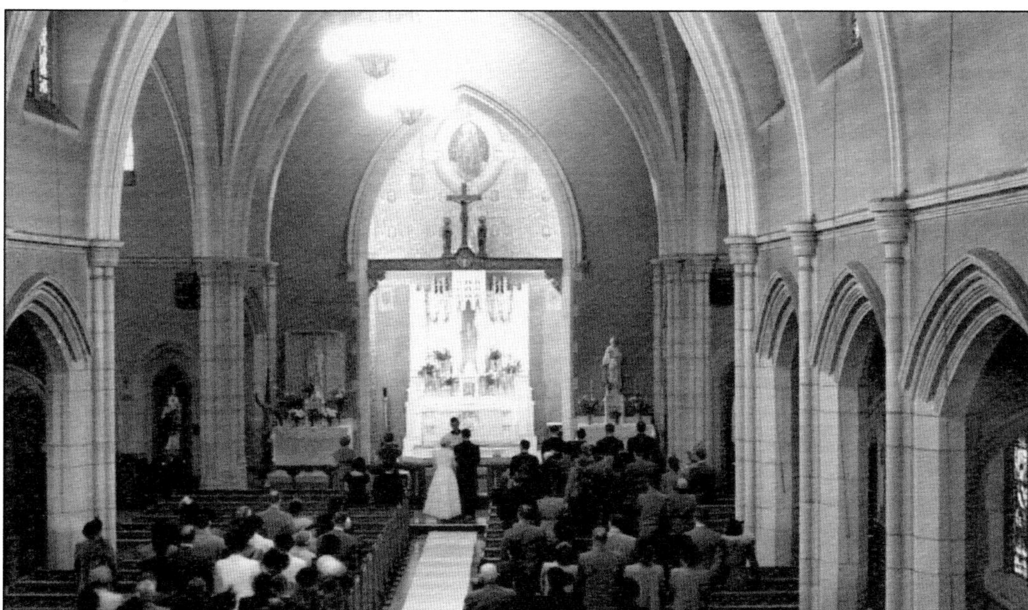

St. Mary's Church, Uxbridge, was the site of the 1950 wedding of Phyllis Augusciak and Stanley A. Smyth III. Lacking their own ethnic parish, some Uxbridge Poles joined St. Mary's. Those who wanted to worship in Polish traveled to Woonsocket, Rhode Island, to attend St. Stanislaus Kostka Roman Catholic Church (founded in 1905) or the Polish National Catholic Church of Our Saviour (dedicated in 1924).

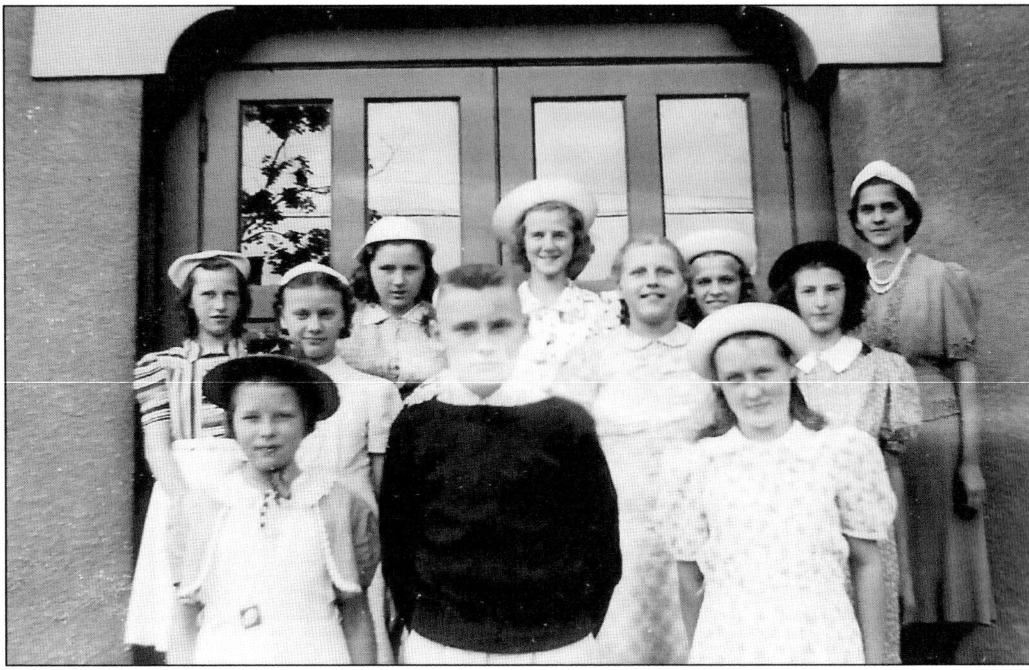

Members of St. Hedwig's Children's Choir, Southbridge, in 1941 include, from left to right, (first row) G. Korzeniecka, F. Dusza, and ? Korzeniecka; (second row) H. Dusza, Sophie Swiacki, and R. Rossman; (third row) E. Planeta, E. Koprowska, C. Taraszkiewicz, B. Domian, and Hedwig Swiacki, choir director, who succeeded her brother as organist in the 1980s. While a student at Mary E. Wells High School, Swiacki was its orchestra director.

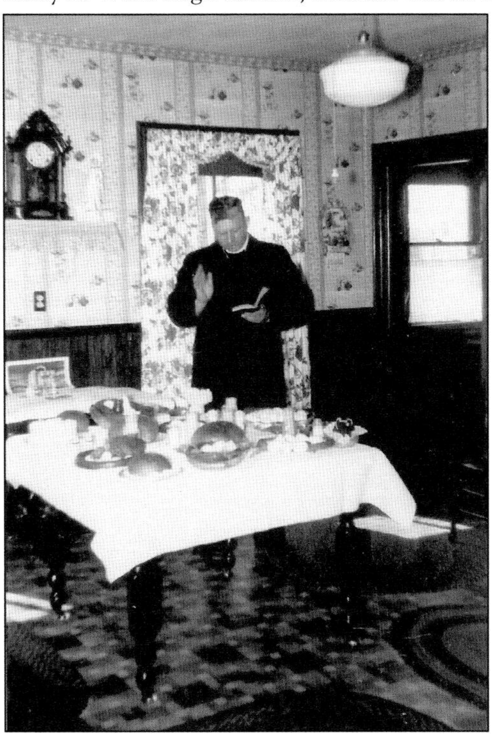

On Holy Saturday in April 1950, Rev. Peter Samorajski of St. Joseph's Parish, Webster, blesses a sampling of Polish Easter food at the home of Aloysius and Apolonia Sroczynski on North Main Street. The traditional foods presented for blessing all have symbolic meaning: ham and kielbasa (abundance), salt (purification), horseradish (bitter sacrifice), both decorated and shelled eggs (life), and a butter, bread, or cake Paschal Lamb, or *Baranek* (Jesus).

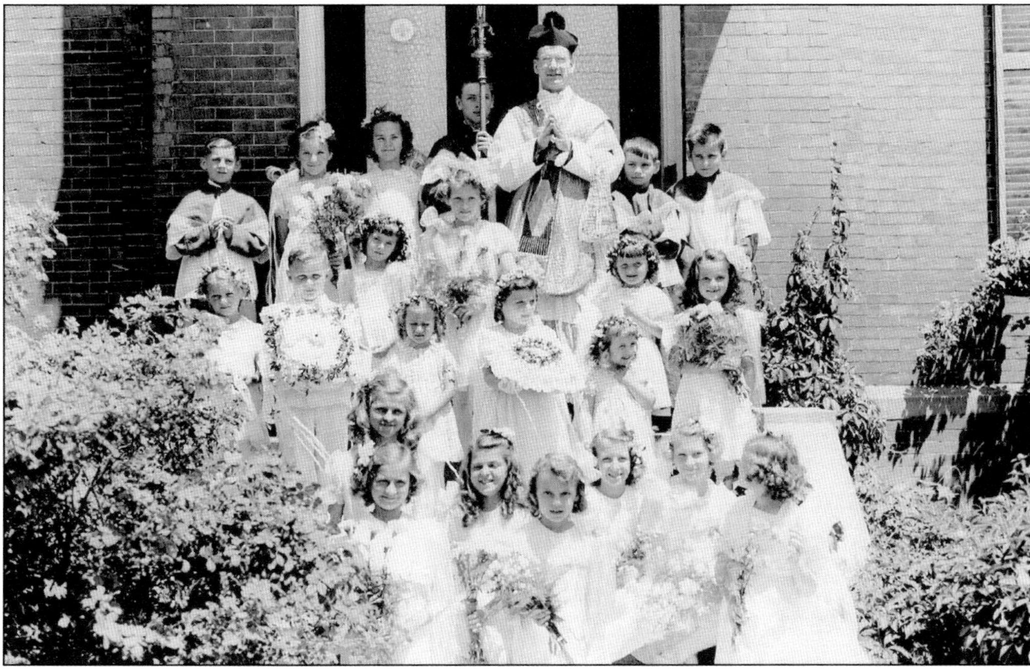

Rev. Casimir Swiacki prepares to join a 1950s "May Crowning" procession with "little angels" and altar boys. Polish parishes honor the Virgin Mary in May with a ceremony in which a girl crowns a statue of Mary with a wreath of flowers. Participants and faithful observers sing hymns along the procession route. Swiacki was then associate pastor of St. Joseph's Church, Webster, serving at St. Andrew Bobola, Dudley.

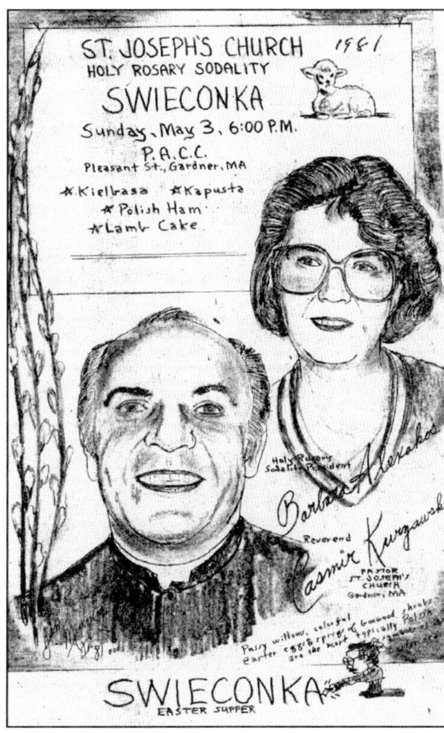

A poster featuring sketches of Rev. Casmir Kurzawski, pastor, and Barbara Alexakos, president of the Holy Rosary Sodality, of St. Joseph's Church, Gardner, announces the sodality's 1981 *Swieconka*, or Easter meal. Held at the Polish American Citizens Club on Pleasant Street, the dinner featured kielbasa, *kapusta* (cabbage), Polish ham, and a lamb-shaped cake. Swieconka signifies both the traditional Polish Easter breakfast and a community Easter meal or party.

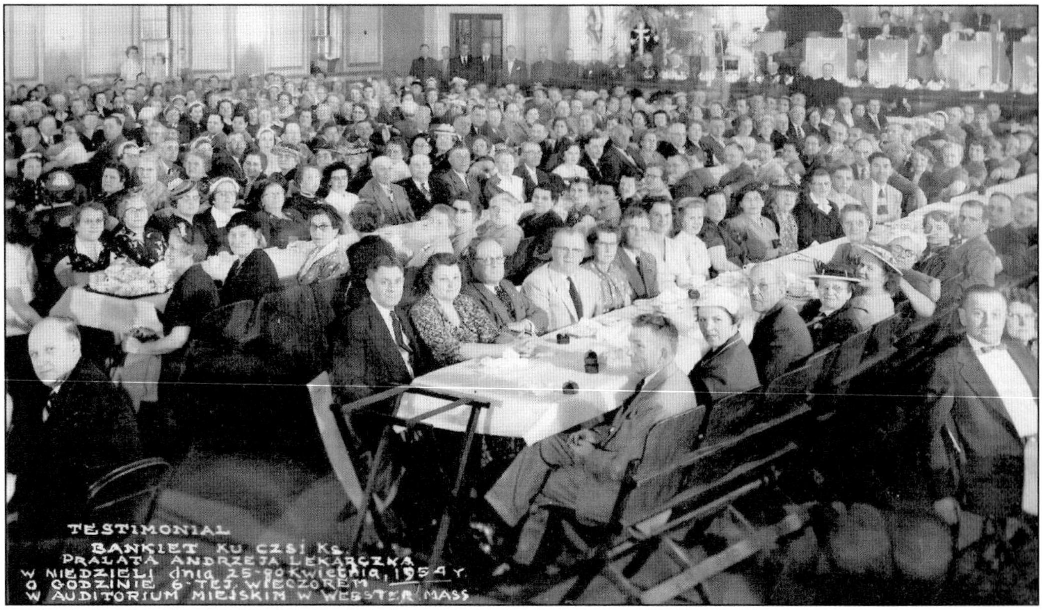

A banquet held at Webster's municipal auditorium in April 1954 honored Rev. Dr. Andrew Lekarczyk, pastor of St. Joseph's Parish. He came to Webster in 1935 from a series of smaller parishes in western Massachusetts. Despite the economic hardships of the Great Depression, Lekarczyk reduced parish debt and expanded facilities. Pope Piux XII raised his status to "very reverend monsignor," and in 1961, John XXIII elevated him to "right reverend monsignor."

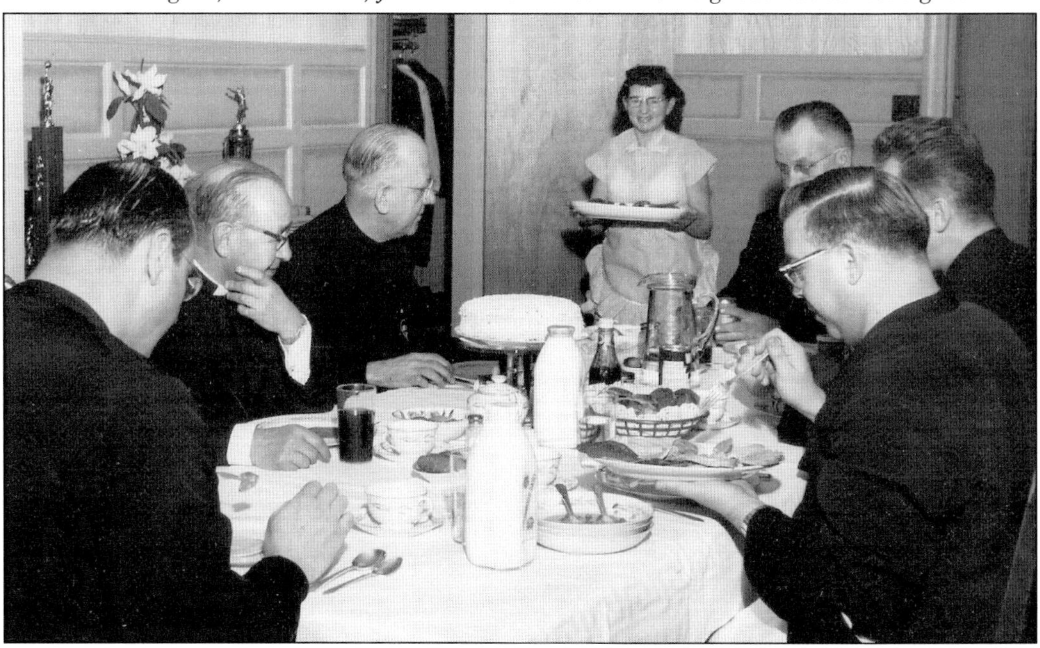

The priests of Our Lady of Czestochowa Parish, Worcester, enjoy lunch with two guests at the rectory around 1960. Seated clockwise from far left are Reverends Chester Janczukowicz, Anthony Nasiatka, and John Chwalek, Msgr. Charles Chwalek, unidentified, and Rev. John Szamocki. Serving the meal is Wanda ?, rectory cook. Rev. John Chwalek, brother of the Worcester pastor, served at parishes in western Massachusetts.

Aleksander Marczewski accepts a bouquet from Monsignor Chwalek, pastor of Our Lady of Czestochowa Parish, following a solo piano concert at Kosciuszko Auditorium in Worcester in 1968. Standing are (from left to right) daughter Elizabeth Marczewski, wife Barbara Lichterowicz Marczewski, Rev. John Szamocki, and son Richard Marczewski. In Poland, Marczewski was a renowned orchestral director, conductor, and composer. In Worcester, he served as organist and choir director at the Polish parish.

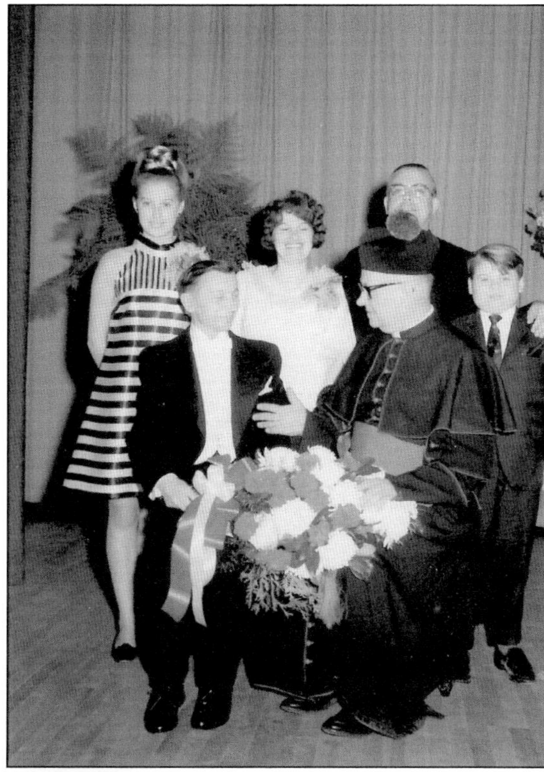

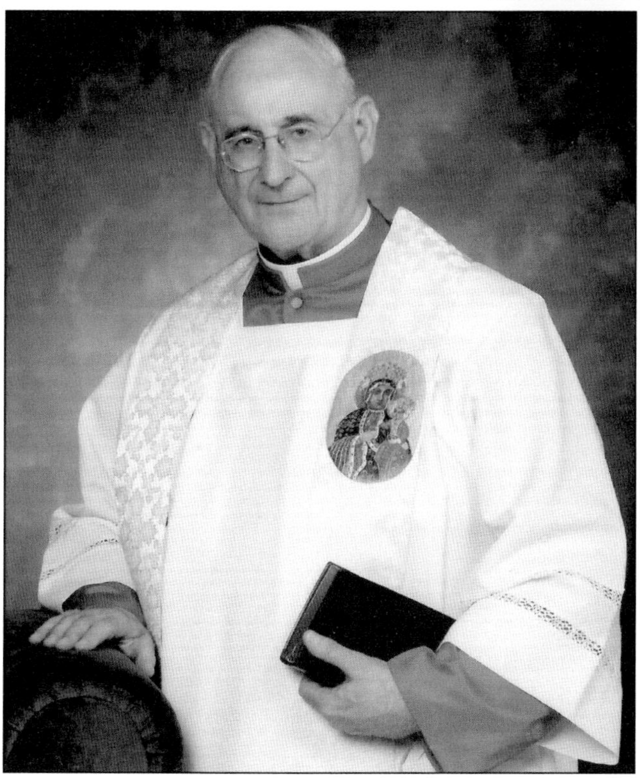

Msgr. Chester Janczukowicz served several parishes: St. Aloysius, Gilbertville; St. Mary's, Uxbridge; Good Shepherd, Linwood; St. Aloysius, Rochdale; St. Mary's, Jefferson; and St. Joseph's, Webster. He was most associated with his home parish of Our Lady of Czestochowa, Worcester, where he served 12 years as associate pastor and school athletic director and 17 years as pastor and school headmaster. Pope John Paul II named him a prelate of honor in 1991.

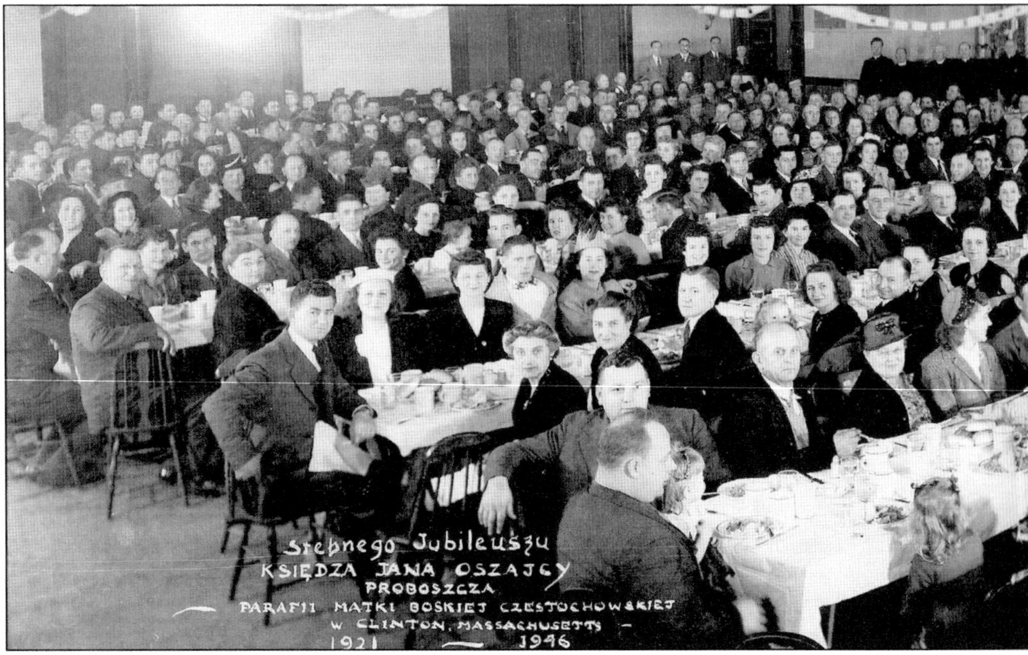

Hundreds of people filled Clinton Town Hall in November 1946 for a banquet honoring Rev. John Oszajcy on his 25th anniversary in the priesthood. Oszajcy was pastor at St. Mary's in Clinton from 1926 to 1929, and from 1935 until poor health forced his retirement in 1952. He organized several church societies, assured completion of St. Mary's School construction, and made substantial improvements to the parish property.

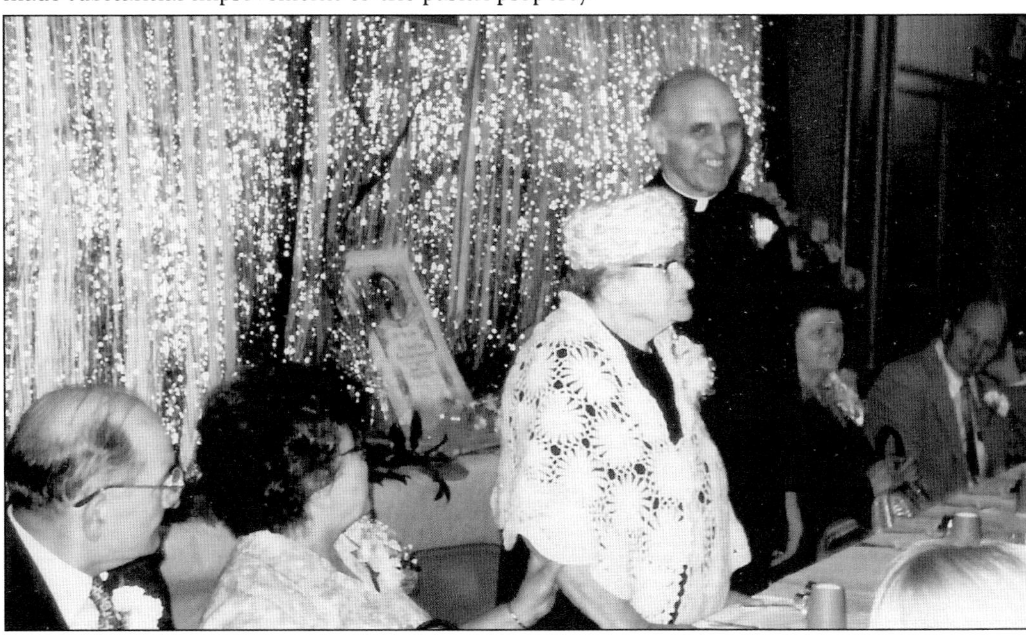

Rev. Joseph Szwach of Clinton smiles as his mother, Katarzyna Szwach of Dudley, stands with him during a celebration of his silver jubilee in 1980. A papal message is displayed behind them. Seated at left are the priest's brother-in-law and sister. The banquet was held in the social hall of Our Lady of Jasna Gora Parish, earlier named St. Mary's.

Overseen by Rev. Peter Samorajski, a new Polish church was built in Clinton and opened in December 1962. Our Lady of Jasna Gora's distinctive exterior incorporates Attic and Spanish architectural elements, modified to suit New England winters. A triptych design of colored brick frames the aluminum doors; at top are six Christian symbols found in the Roman catacombs. The equal-armed cross signifies everyone's equality in God's eyes.

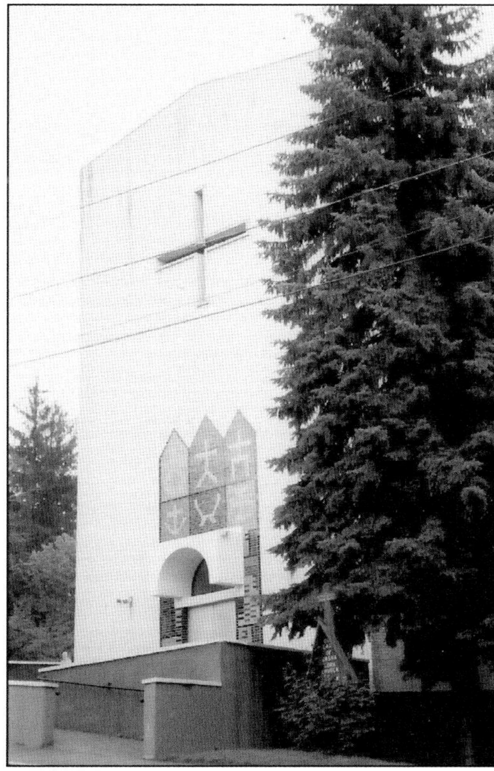

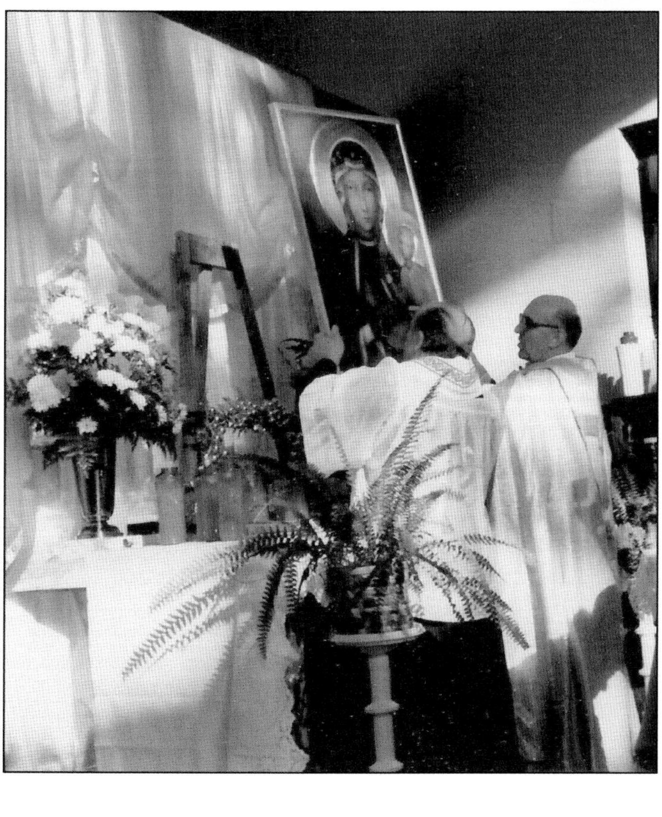

Rev. Joseph Szwach (right) installs an icon of the Black Madonna at the rear of Our Lady of Jasna Gora Church, Clinton, around 1982. Since Roman Catholicism was introduced in Poland in 966 CE, the Virgin Mary has been revered as the symbolic Queen of Poland. Her image as the Black Madonna is associated with both the city of Czestochowa and its famous pilgrimage destination, the Jasna Gora monastery.

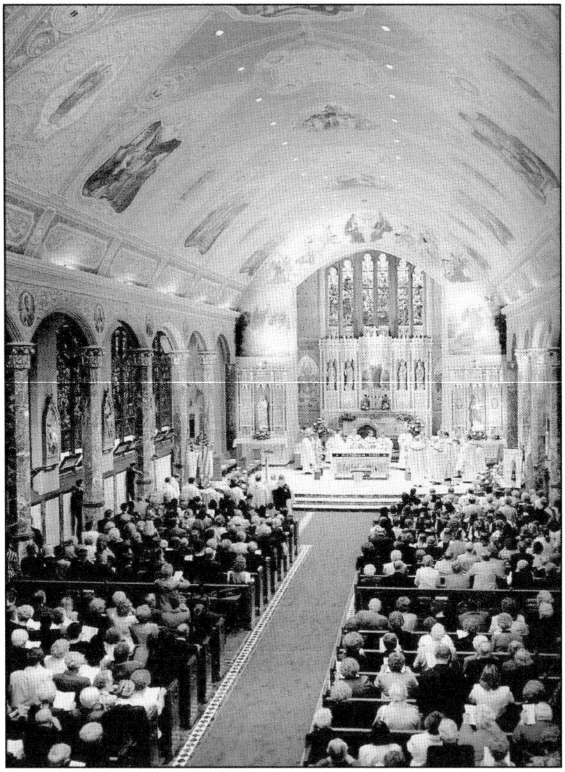

Following an extensive renovation program initiated three years earlier by Msgr. Anthony Czarnecki, St. Joseph's Church was rededicated by Bishop Daniel Reilly in October 1997. Pope John Paul II conferred the title of basilica on the church in 1998. The title is bestowed upon churches in recognition of their antiquity, dignity, or historical or devotional significance. Here it honored St. Joseph's historical importance as the first Polish church in New England.

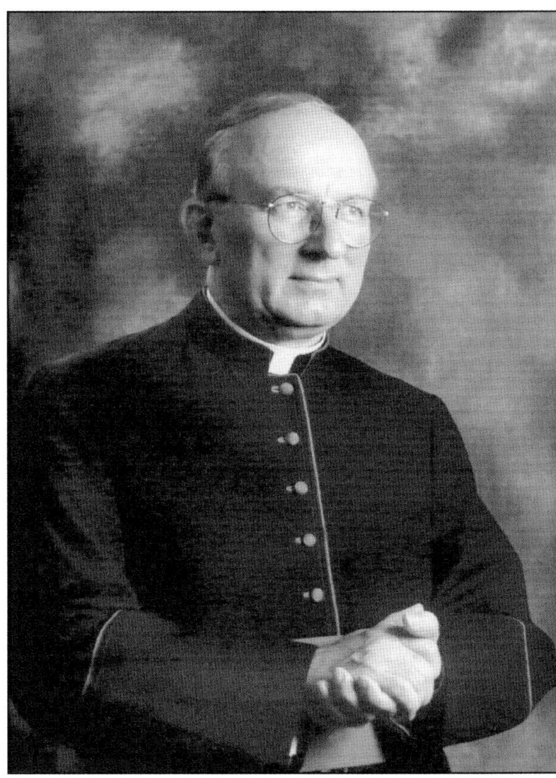

Monsignor Czarnecki emigrated from Poland in 1971 to accept an assignment at Our Lady of Czestochowa Parish in Worcester. He subsequently served as associate pastor at St. Andrew Bobola in Dudley, then in Washington, D.C., for the National Conference of Catholic Bishops. In 1993, he returned to Worcester Diocese to become pastor of St. Joseph's Parish in Webster. The community has a substantial new Polish population.

Rev. Thaddeus Stachura has served extensively in Worcester Diocese's two largest Polish parishes: as associate pastor at St. Joseph's, Webster, 1971–1978; prelate at Our Lady of Czestochowa, Worcester, 1978–1983; pastor at St. Joseph's, 1983–1993; and pastor at Our Lady of Czestochowa, 1993–present. He has also served at St. Mary's, Uxbridge, and St. Catherine of Sweden, Worcester. Worcester's Polish Quo Vadis Club named him Man of the Year in 1989.

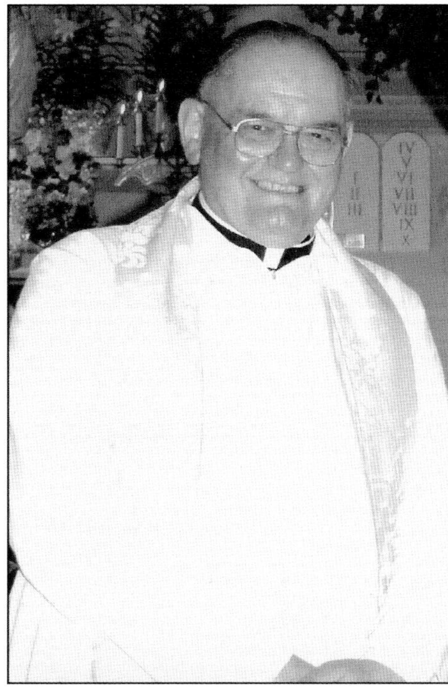

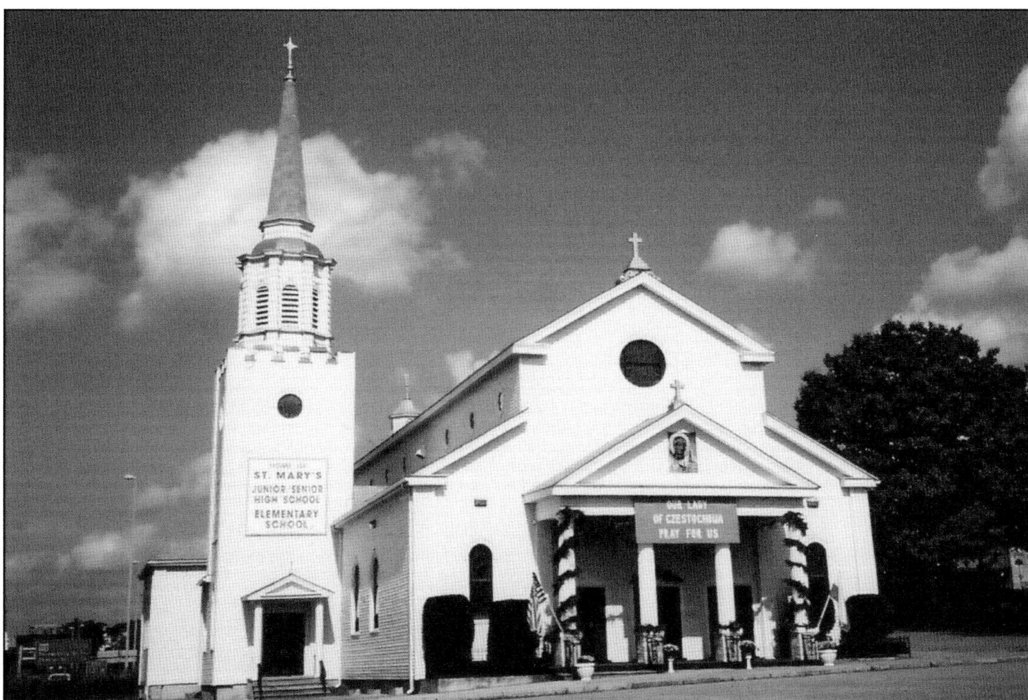

Adorned for its centennial celebration in October 2003 is Our Lady of Czestochowa Church in Worcester. The church was remodeled and expanded in 1959–1960, partly by plan and partly in necessary adaptation to Interstate 290 construction. With English and Polish still alternating on the mass schedule, the parish today is a magnet for new young families from Poland as well as for the descendants of its founders.

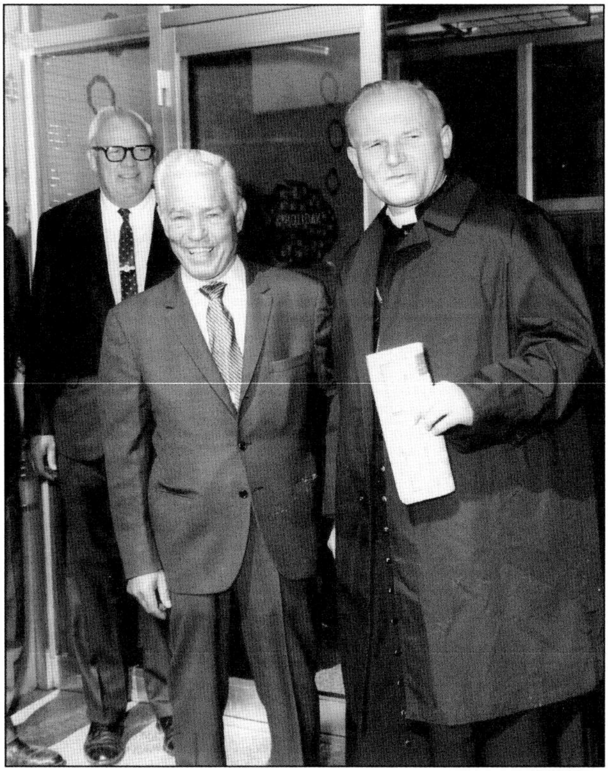

Longtime Fitchburg legislator and mayor George Bourque (left) and an unidentified man accompany Karol Cardinal Wojtyla as he steps outside a public building during his first visit to Massachusetts in 1969. Wojtyla returned to the state in 1976 and as Pope John Paul II in 1979. Busloads of Polish Americans traveled to the Boston area to hear him speak or simply witness those historic appearances.

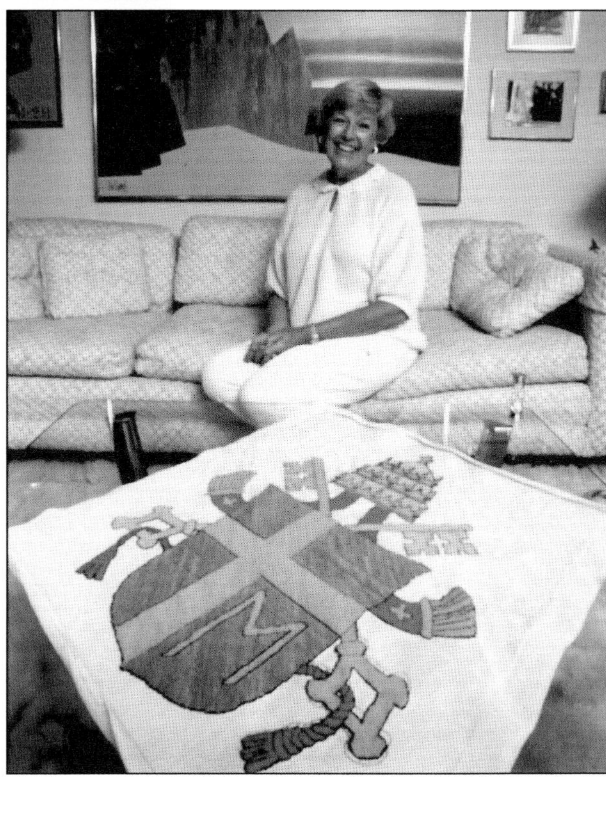

Worcester native Therese Roszko Abdella displays the chair covering she created for Pope John Paul II's 1987 tour of the United States. An experienced needlepoint artist, she drew the papal coat of arms freehand, selected appropriate yarns and colors, and then manifested the crest in 121,559 stitches. The needlepoint crest adorned the back of the papal chair the Holy Father used in his Miami meeting with 500 American priests.

Three

PASSAGES

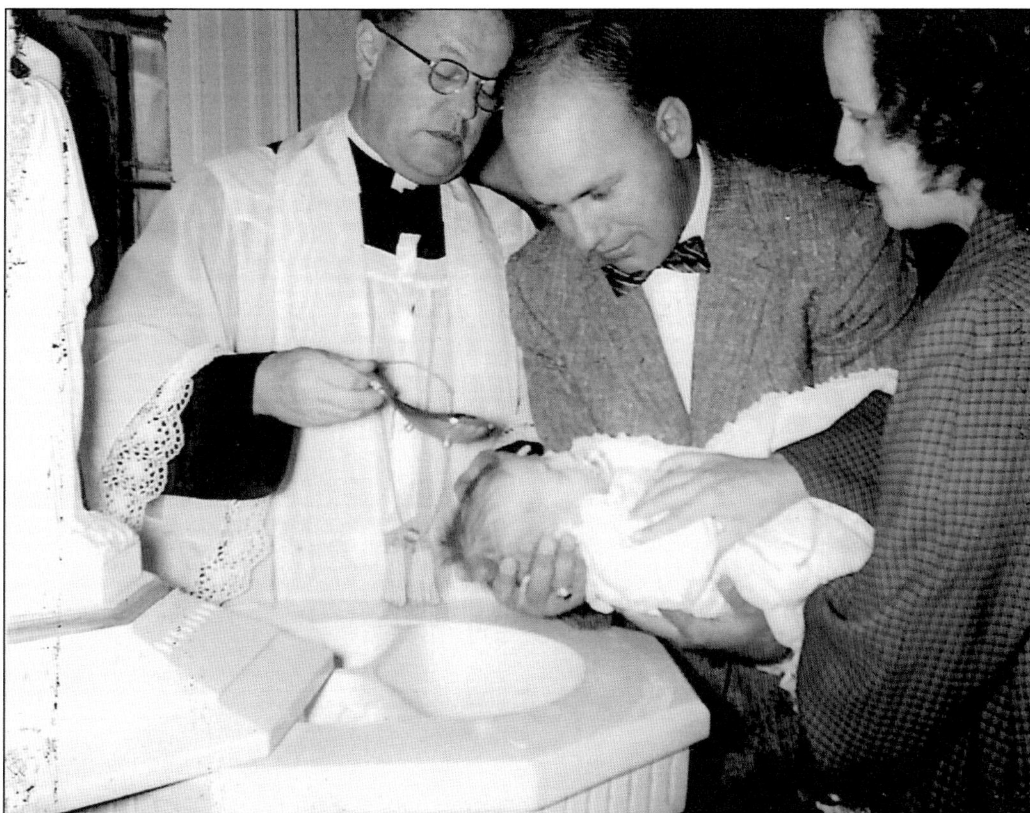

Baptism, first communion, and confirmation represent sacred rites of passage in the spiritual life of a Roman Catholic. Here Rev. John Kochanowski baptizes Richard Wolosz, son of Henry and Mary Wolosz, at Our Lady of Czestochowa Church in August 1957. Holding the infant are godparents Stanley Wolosz and Stella Kosciusko. Three generations of the Wolosz family have been baptized in the Worcester church.

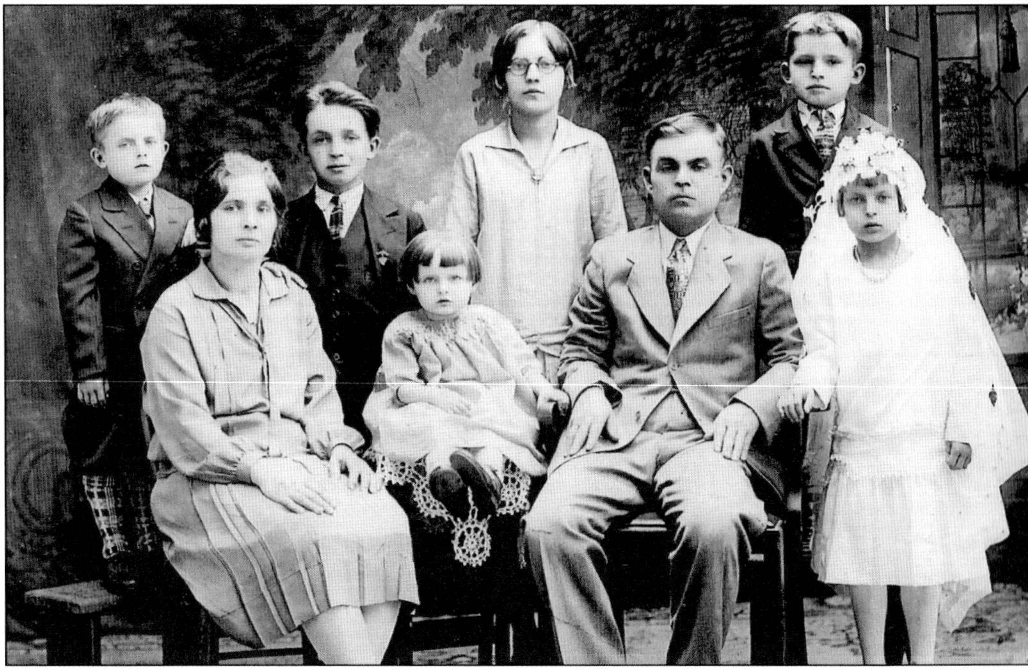

An extended family celebrates Sophie Misiaszek's First Holy Communion at St. Aloysius Church, Gilbertville, around 1928. From left to right are (first row) aunt Josephine Lichwala, sister Rose Misiaszek, father Karol Misiaszek, and Sophie Misiaszek; (second row) brother Edward Misiaszek, cousin Joseph Lichwala, sister Felicitia Misiaszek, and cousin John Lichwala. Sophie's mother, Mary Mikolajczyk, died about two years earlier.

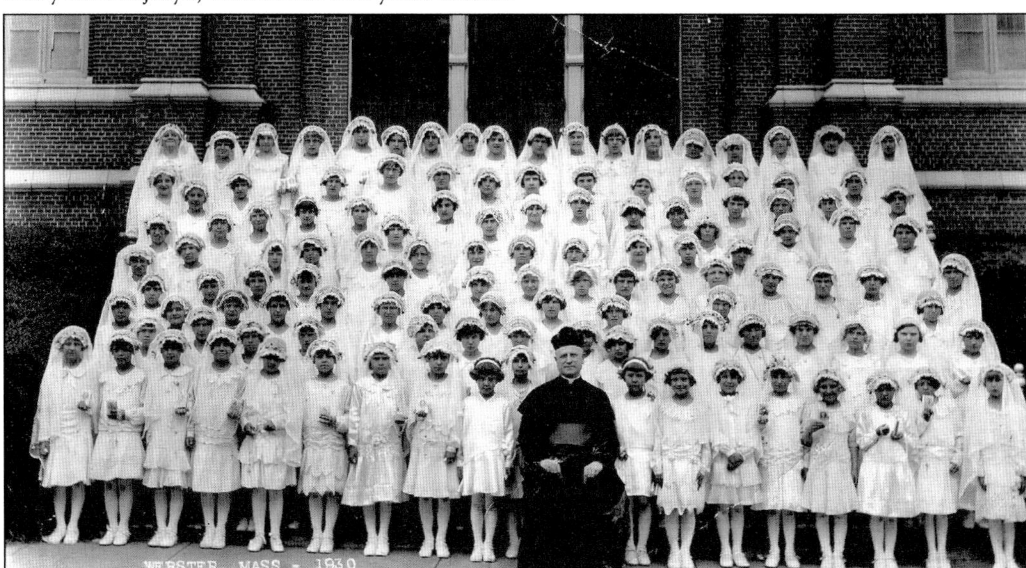

About 150 girls dressed in white for First Holy Communion stand outside St. Joseph's Church in Webster in May 1930. Seated in front is their pastor, Msgr. Anthony Cyran, who that February had made history as the first Polish priest in New England to be invested with the robes of a monsignor. Between 1910 and 1933, Cyran oversaw completion of the parish convent, new brick church, school, and rectory.

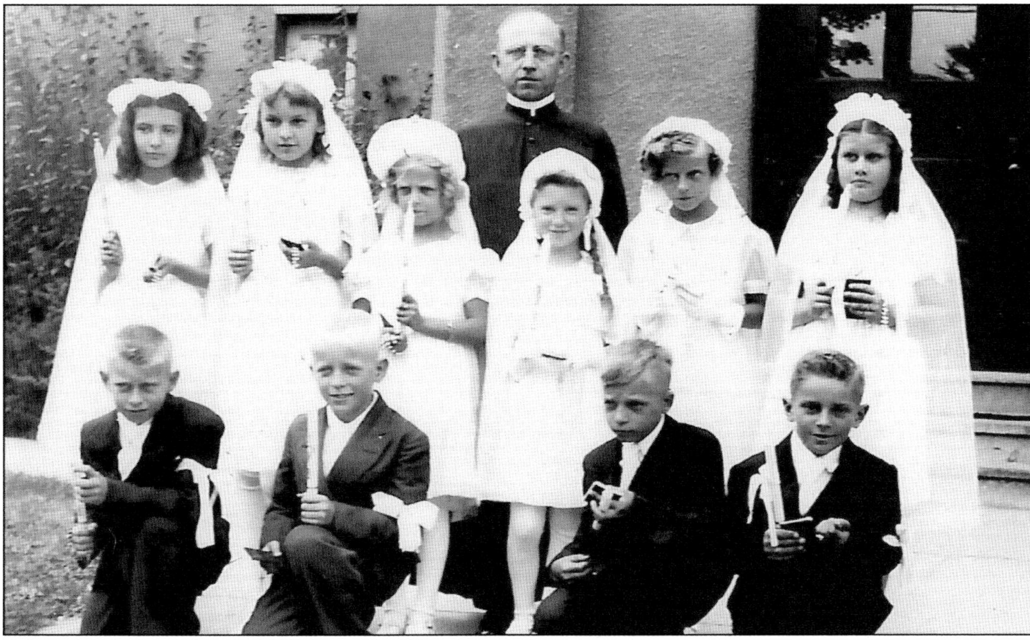

Rev. Martin Hanyz, pastor of St. Hedwig's Parish in Southbridge, stands with children making their First Holy Communion in 1944. Communicants from left to right are (first row) Ed Zelazo, John Swirbliss, Richard Waskiewicz, and Steve Kupiec; (second row) Ann Noga, Patricia Guzewicz, Dorothy Piasta, Gloria Lehonczak, Jean Swirbliss, and Margaret Polakowski. Hanyz was St. Hedwig's pastor from 1918 until his retirement in 1968.

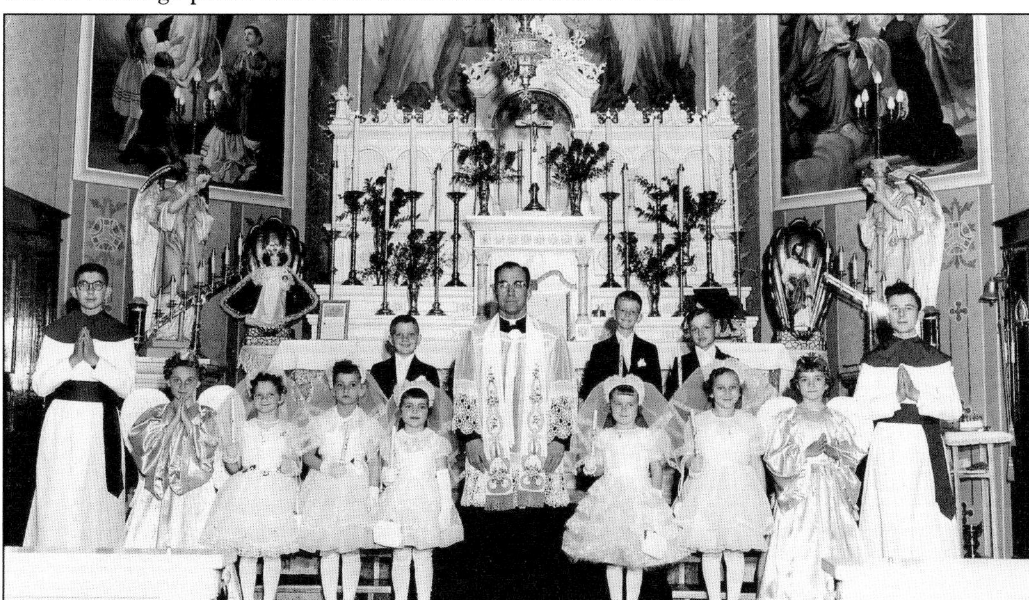

The 1956 First Holy Communion class of St. Stanislaus Church, West Warren, poses with Rev. Aleksander Struczko, pastor. From left to right are (first row) altar boy Richard Ligarski, "angel" Betty Tokarz, Janice Kwasniak, Sandra Wegzryn, Patricia Lizak, Sylvia Sablak, Barbara Korzec, "angel" Linda Niemiec, and altar boy Bernard Kulis; (second row) James Skowrya, Reverend Struczko, Edward Wozniak, and Richard Borowiec.

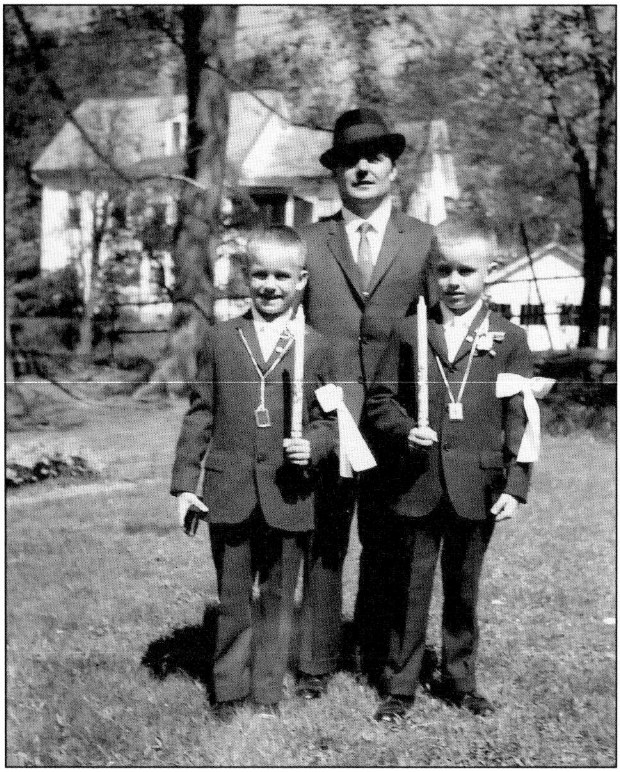

Identical twins Daniel (left) and Ronald Kaczynski stand with their father, Henry Kaczynski, at the family home on Walnut Street, Gardner, in May 1964, after the boys made their First Holy Communion at St. Joseph's Church. Their ribbon armbands, candles, scapulars, medals, and boutonnieres are traditional boys' accessories on this occasion.

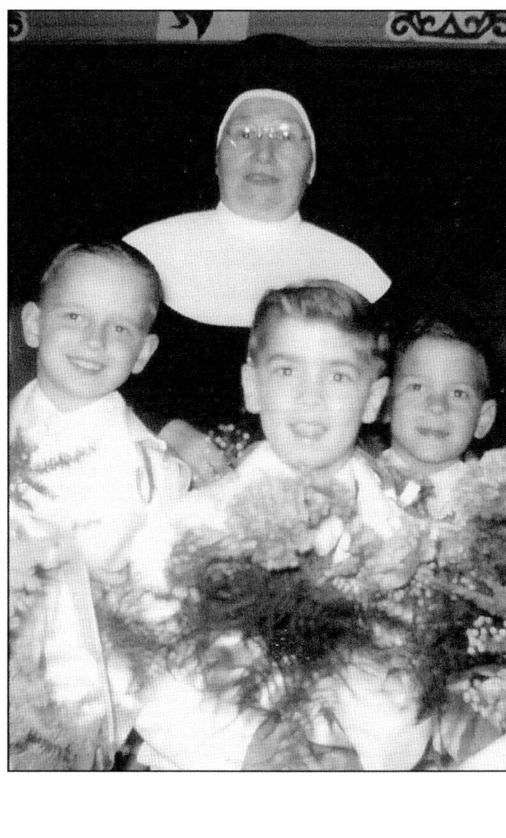

Sr. Mary Remigina prepares three boys to serve as "angels" leading the 1961 First Holy Communion class into Our Lady of Czestochowa Church. Holding their bouquets are, from left to right, unidentified, Kenneth Wolanin, and John Giza. The parish tradition was for kindergarten and first-grade girls and boys to precede the second-grade communicants in a procession down Richland Street and into the church.

Eight-year-old Catherine Nieszczezewski and Sr. Mary Ursula of the Felician Order pose in the upper yard of St. Joseph's School, Webster, for a May 1967 First Holy Communion photograph. Pictured in the background is the convent. Nieszczezewski lived with her family on Charlton Road, Dudley, and graduated from Shepherd Hill Regional High School, Dudley.

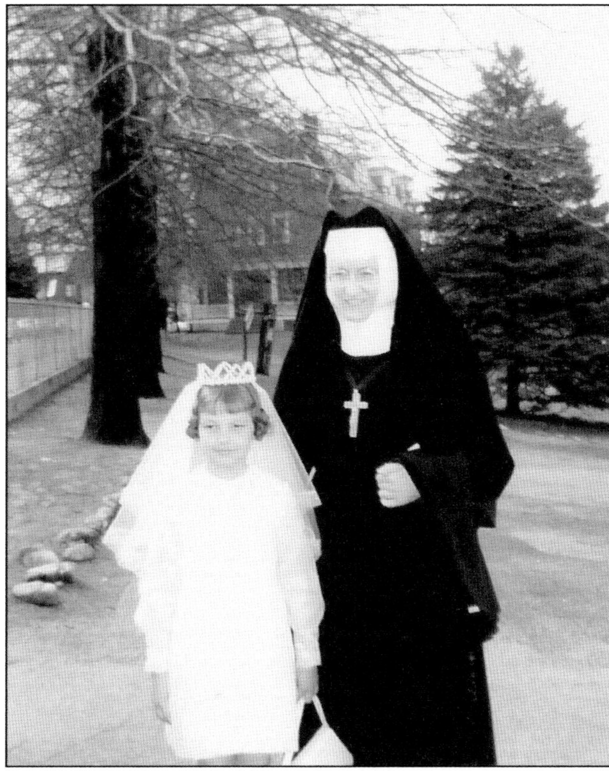

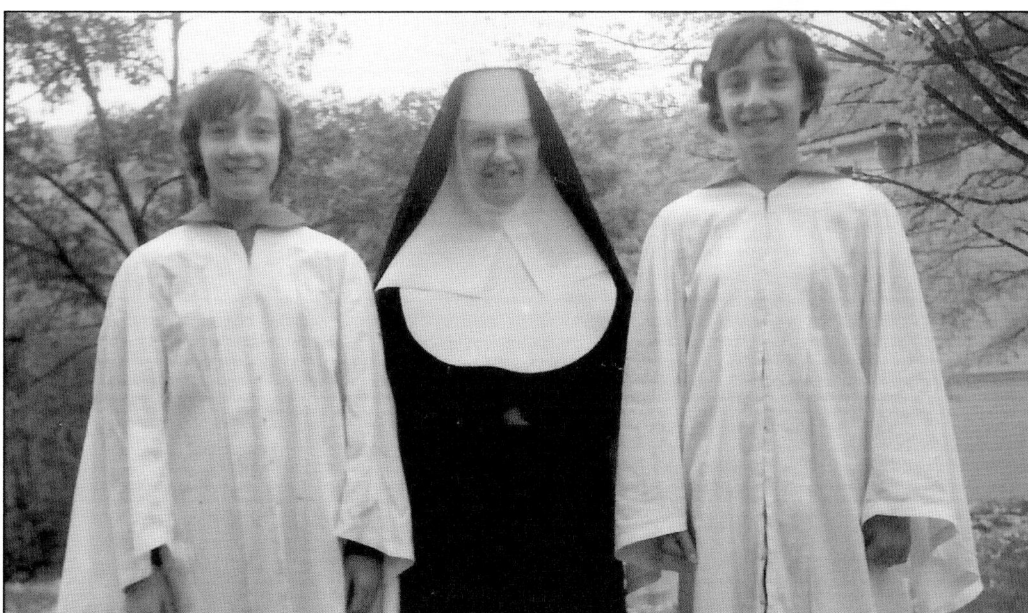

An unidentified Sister of Mercy joins twins Elaine (left) and Arlene Miarecki on confirmation day at St. Aloysius, Gilbertville, around 1968. The Sisters of Mercy taught at St. Aloysius School from 1952 until it closed in 1970. They were the last of three orders to teach there. The Sisters of St. Anne arrived in 1889 and remained for 19 years; the Faithful Companions of Jesus served from 1908 to 1952.

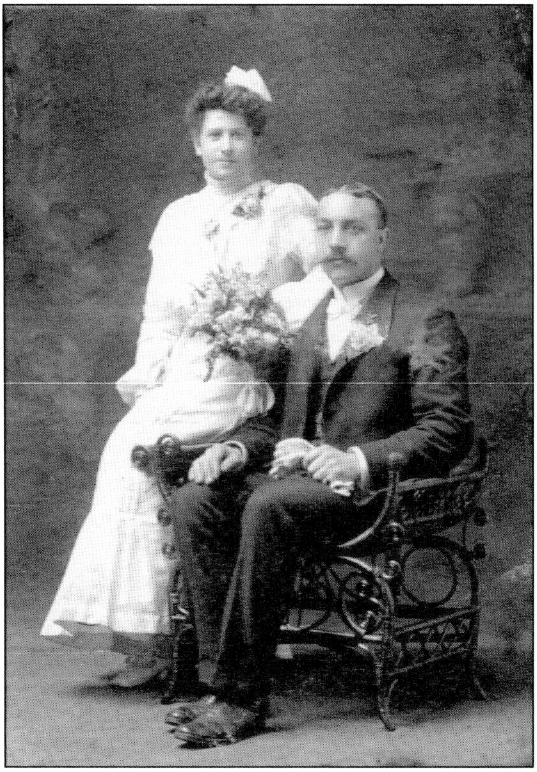

Franceszka Borowska and Stanislaw Galkowski are pictured during their engagement in 1902. Both were born in Rypin district, Plock province, Russian Poland, and were among the founders of Our Lady of Czestochowa Parish. They married in June 1906 and had seven children: Joseph, Helen, Charles, Phyllis, Theodore, Henry, and Eugene. The Galkowskis were active in the Polish Roman Catholic Union and several parish societies.

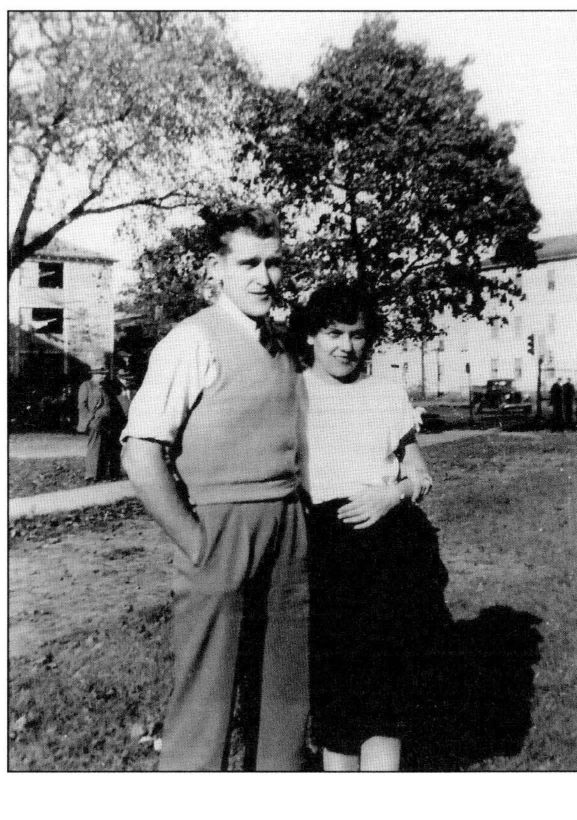

Daniel Lucas stands with his arm around his fiancée, Jane Prokopowicz, in Worcester's Crompton Park in 1946. They were married at Our Lady of Czestochowa Church in 1947. He served in the Worcester Police Department, retiring as a sergeant; she was a skilled seamstress and also worked at Astra Pharmaceuticals. They built a home on Harwich Street, where they raised children Mary Jane, Donald, and Nancy and hosted countless family gatherings.

Karolina Szymaszek and Wojciech Krawczyk were married on January 26, 1903, at St. Joseph's Church, Webster. He was born in Zdziarzec, northeast of Tarnow, Galicia. After their marriage, the couple moved to Lowell, where their four children, Louis, Mary, Bronislawa, and Aniela, were born. Karolina died in the influenza epidemic of 1918–1919; her widower remarried and moved to Lynn.

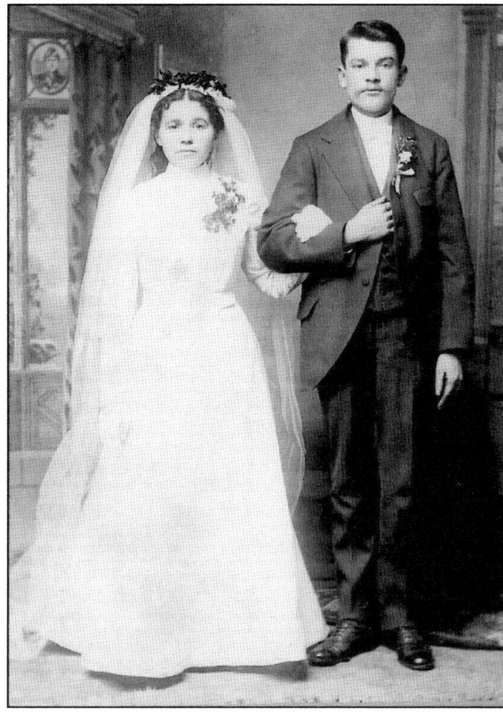

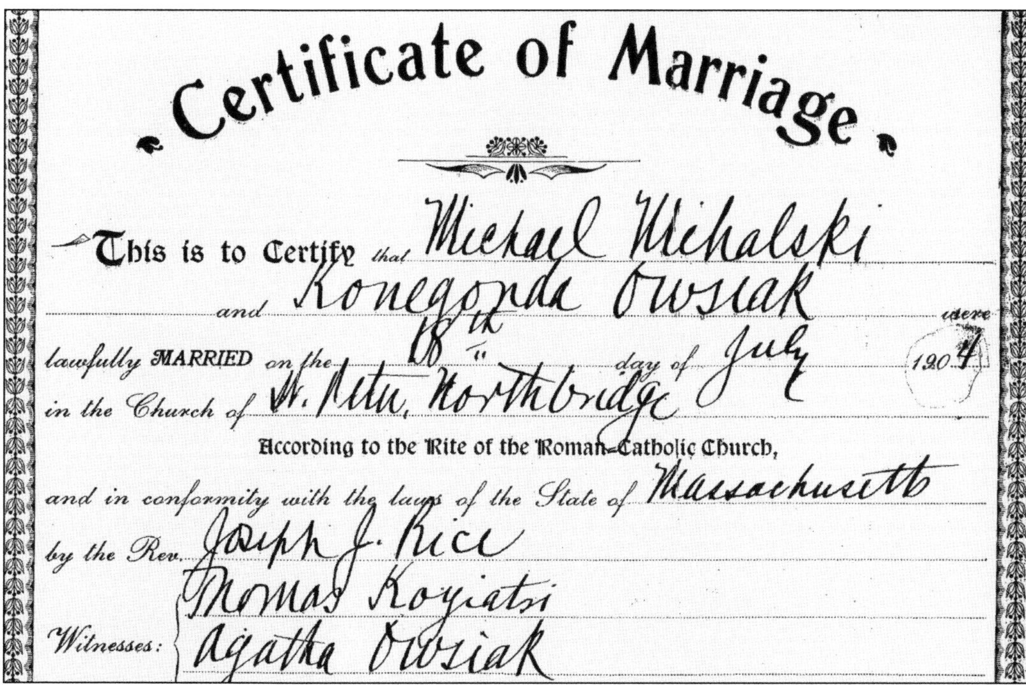

Certificate of Marriage

This is to Certify that Michael Michalski and Konegonda Owsiak were lawfully MARRIED on the 18th day of July 1904 in the Church of St. Peter, Northbridge According to the Rite of the Roman Catholic Church, and in conformity with the laws of the State of Massachusetts by the Rev. Joseph J. Rice

Witnesses: Thomas Koyiatsi, Agatha Owsiak

A marriage certificate issued by St. Peter's Church, Northbridge, confirms the July 18, 1904, wedding of Michael Michalski and Kunegunda Owsiak. According to newspaper reports, the Michalskis were the first Polish couple to be married at St. Peter's, which opened in January 1904. The bride was born in Warzyce, near Przemysl, and the groom in the Jaslo district of Tarnow, Galicia. They owned a farm on Spring Hill Avenue, Northbridge.

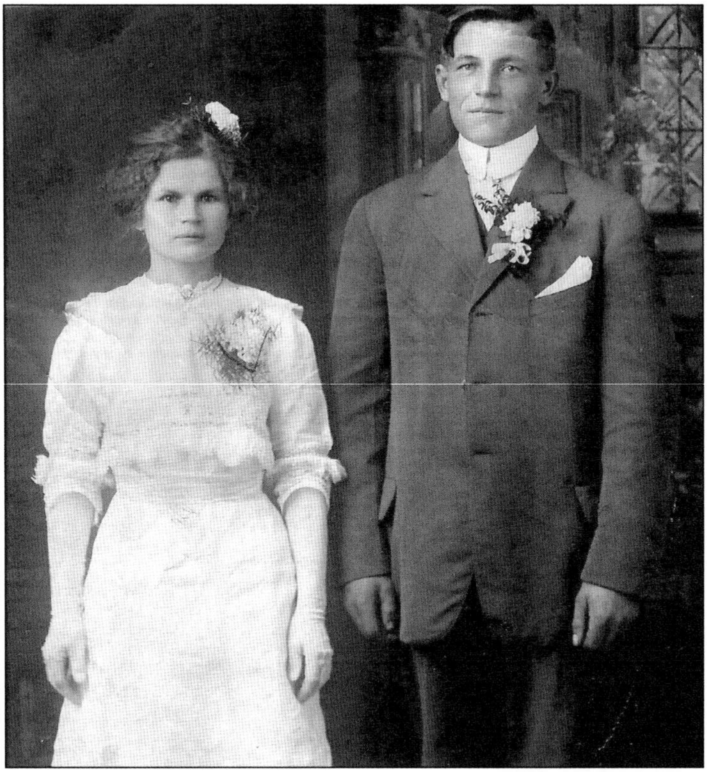

Catherine Chodor and Adam Repik, both immigrants from Galicia, appear to have been wedding attendants when this photograph was taken around 1912. They were married at St. Joseph's Church, Webster, in February 1914, and had six children: John, Theodosia, Karol (Charles), Bronislawa (Beatrice), Mary, and Antonia. The Repik family resided in Dudley. Adam Repik was employed at Stevens Linen and Anglo Fabrics and was active in Polish heritage organizations.

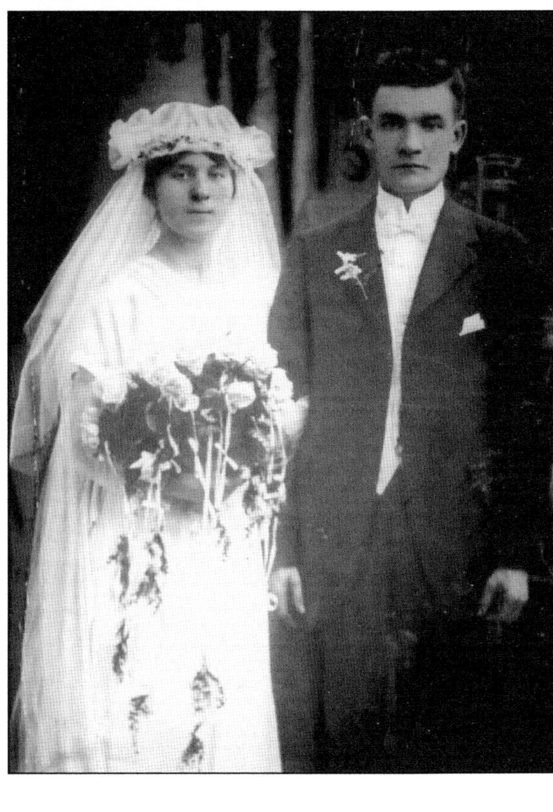

Joanna Dembczak, a Czestochowa native, and Stephen Milewski, born in Kalisz, married in 1917 at Our Lady of Czestochowa Church, Worcester. They lived on Suffield Street where two sons were born. In 1920, the Milewskis returned to Poland where they had three more children. In 1936, son Edmund returned to Worcester; the rest of the family remained in Poland. A baker at Town Talk Bread, Edmund lived on Wabash Avenue.

Wladyslaw Czabaj and Wiktorya Glista exchanged wedding vows in 1919 at St. Aloysius Church, Gilbertville. They lived on South Main Street, where they owned and operated Czabaj Market. He was born in 1899 in Tarnow; she was also born in Galicia, in 1898. In 1948, Matthew and Adryanna, two of their four children, built a new grocery store next door to the original market and operated it until 1997.

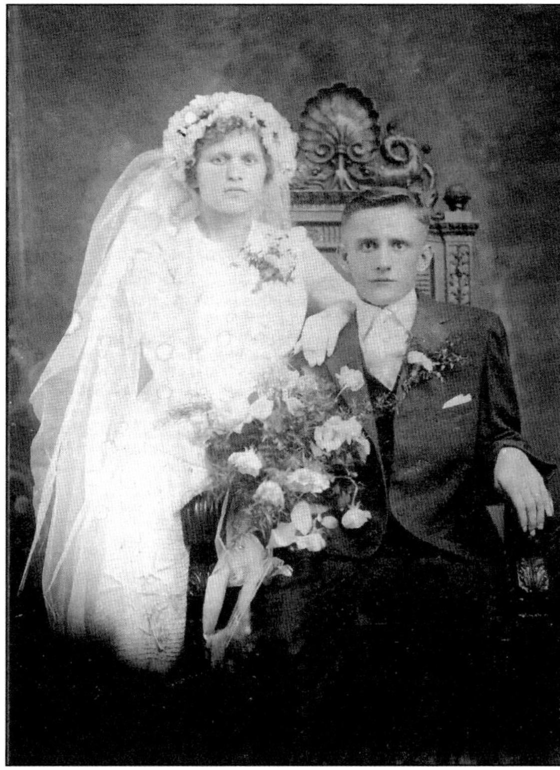

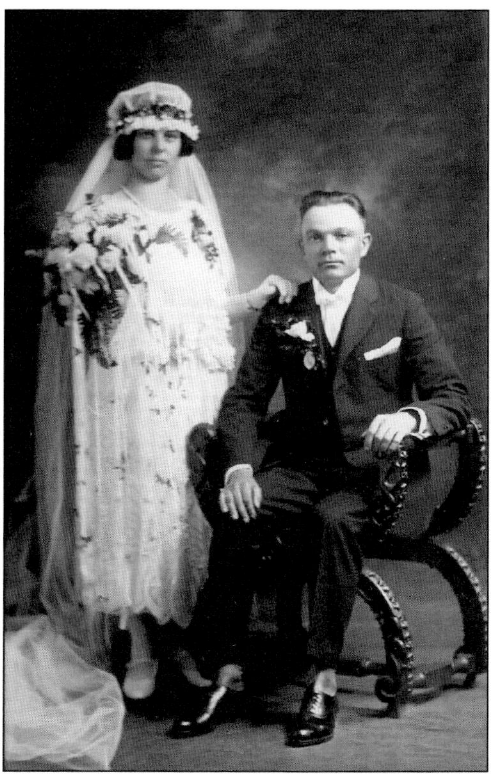

Zofia Linek and Tomasz Obara, who emigrated separately from Grodzisko in 1912, were married in 1923 at St. James Church, South Grafton. They lived on Farnum Street and had one daughter, Stasia. Before their marriage, Obara was a widower with five children, including a set of twins. When his first wife, Anna Piekos, became ill, she returned to Poland, leaving the twins with him.

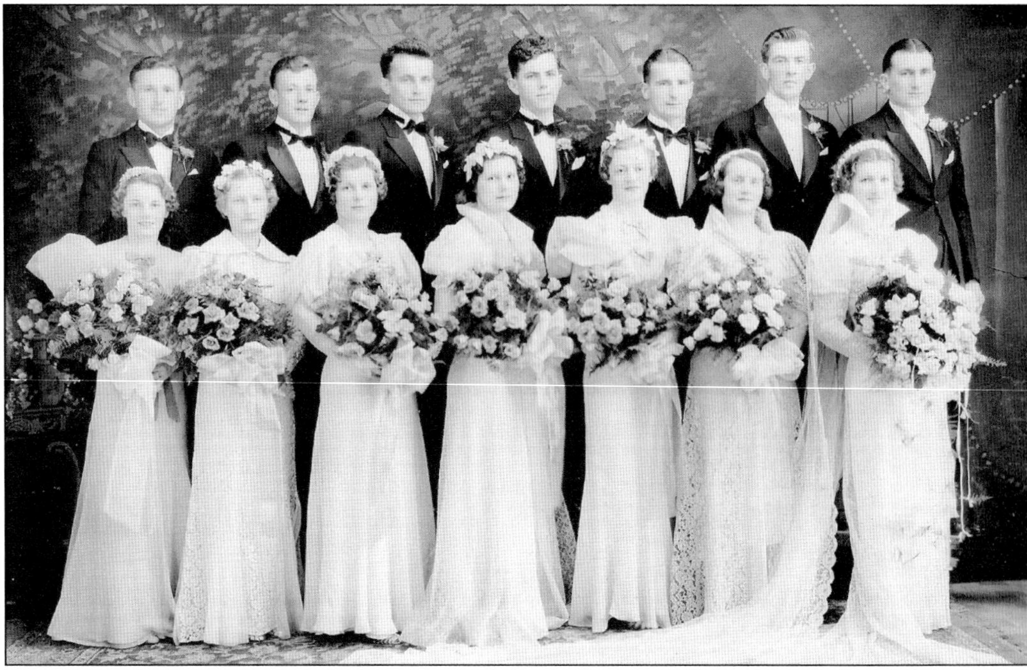

Anita Majka and Francis Wypych were married on June 26, 1937, at St. Aloysius Church, Gilbertville, with a dozen attendants in their wedding party. Identified in the first row are Josephine Kardas (third from right), Mary Wypych (second from right), and bride Anita Majka at far right. In the second row are Joseph Misiaszek (second from left); Steven Paydos (fourth); Matthew Majka, the bride's brother (second from right); and groom Francis Wypych at far right.

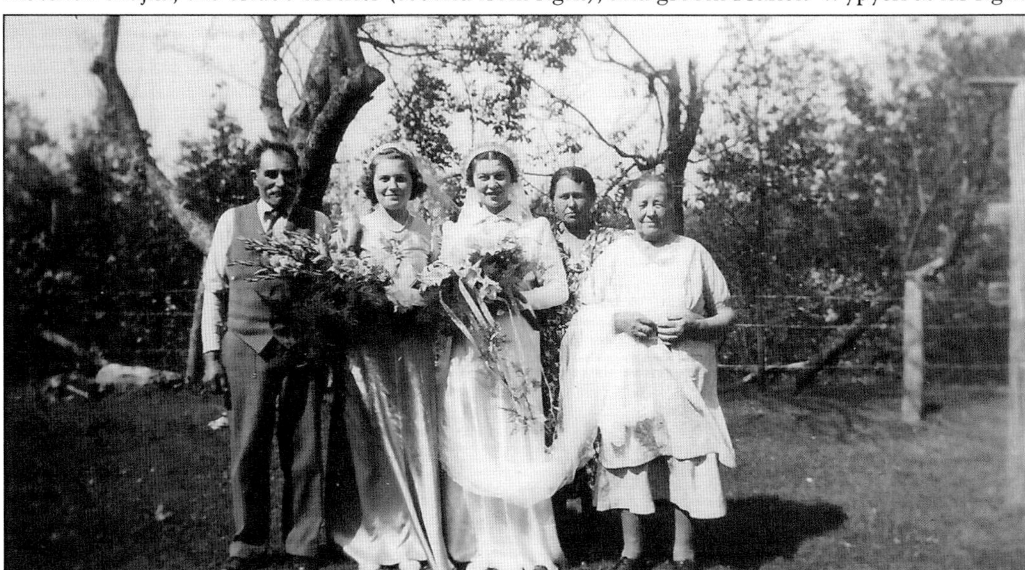

Sophie Makowski and Rudolph Rinfrette were married three days after the great New England hurricane of September 1938. Their reception was at the Makowski farm in Douglas, where a damaged barn and downed trees kept the bride's father, John, too busy to join in this photograph. From left to right are the bride's grandfather Antoni Sadowski; sister Genevieve Makowski; Sophie Rinfrette; mother Alexandra Makowski; and grandmother Josephine Sadowski.

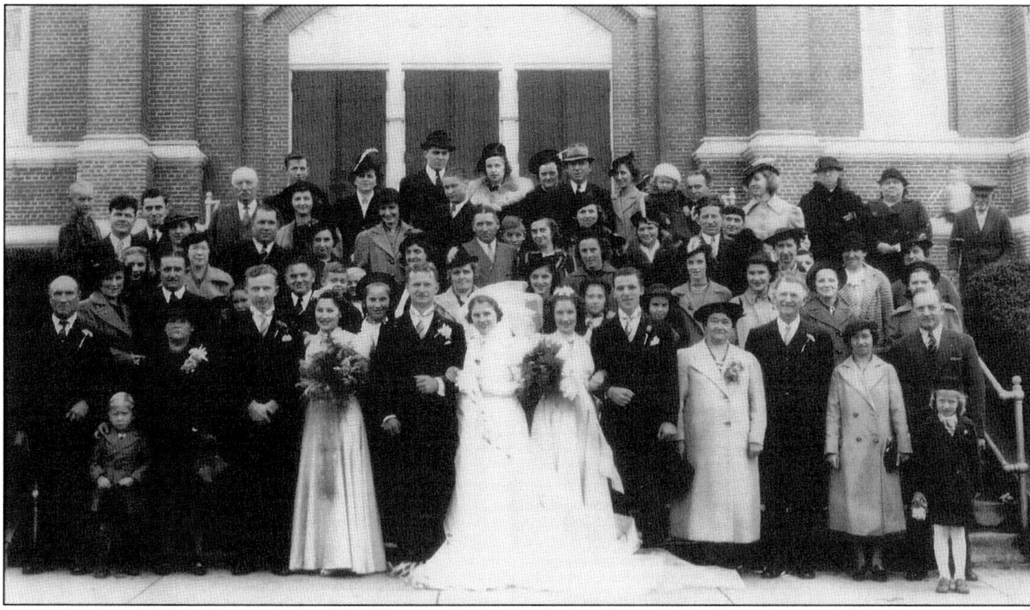

Family and friends surround Theodore Nawrocki and Bernice Pikora after their 1939 wedding at St. Joseph's Church, Webster. From left to right are (first row) John Pikora, Joseph Pikora Jr., Annie Pikora, Walter Nawrocki, Pearl Pikora, the bridal couple, Rose Pikora, Matthew McManus, Hattie Nawrocki, Victor Nawrocki, Annie Kozlowski, Jack Kozlowski, and unidentified. Behind are members of the Pikora, Nawrocki, Radula, Suchocki, Piniarski, Panek, Patrowicz, Prokopowicz, Ceppetelli, Sager, Pluta, Angelo, Duval, Budzinski, Milas, and Heneault families.

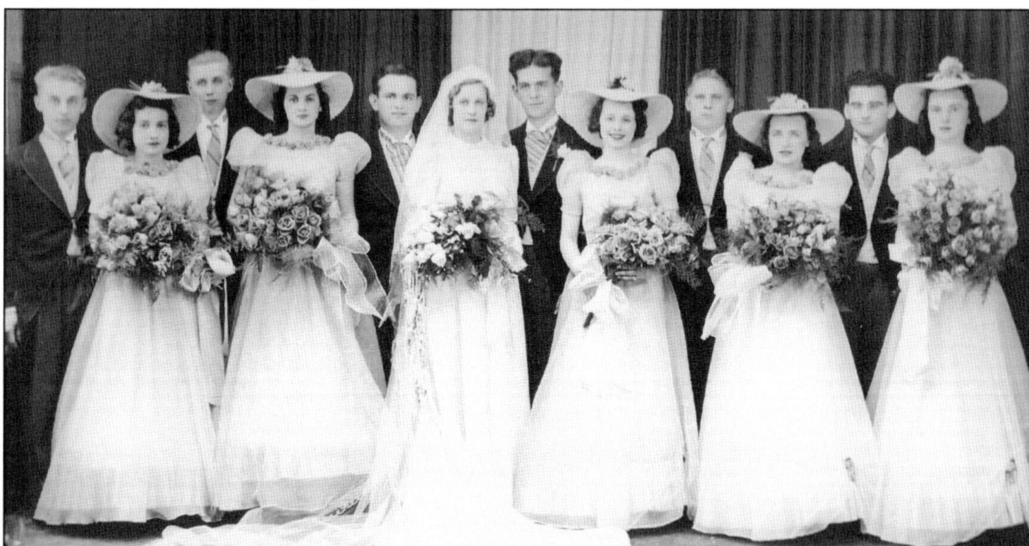

Joseph Baniukiewicz and Jennie Brodzik were married on April 29, 1939, at Our Lady of Czestochowa Church, Worcester. From left to right are Peter Piascik, the groom's cousin; unidentified; Costay Brodzik, the bride's brother; Helen Baniukiewicz, the groom's cousin; Stanley Baniukiewicz, the groom's brother and best man; Jennie and Joseph Baniukiewicz; Theresa Gutkoski, the maid of honor; Stanley Soliwoda, the bride's cousin; Irene Piascik and Tadeusz Baniukiewicz, the groom's cousins; and unidentified.

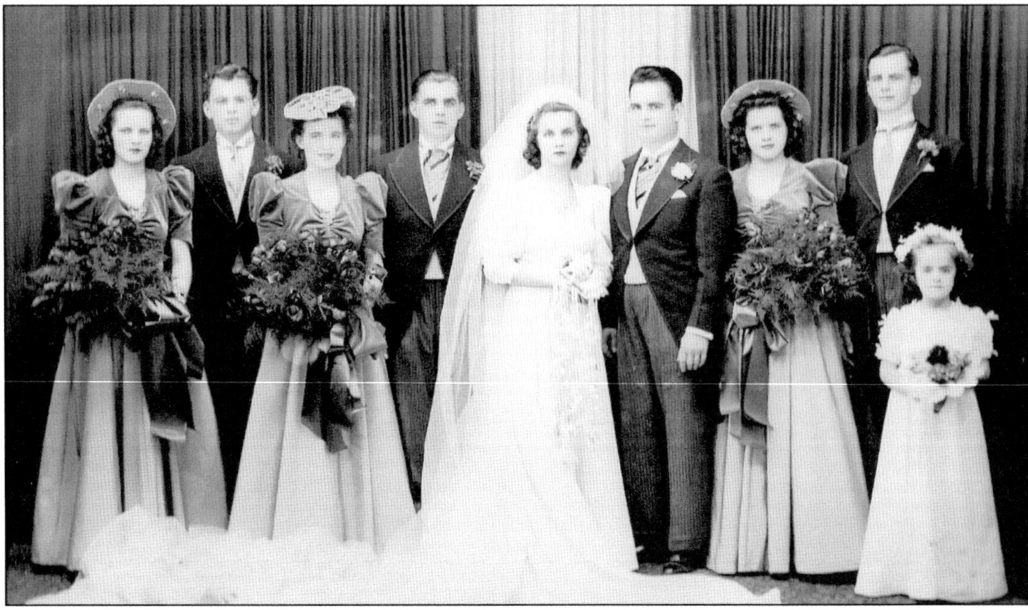

In 1941, Stanley Baniukiewicz and Cecelia Siminski were married at Our Lady of Czestochowa Church, Worcester. Pictured from left to right are Stella Kasprzak, the bride's cousin; Charles Baniukiewicz, the groom's cousin; Irene Piascik, the groom's cousin and maid of honor; Peter Siminski, the bride's brother and best man; the bridal couple; Rose Siminski, the bride's sister; Eugene Baniukiewicz, the groom's brother; and Theresa Baniukiewicz, the groom's sister and flower girl.

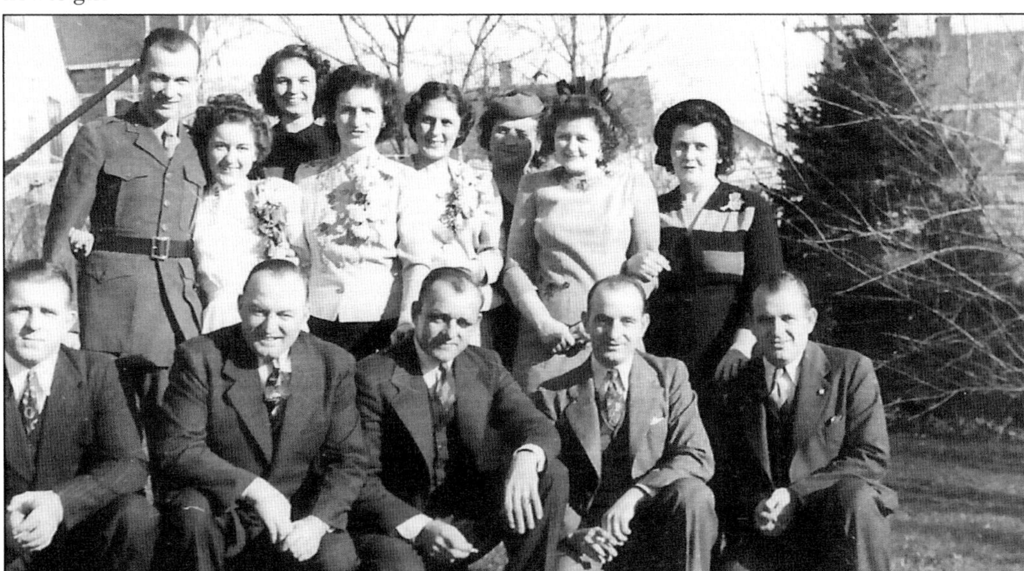

The sun shines on the Kapulka siblings and their spouses after a wedding in Worcester in November 1945. From left to right are (first row) Joseph Kapulka, George McKeon, Michael Kapulka, John Kapulka, and Francis Kapulka; (second row) groom Richard Moffett, bride Theresa Kapulka, Mary Kapulka, Dorothy Moore Kapulka, Julia Kapulka McKeon, Alice Vacca Kapulka, Violet Smith Kapulka, and Helen Duffy Kapulka. Parents George and Anna Barna Kapulka died in the 1930s.

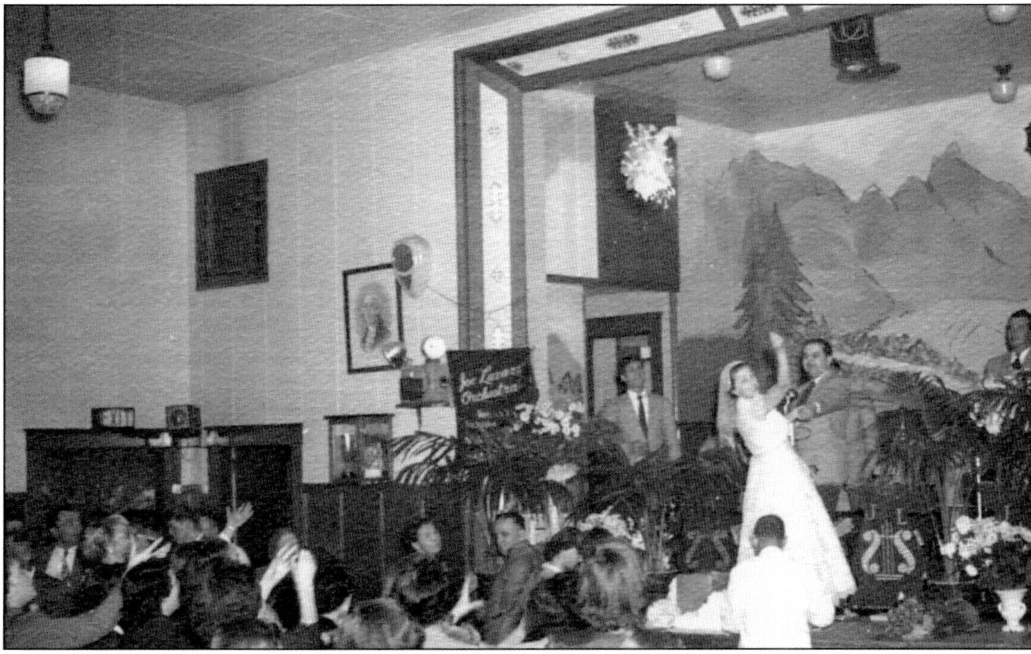

Single women in the crowd press forward in hopes of catching the bouquet tossed by new bride Phyllis Smyth during a wedding reception at the Polish American Social and Civic Corporation hall in Uxbridge. Phyllis Augusciak and Stanley A. Smyth III were married in St. Mary's Church, Uxbridge, on October 14, 1950. A popular site for celebrations, the hall is a landmark in the town's Polish Hecla Street neighborhood.

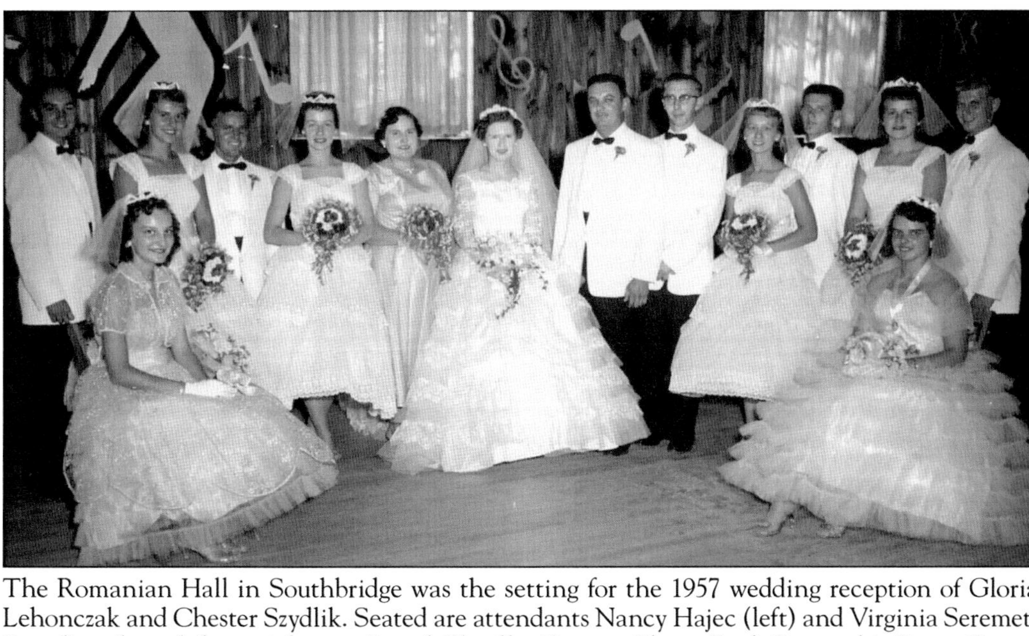

The Romanian Hall in Southbridge was the setting for the 1957 wedding reception of Gloria Lehonczak and Chester Szydlik. Seated are attendants Nancy Hajec (left) and Virginia Seremet. Standing from left to right are Raoul Plouffe, Norma Ohop, Fred Czyzewski, Betty Canty, Dorothy Lehonczak, the bride and groom, Joseph Lehonczak, Shirley Szydlik, Joseph Barys, Joan Berthume, and Ed Zelazo.

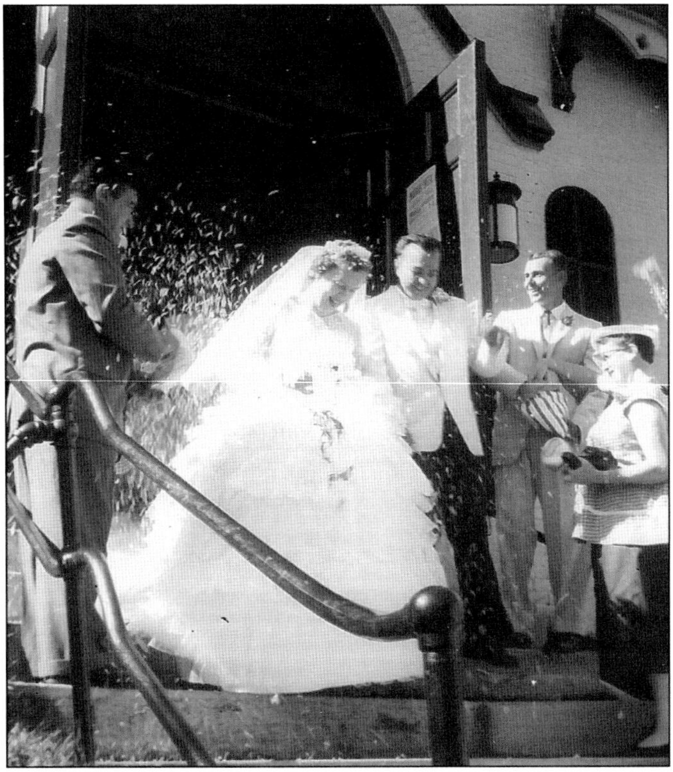

Wedding guests toss confetti over Helen Jogis and John Miarecki as they exit St. Aloysius Church, Gilbertville, after their August 1958 marriage. The Miareckis resided on Birch Street and had three daughters. She was a screen printer at Silk Screen Service Company, Ware. He had served in the Korean War as a staff sergeant in the U.S. Army.

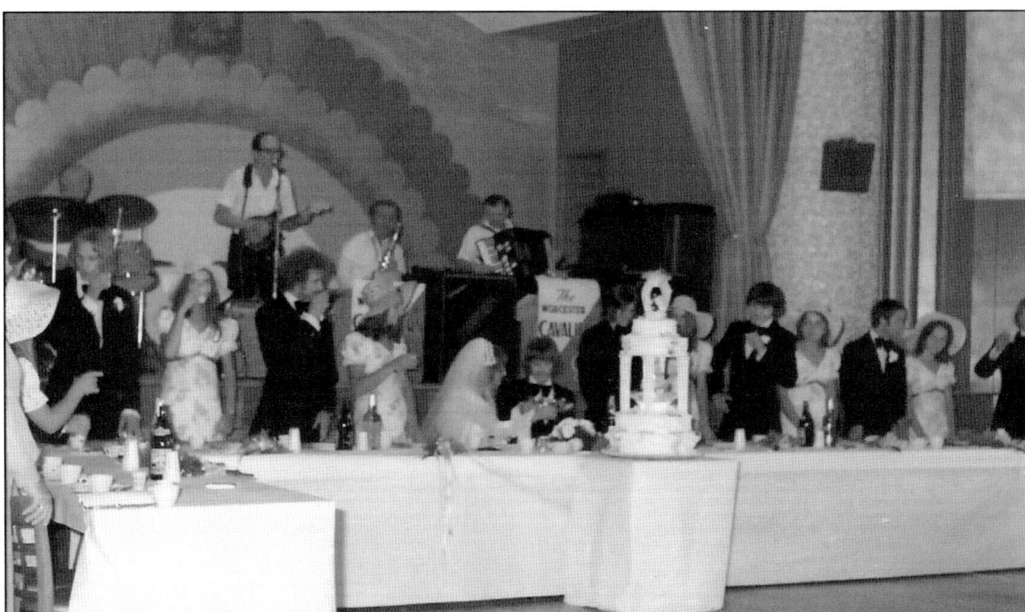

Members of the wedding party toast bride Jolanta Kozaczka and groom Stanley Sobiech (both seated at center) at a reception held at the White Eagle Hall in Worcester in 1974. Pictured from left to right are Leszek Snopko, Janet Shouris, Louie Jachimczyk, Bozena Kozaczka, the bride and groom, Jan Sobiech, Janina Sobiech, Zbiszek Wesolowski, Anna Swieszkowski, Andrzej Kozaczka, Halina Sawicki, and Roman Sobiech. On stage are the Worcester Cavaliers.

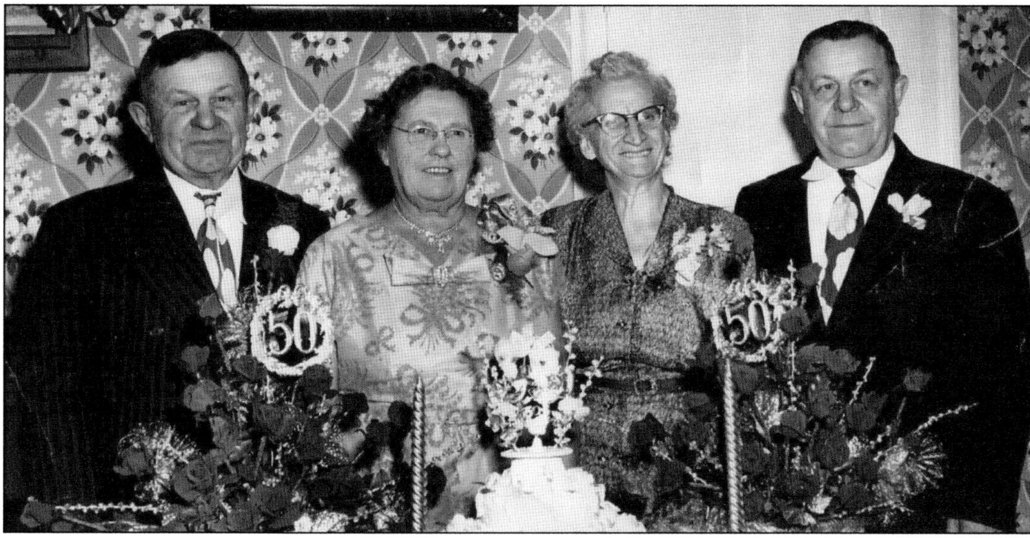

John and Alexandra Sadowski Makowski (couple at left) celebrated their 50th wedding anniversary in 1960 with a reception at Sokol Hall in Douglas, attended by their 10 children, 30 grandchildren, and 3 great-grandchildren. The Makowskis were married in Providence, Rhode Island, in February 1910 and moved to Douglas in 1918. Shown with them are John's sister-in-law and brother, Stella Kacinski Makowski and Michael Makowski.

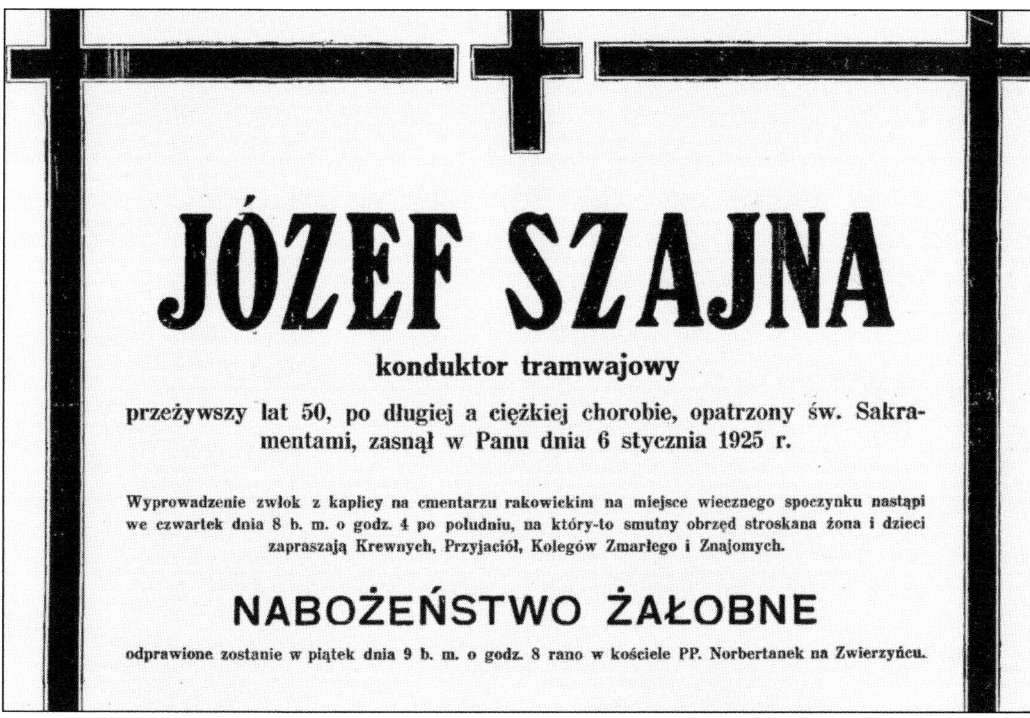

JÓZEF SZAJNA

konduktor tramwajowy

przeżywszy lat 50, po długiej a ciężkiej chorobie, opatrzony św. Sakramentami, zasnął w Panu dnia 6 stycznia 1925 r.

Wyprowadzenie zwłok z kaplicy na cmentarzu rakowickim na miejsce wiecznego spoczynku nastąpi we czwartek dnia 8 b. m. o godz. 4 po południu, na który-to smutny obrzęd stroskana żona i dzieci zapraszają Krewnych, Przyjaciół, Kolegów Zmarłego i Znajomych.

NABOŻEŃSTWO ŻAŁOBNE

odprawione zostanie w piątek dnia 9 b. m. o godz. 8 rano w kościele PP. Norbertanek na Zwierzyńcu.

This *klepsydra*, a traditional Polish poster used to publicly announce a death, invites friends and relatives to the funeral services of Jozef Szajna in Krakow. It reports that Szajna, 50, a tram conductor, died on January 6, 1925, after a long, difficult illness, and was to be buried at historic Rakowicki Cemetery. Family in Poland sent a copy of the klepsydra to Jozef's youngest brother, Antoni Szajna, in South Grafton.

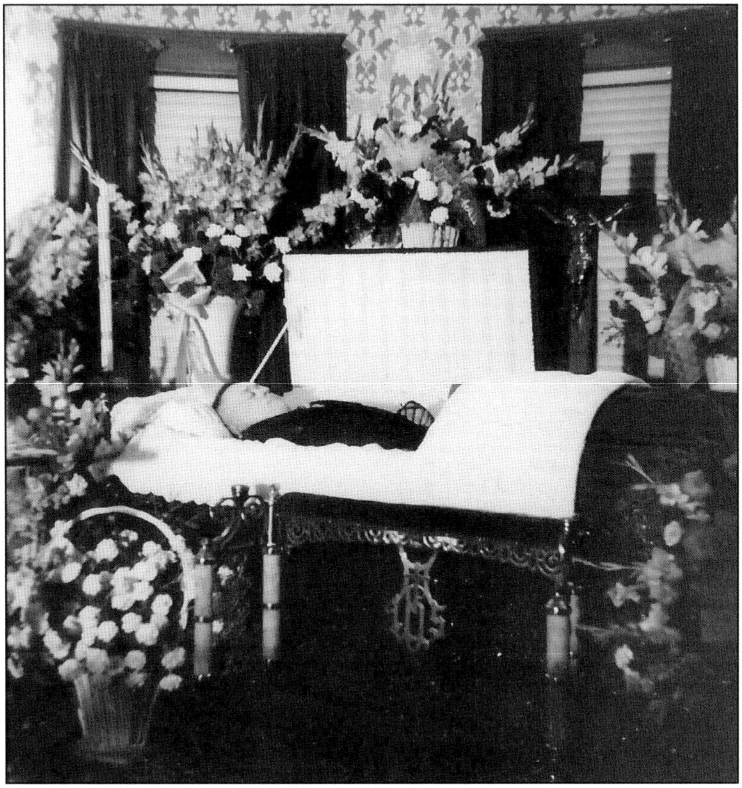

A home wake in Worcester in 1951 shows Julius Prokopowicz on view in an open coffin. Candles, crucifixes, and floral arrangements fill the parlor of the family's home in a Millbury Street three-decker. The funeral Mass was held at Our Lady of Czestochowa Church. Burial at Notre Dame Cemetery was arranged by funeral director Isador Mikoloski. Alexander Jozefowski and Lucian and Henry Karolkiewicz operated Worcester's other Polish funeral homes.

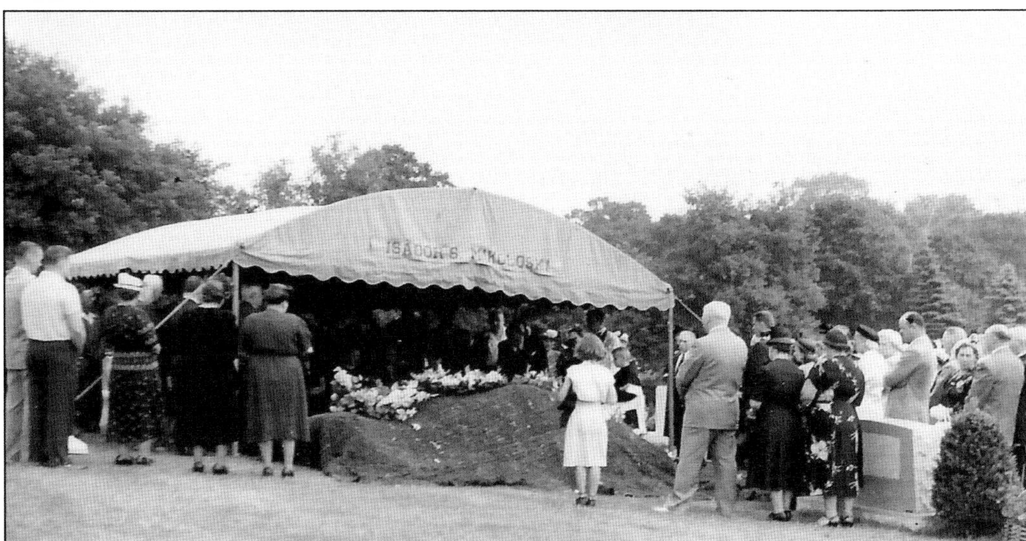

A tent shields mourners from the weather during burial services for Julius Prokopowicz at Notre Dame Cemetery, Worcester, in July 1951. Notre Dame and St. John's Cemeteries serve the city's ethnically diverse Catholics. St. Joseph's Parish in Webster established the first Polish cemetery in central Massachusetts, purchasing land in 1889. Worcester Diocese has two other Polish cemeteries: St. Joseph's, Gardner, developed in 1933, and St. Hedwig's, Southbridge, established in 1962.

Four

FAMILIES

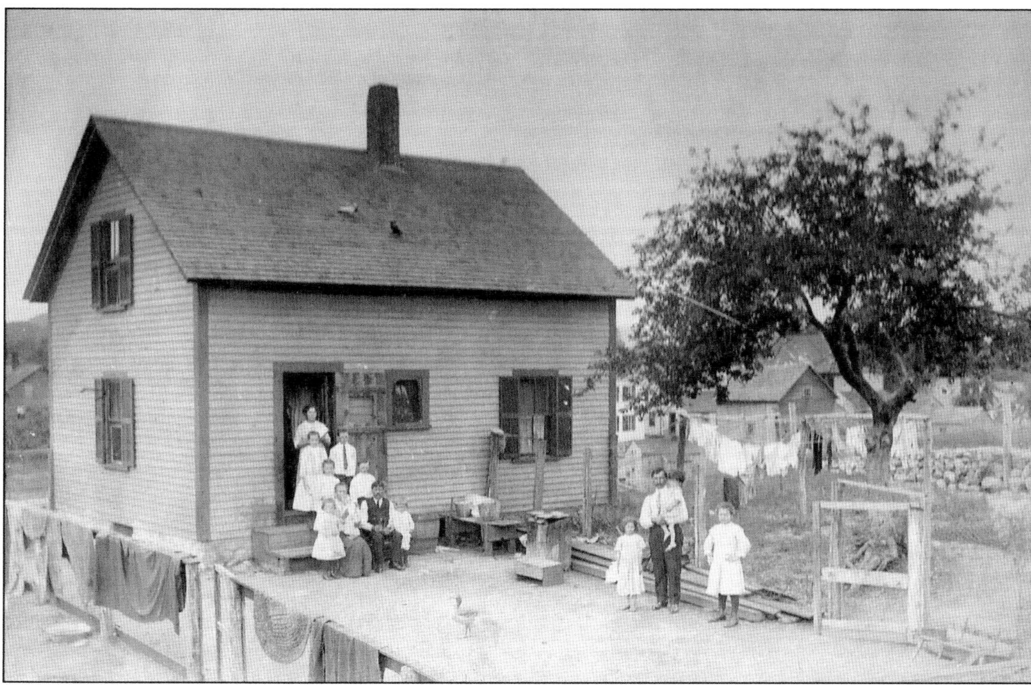

The Planeta and Gancarz families stand outside the Planeta home in West Warren in 1914. In the doorway are the Planetas, from left to right, (first row) Emily, Salomea holding baby Cecilia, Jacub, and Stephen; (second row) Mary and Walter; (third row) Sophie and Michael. Magda ?, a catechism teacher, stands behind them. Standing by the fence are (from left to right) Emily, Aloysius holding Anna, and Josephine Gancarz.

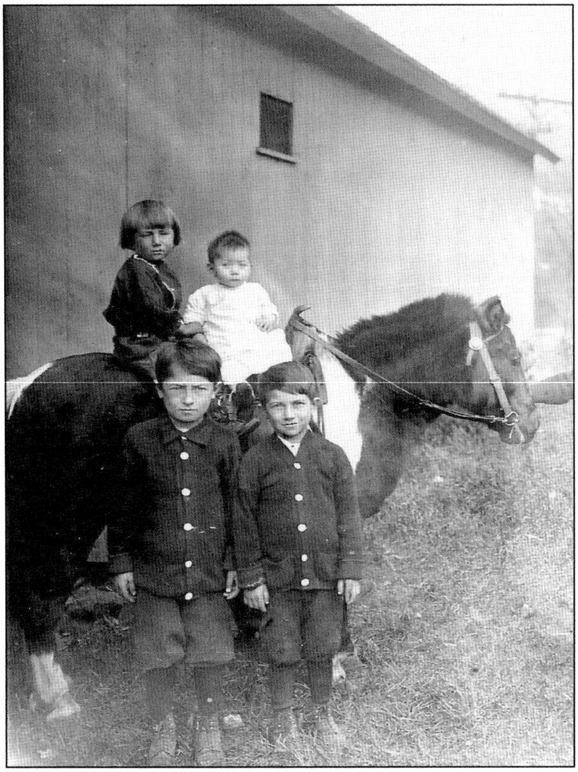

The children of Peter and Mary Pajdos Wypych pose with a pony around 1912. Standing are sons Michael (left) and John; seated are Frank (left) and baby Helen. The Wypychs resided on Bridge Street, near a covered bridge, in the "Patch," Gilbertville's Polish immigrant neighborhood. In this era, itinerant photographers with ponies as live props walked house to house, offering their services for $1 or so.

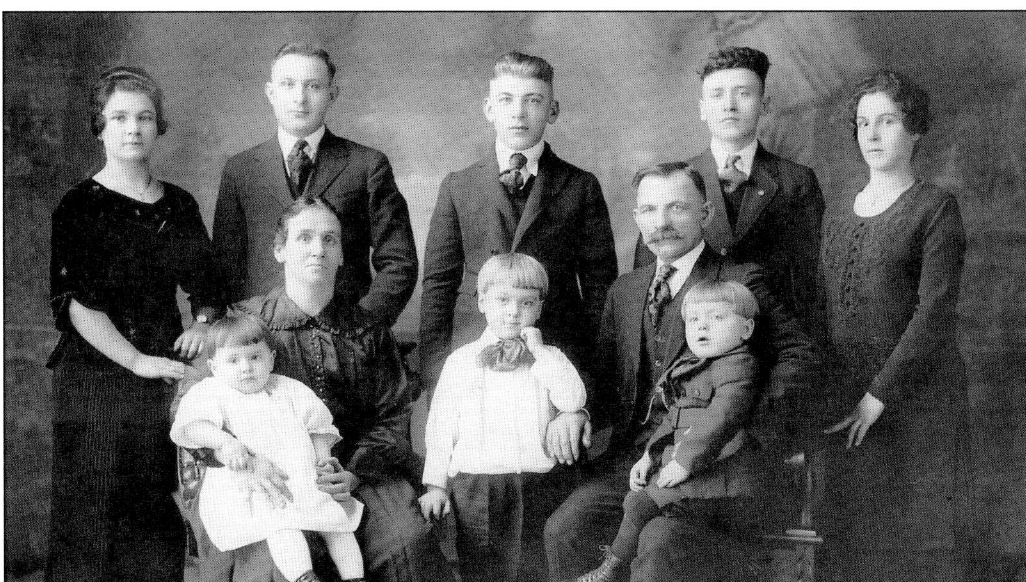

Salomea and Joseph Saletnik (seated) made several trips from Tarnow, Galicia, to establish their three adult children in America. Typifying "chain migration," the Saletniks chose Southbridge because of family and friends already there. Joining the couple in this 1921 photograph are, from left to right, (first row) grandchildren Stella, Henry, and Stephen Skowron; (second row) Aniela Saletnik and husband Stanislaw Stoklosa; John Saletnik; and Vincent and Mary Saletnik Skowron.

Adam and Julia Kawecki Sieniawski emigrated from the Ulanow area of Galicia around 1913 and settled in Worcester. The Sieniawskis were members of the Polish Political Independent Club, Polish National Alliance, and White Eagle Association; Julia also belonged to Zwiazek Polek and St. Ann's Sodality of Our Lady of Czestochowa Parish. Adam was a painting contractor, an occupation shared by his son Andrew.

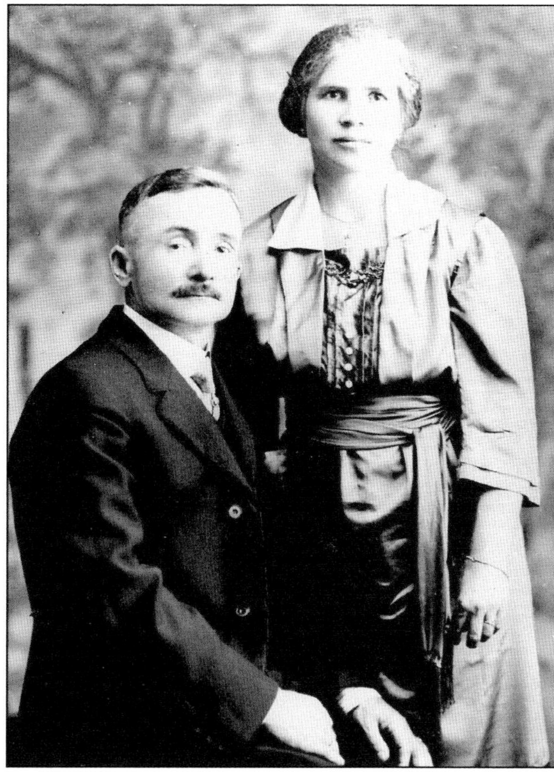

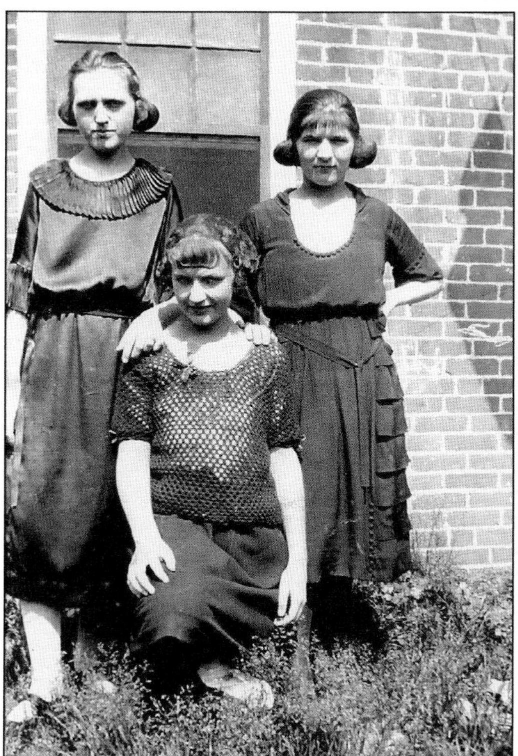

Looking stylish and serious are three young women who grew up in Webster and Dudley. From left to right are Frances Gryszkiewicz Sharameta, Martha Borus, and Anna Kubarski. The daughter of Paul and Josephine Pobrowski Gryszkiewicz, Frances married Charles Sharameta in 1918. The couple lived in Worcester and worked as cooks; he opened Charles Lunch on Millbury Street in 1923.

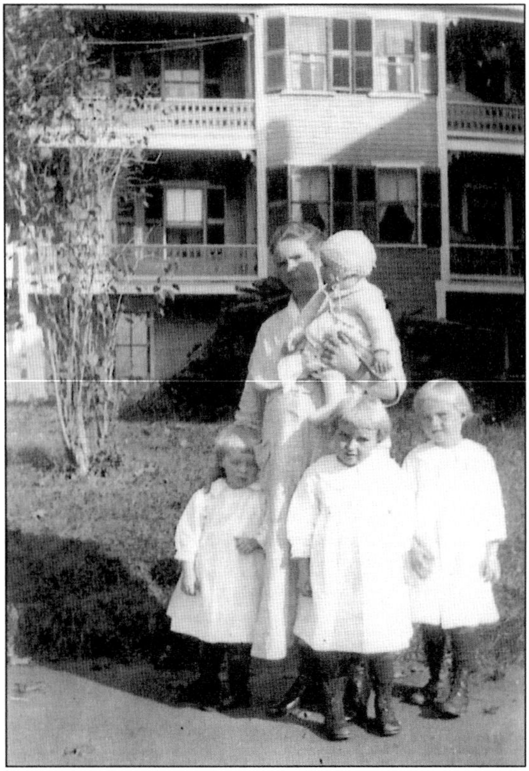

Felicia Dzieniszewicz Nawrocki holds her infant son Walter in this 1923 photograph while her three daughters stand in front. From left to right are Alice, Harriet, and Johanna. The family of Wladyslaw and Felicia Nawrocki resided at 266 High Street, Webster. He worked as a shearer for American Woolen Company.

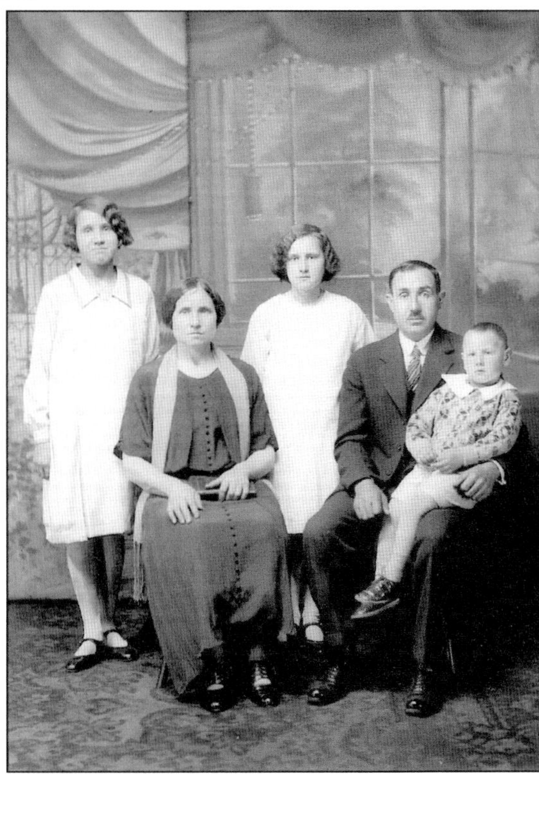

The Janczukowicz family, who resided on Worcester's Vernon Hill, poses for a studio portrait around 1926. Seated are Teofila and Joseph, holding their son Chester; standing are their daughters Josephine (left) and Mary. Joseph Janczukowicz and Teofila Klewiec were both born in Wilno province, Russian Poland, and emigrated in 1912. He worked as a heat treater at Reed and Prince Manufacturing Company and was a member of Polish National Alliance Lodge 758.

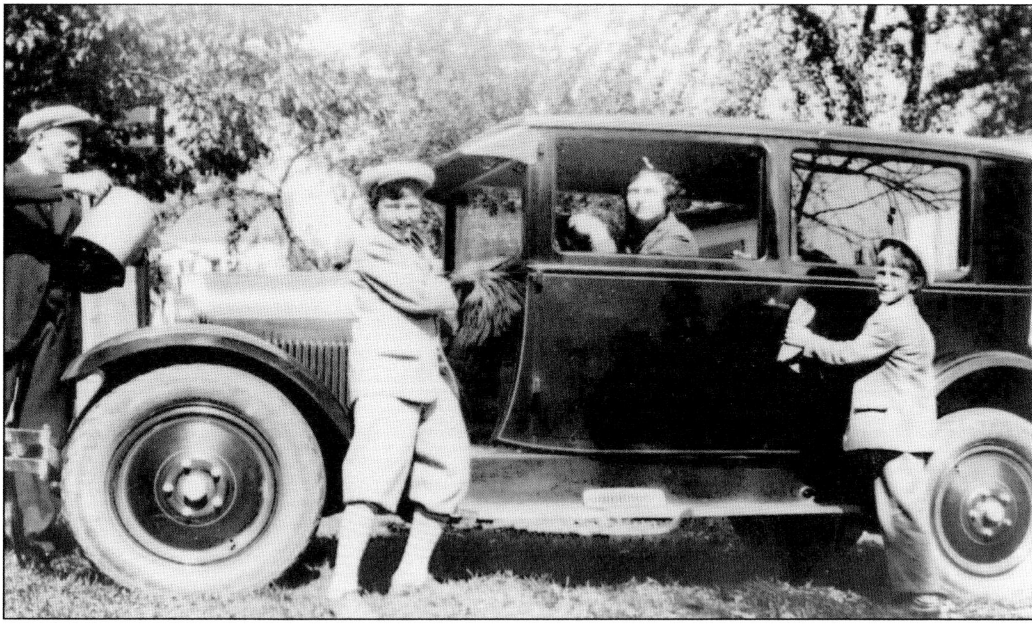

Anthony Michniewicz tends to the family's first new car, a 1925 Dodge that cost about $500, while his wife, Anna Narkevicius Michniewicz, sits in the driver's seat. Sons Anthony (left) and Stanley give the car a shine. The 1930 census lists the family living on Pleasant Street in Gardner, with both parents working at a chair factory. He was a Polish immigrant from the Wilno area, and she was Lithuanian.

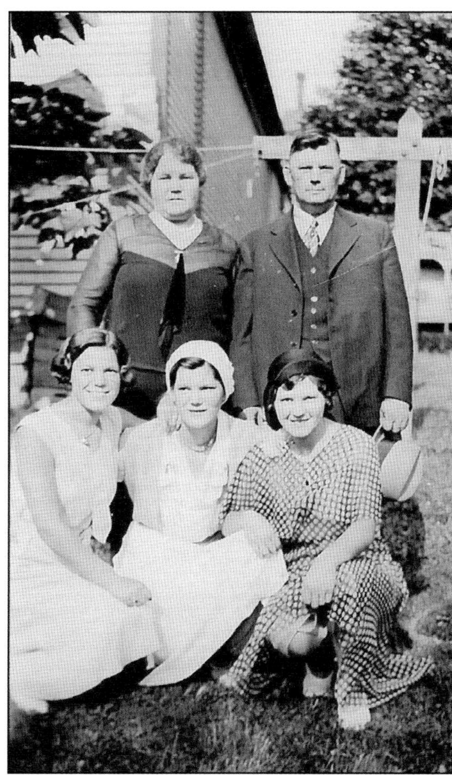

Kneeling from left to right are Stella, Elizabeth, and Nellie Bonk, around 1924. Standing proudly behind them are their parents, Catherine and John Bonk of Gardner. Stella and Nellie Bonk both played sports at Gardner High School. Nellie was awarded hockey and basketball numbers, and Stella once scored 30 points in a Gardner High School basketball victory over Orange High School.

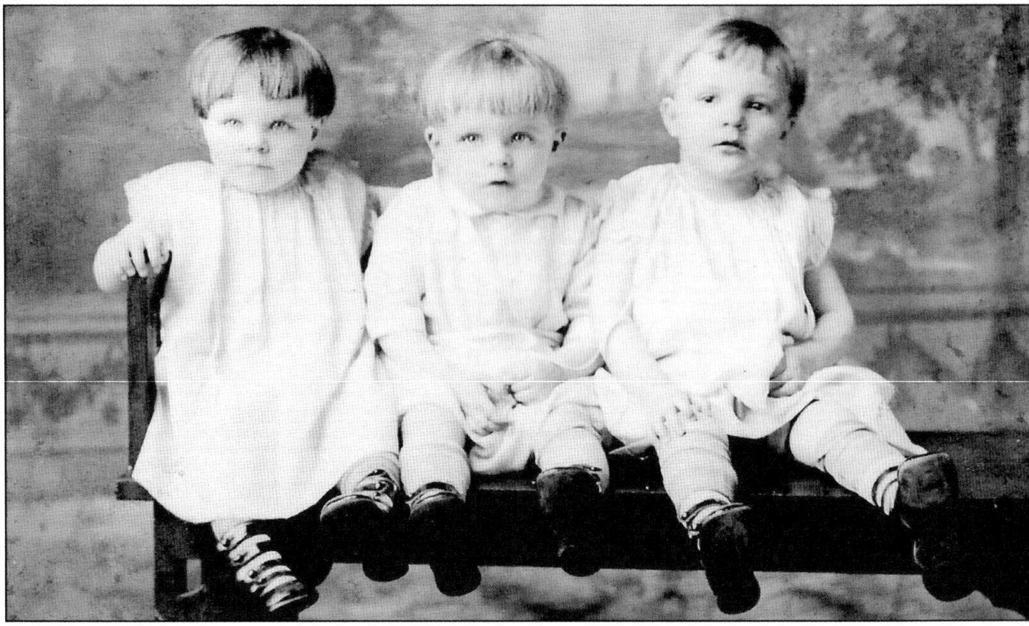

The first triplets born in the Webster-Dudley area were, seated from left to right, Anna, Joseph, and Marie Sielawa, born on April 29, 1927, to Ignatius and Helen Kozlowski Wisniewski Sielawa. When the children were a year old, the family moved to a newly built home at 6 Sixth Avenue, Dudley. The triplets graduated from St. Joseph's School and Bartlett High School and worked at local companies.

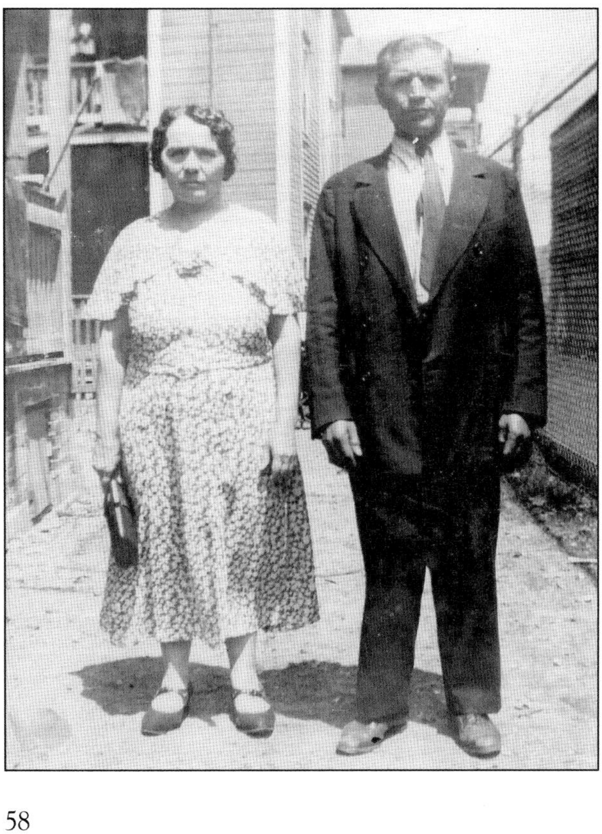

Mary Polka and Felix Hmura stand on Lamartine Street in Worcester's Polish "Island" neighborhood around 1933. At right is Parker Manufacturing Company. Felix worked at Standard Foundry and was also a carpenter. The Hmuras were the parents of six children: Walter, Francis, Julia, Helen, Ann, and Anthony. Late in life, Mary received a key to the city from Mayor Sara Robertson at a Polish Lithuanian ethnic festival at Crompton Park.

Stanislawa Ruscik (left) and her husband, Peter Budnik, enjoy a visit with her sister Stefania Ruscik Prokopowicz of Worcester at their Spencer farm in 1939. The Budniks were married around 1915 and had seven children: Jean, Stanley, Mary, Helen, Joseph, Josephine, and Edward. They lived in Worcester for several years before buying the farm. The Ruscik sisters were born in Gierniki in Szczuczyn parish, east of Grodno in Russian Poland.

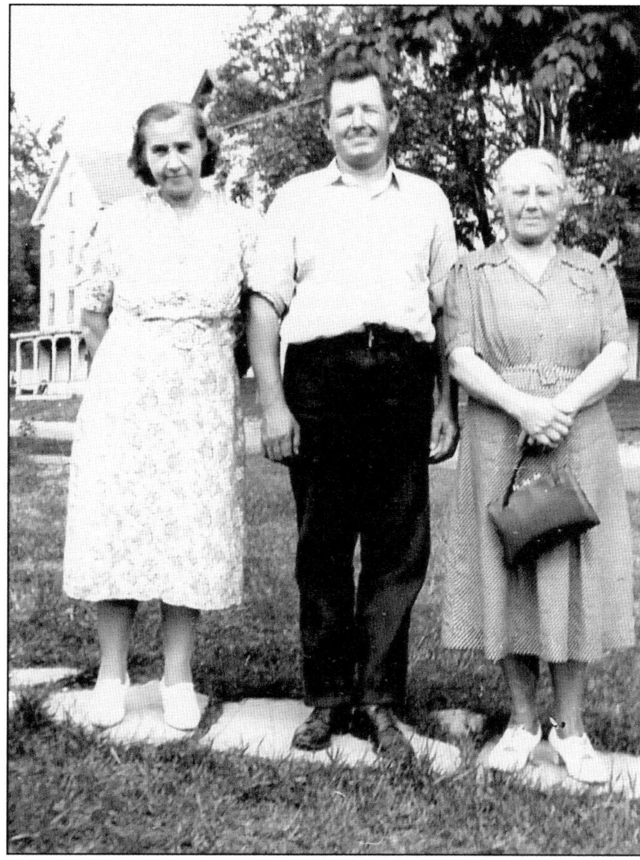

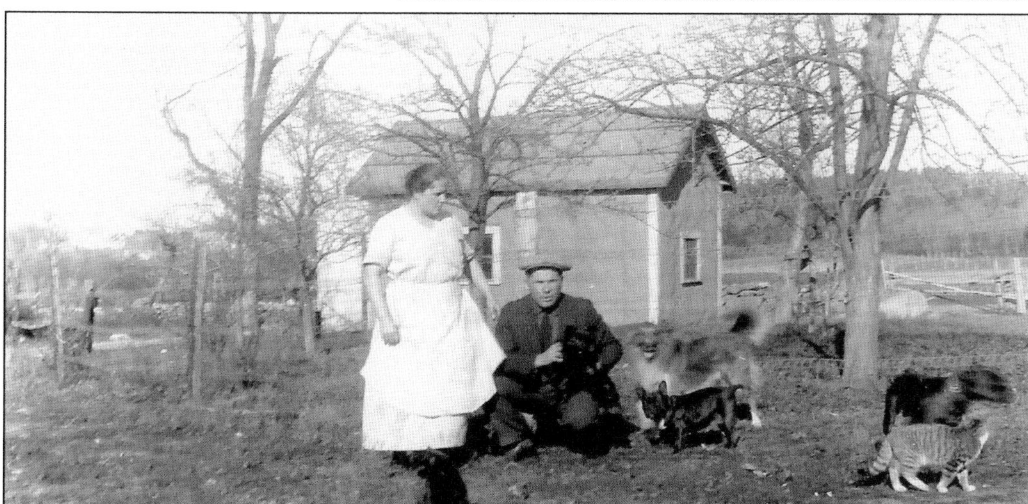

Pets mill around Mary Piekos and her husband, Antoni Szajna, at their home in the Farnumsville section of South Grafton. Like many Poles who settled there in the early 1900s, the Szajnas were natives of Galicia. They worked as weavers at a local cotton mill before purchasing property on Providence Road, where they farmed and operated the Klondike Inn. After Mary died in the 1930s, Antoni married Jane Socha.

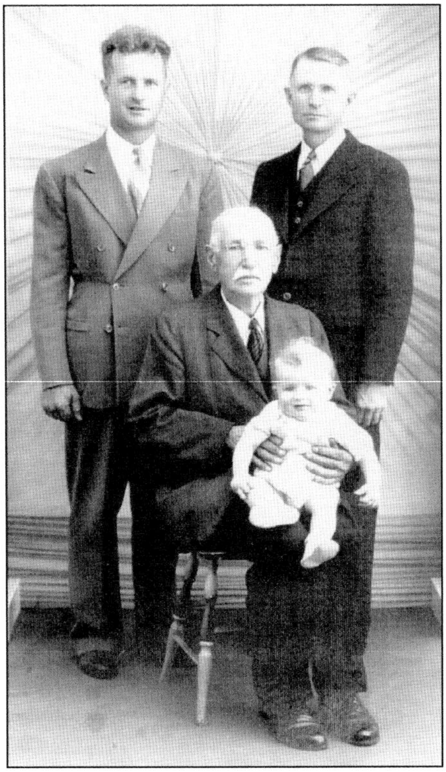

Four generations of first sons in the Nawrocki family of Webster-Dudley pose together in 1941. Seated is Wladyslaw Nawrocki, holding his great-grandson Richard Nawrocki. Standing are his grandson Theodore Nawrocki (left) and son Victor Nawrocki. The Nawrockis immigrated from the Poznan area of German Poland around 1892. Wladyslaw and Victor both worked as spinners in a woolen mill. Theodore worked as a bus driver.

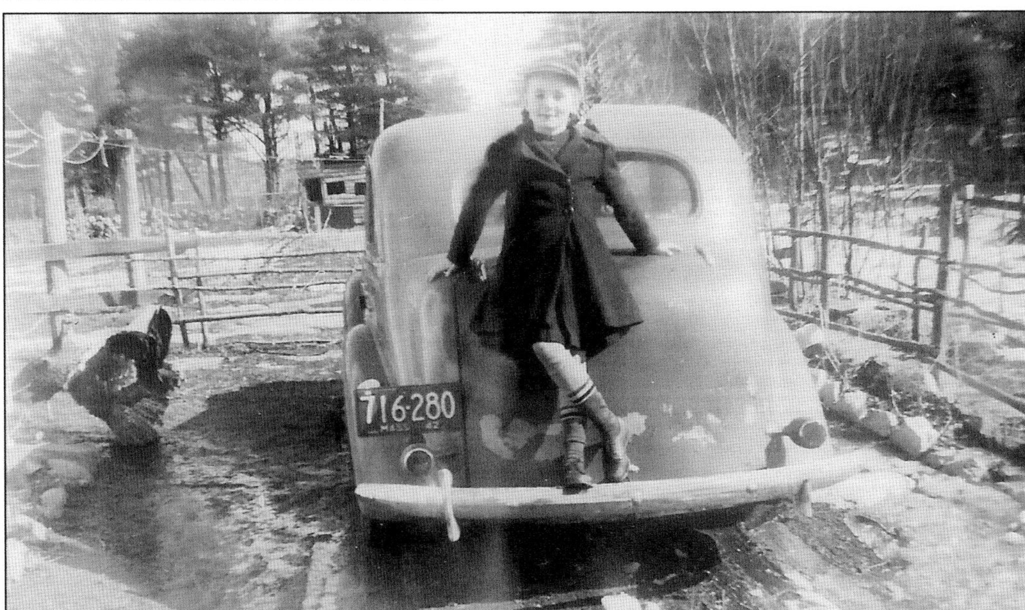

Rita Mosczynski perches on a car bumper on the family farm in Douglas in 1942. The youngest of five children of Konstanty and Gabryela Mosczynski, she grew up to graduate from Douglas High School and Boston College. Rita taught at Park Elementary School, Webster, for over three decades. She also enjoyed farming—a love she passed on to her daughter Susan, who runs the family farm today.

Leopold and Helen Pieniazek Matyszczyk and their children are pictured at their Sterling Street home in Worcester in 1955. In front, from left to right, are daughters Elaine and Mary Ann, Helen holding son Richard, and son Paul. Standing behind are son Lee (left) and Leopold. Leopold was a cost accountant at U.S. Steel Corporation, Worcester, and Helen worked at Coughlin Electric Company on Main Street.

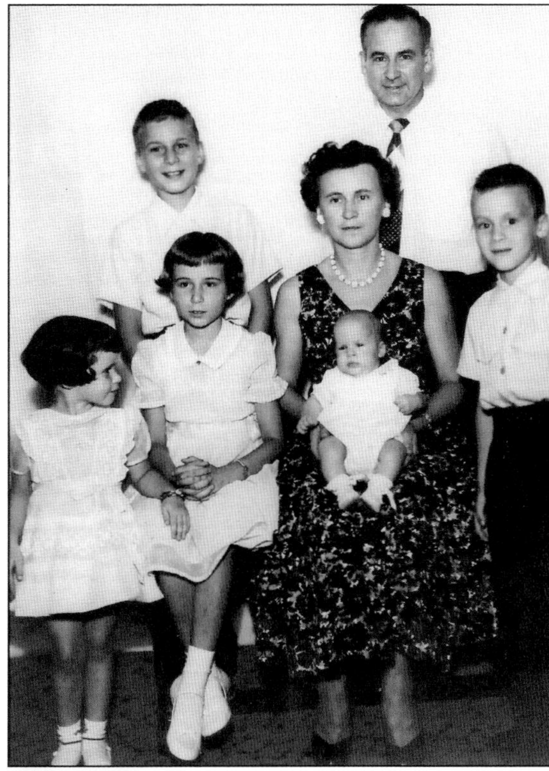

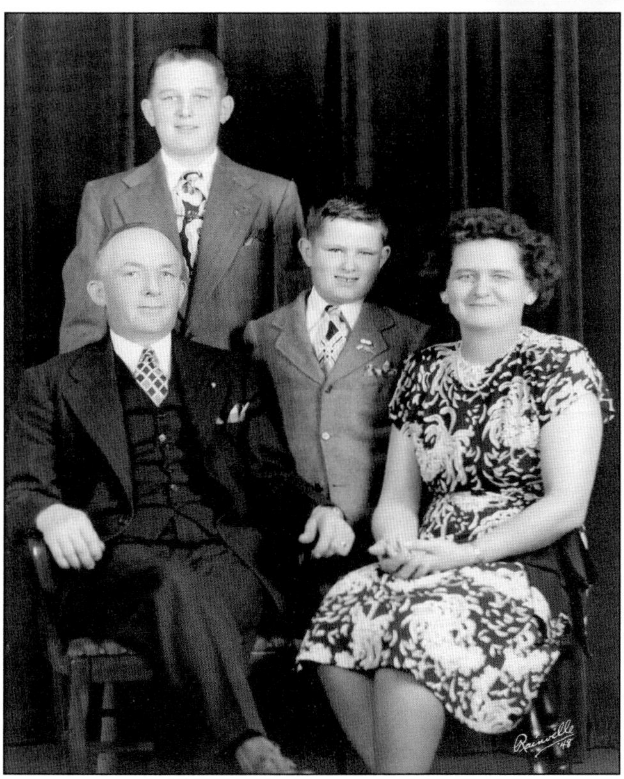

Seated for a 1948 portrait are Joseph Wojnar and his wife, Jennie Bien Wojnar. Standing are their sons Walter (left) and Eugene. Joseph Wojnar was born in Northbridge; his family returned to Poland when he was two years old. He came back to the United States in 1925. The Wojnars were shareholders in South Grafton's Polish National Home Association.

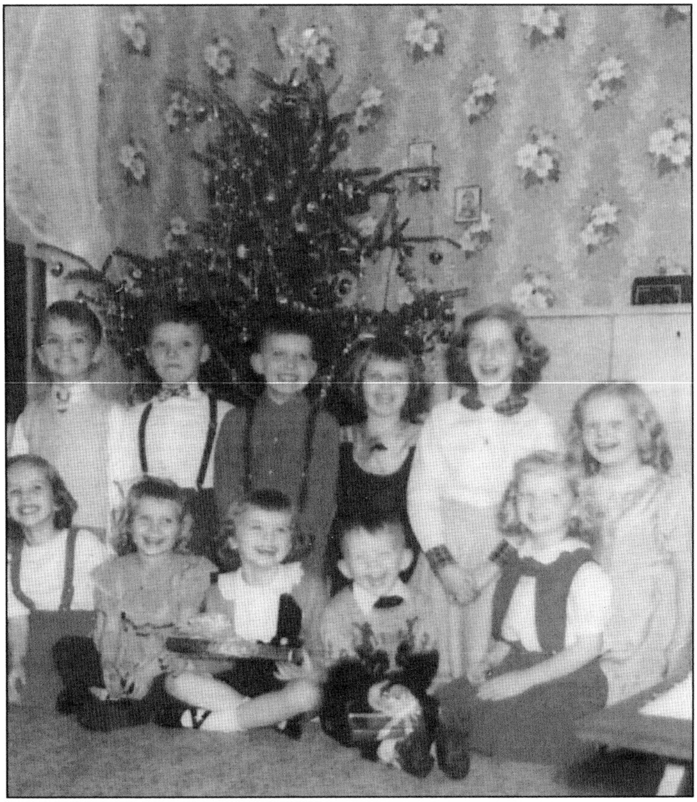

Cousins take a moment during their Christmas Eve 1950 visit at the Ward Street home of their grandparents Peter and Maryanna Kasprzak Siminski. From left to right are (first row) Diane Baniukiewicz, Kathy Siminski, Karen Baniukiewicz, John Misiewicz, and Joan Jankowski; (second row) Stanley Baniukiewicz, Richard Kisiel, Robert Siminski, Tina Siminski, Lucia Siminski, and Anita Jankowski.

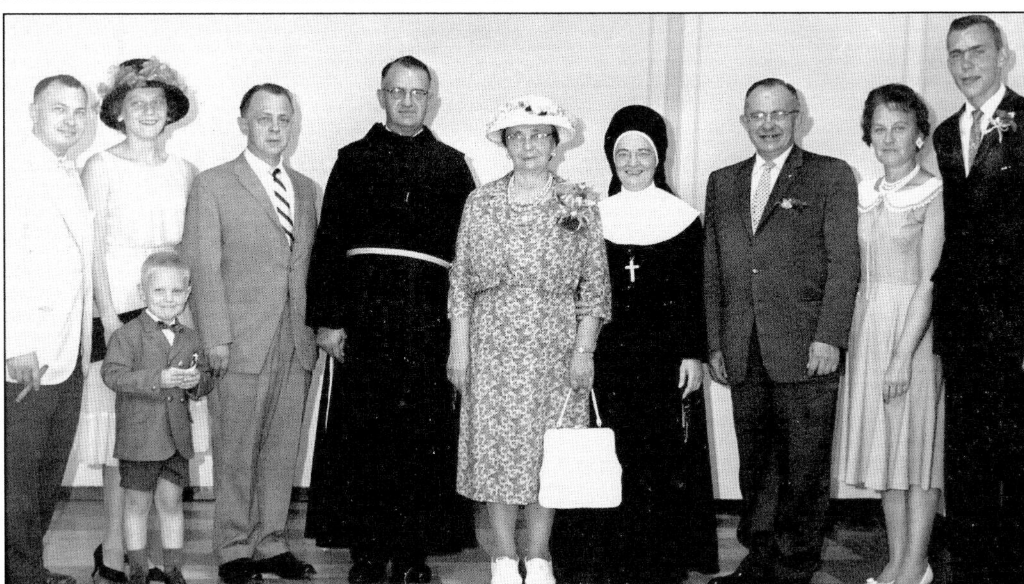

The Bartosiewicz family of Worcester celebrates a milestone in 1961. Standing from left to right in the parish hall are John Bartosiewicz Sr., Genevieve Bartosiewicz, young John Bartosiewicz Jr., Frank Bartosiewicz, Brother Emmanuel Bartosiewicz, OFM, Catherine Bartosiewicz, Sr. Mary Aquila Bartosiewicz, Napoleon Bartosiewicz, Albina Bartosiewicz, and John Bartosiewicz. Sister Aquila was celebrating her 25th anniversary as a sister of the Holy Family of Nazareth.

Sophia Wlodkowska Piascik stands outside her home on Sterling Street, Worcester, in the 1960s. She and her husband, Alexander, were both Lomza natives who immigrated around 1907. They were the parents of four children: Alexander, Peter, Irene, and Rita. Like many of the city's Poles, they moved several times over the decades, usually from one three-decker to the next. Their addresses included Millbury, Scott, and Harlem Streets and Perry Avenue.

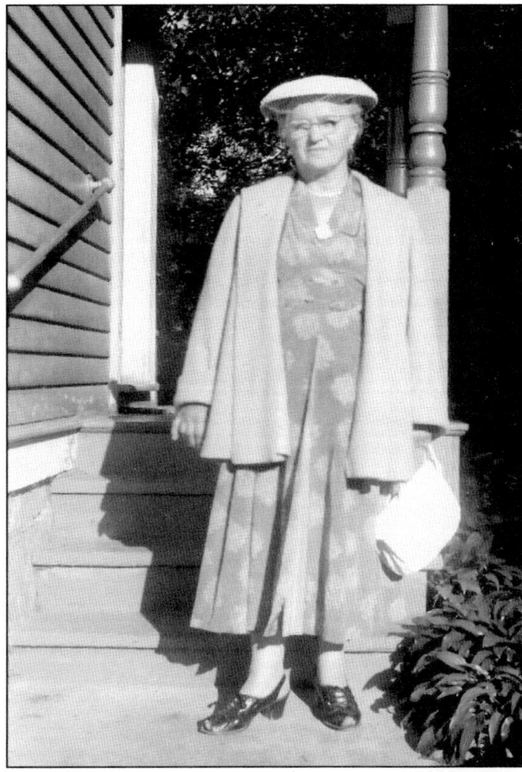

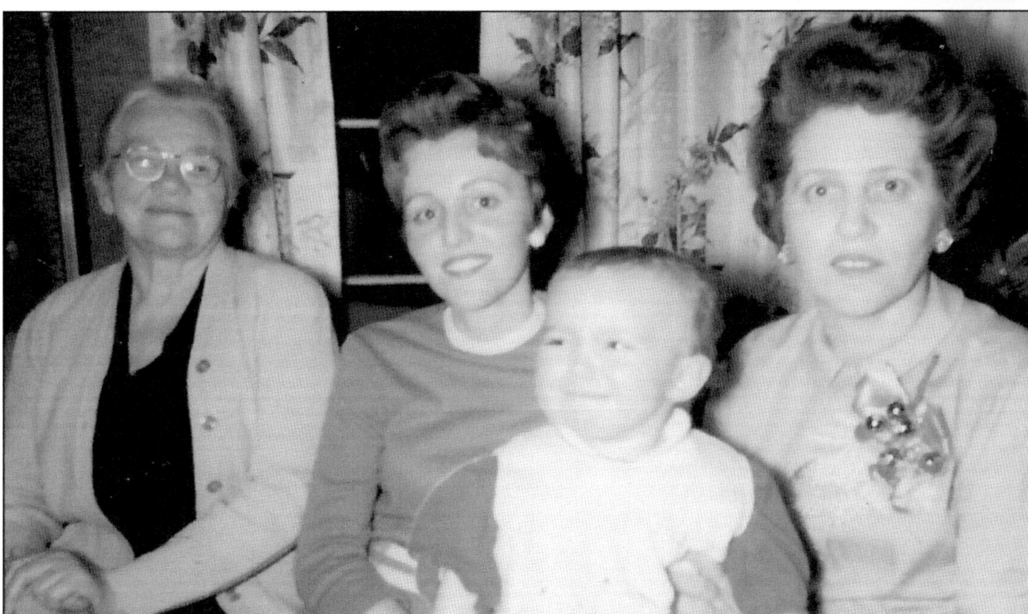

Seated together at the Sova Cichonski home on Dudley Avenue, Whitinsville, in 1964 are four generations of females. From left to right are Karolina Kramarz Sova Cichonski, her granddaughter Bonnie Bailey Domey, great-granddaughter Monica Domey, and daughter Stella Sova Bailey. Karolina Cichonski was born in Jaslo, Galicia, in 1888; she was a founding member of the local Polish National Alliance.

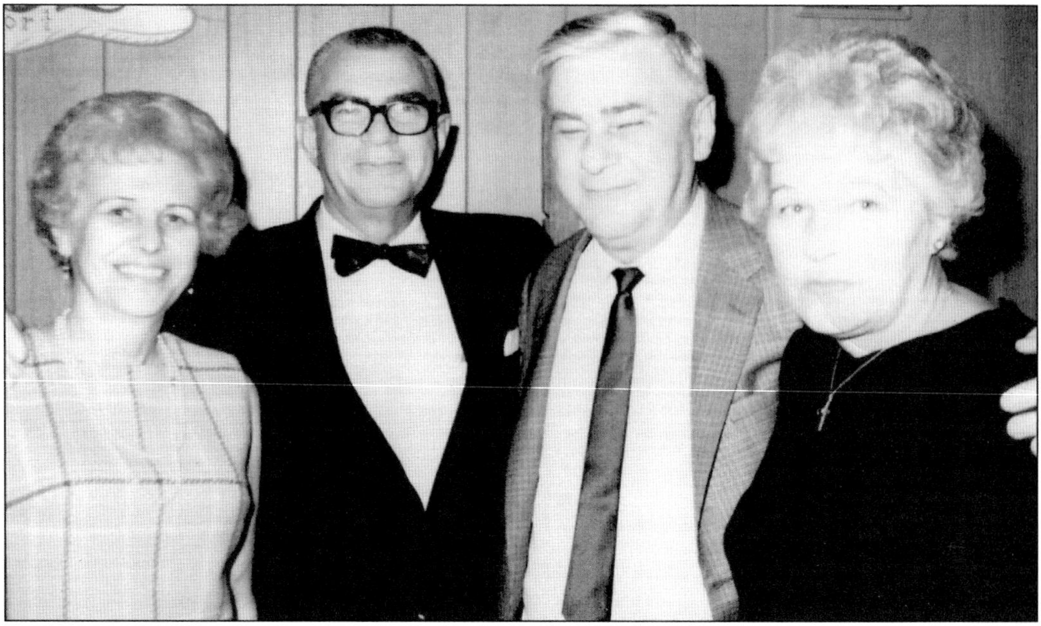

Enjoying a celebration at Charles Restaurant, Worcester, in 1968 are, from left to right, siblings Josephine Prokopowicz Proko, Joseph Prokopowicz, John Prokopowicz, and Pauline Prokopowicz Londergan. Their parents, Alexander and Stefania Ruscik Prokopowicz, immigrated from Szczuczyn, Wilno, and settled on Meade Street in 1913. Josephine was a school department bookkeeper; Joseph, an overseas commissary supervisor; John, a steel union negotiator; and Pauline, a homemaker. Their brother Adolph died in 1952.

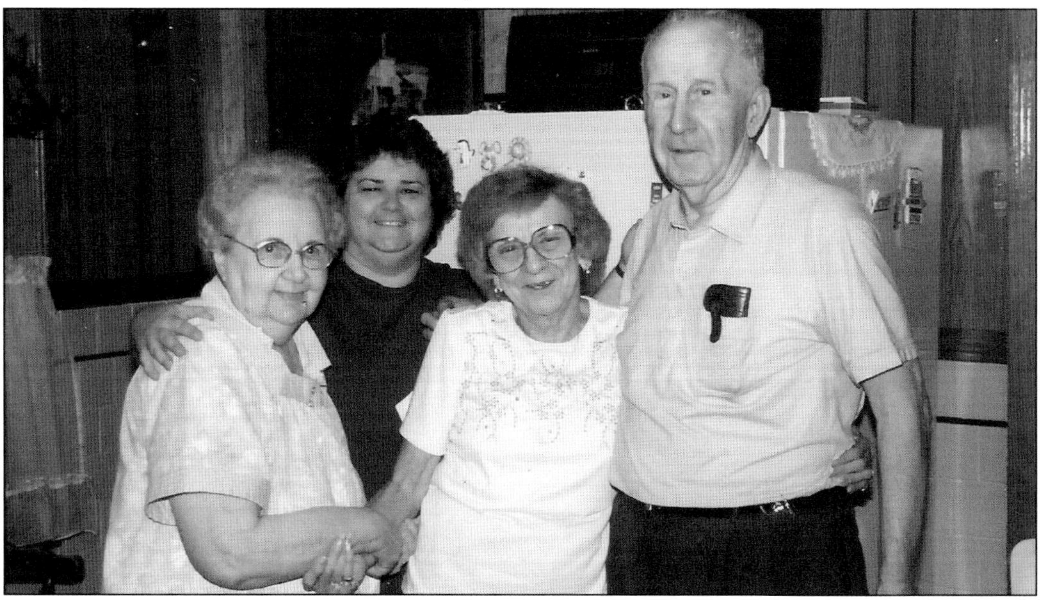

Bessie (far left) and Bernard Krupinski enjoy a visit at their Worcester home with his niece Donna Colyer (second from left) and his sister Angela Krupinski Colyer (third from left) in 1979. Bernard Krupinski was a Millbury Street retailer who owned and operated Circle Shoe Store for about 30 years. The Krupinski siblings were born and raised in Webster, the children of Peter and Michalena Chmielewska Krupinski.

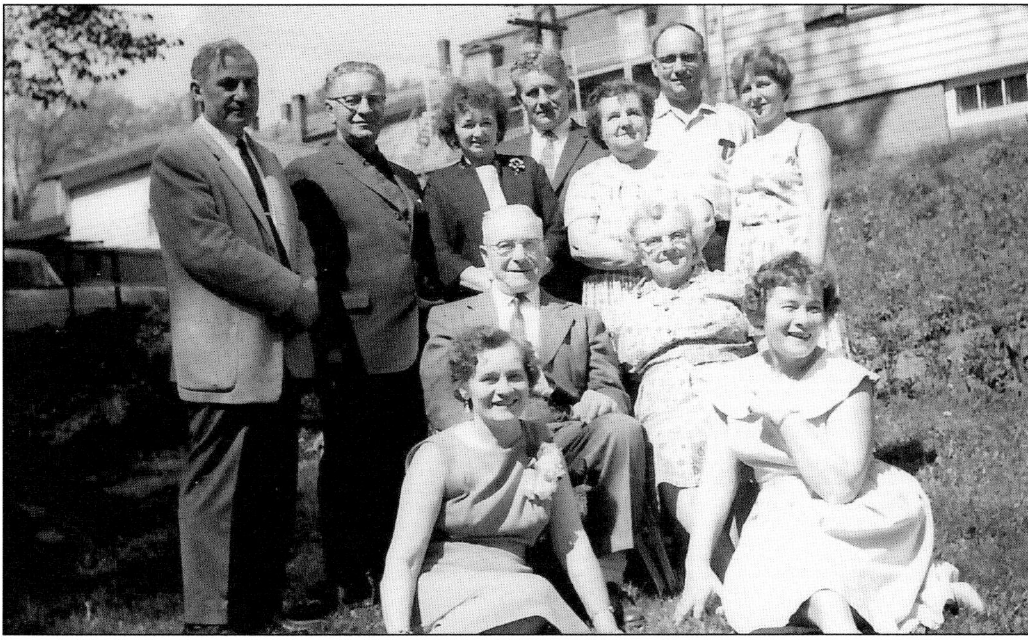

The Lepkowskis get together in Gardner around 1960. Seated on the ground are Irene Kaczynski (left) and Jennie Siarnacki and on lawn chairs, Joseph and Jadwiga Lepkowski. Standing from left to right are Frank Siarnacki, Stanley Lepkowski, Sophie Lepkowski, Eddie Lepkowski, Jennie Bogdanowicz Lepkowski, Carl Carlson, and Eleanor Carlson. The Lepkowski family originated in the Lomza region of Russian Poland. The women were active in the Polish Women's Political Club.

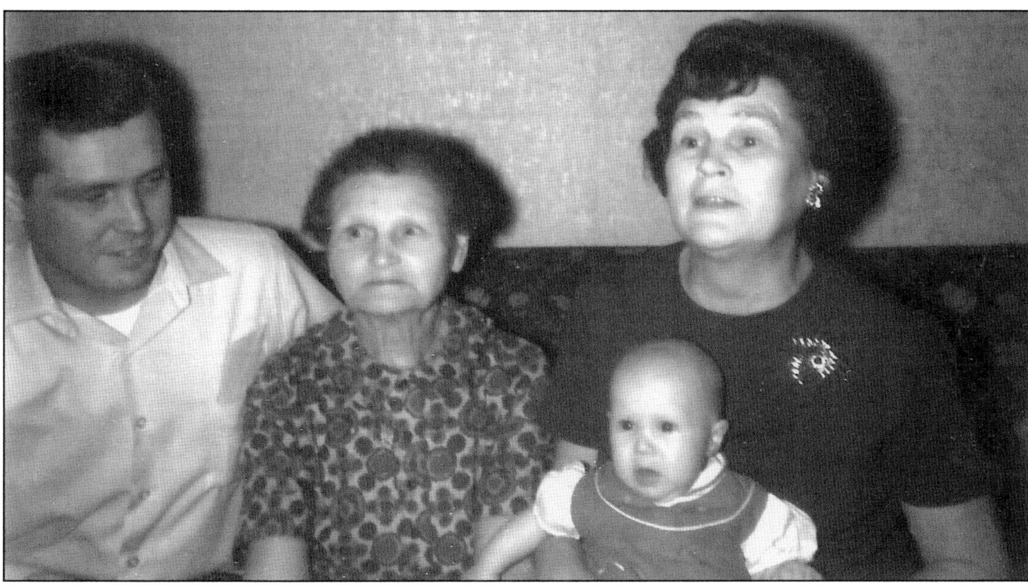

Four generations of the Ostrokolowicz family meet at the home of Rose Charazewicz Poplawski on Negus Street, Webster, in December 1967. Pictured here is Rose Poplawski, with her grandson Edward Ostrokolowicz, daughter Helen Ostrokolowicz, and great-granddaughter Debra Ostrokolowicz. Poplawski and her husband, Charles, operated a Polish bakery in Webster, where their whole family worked. They lived in an apartment above the bakery.

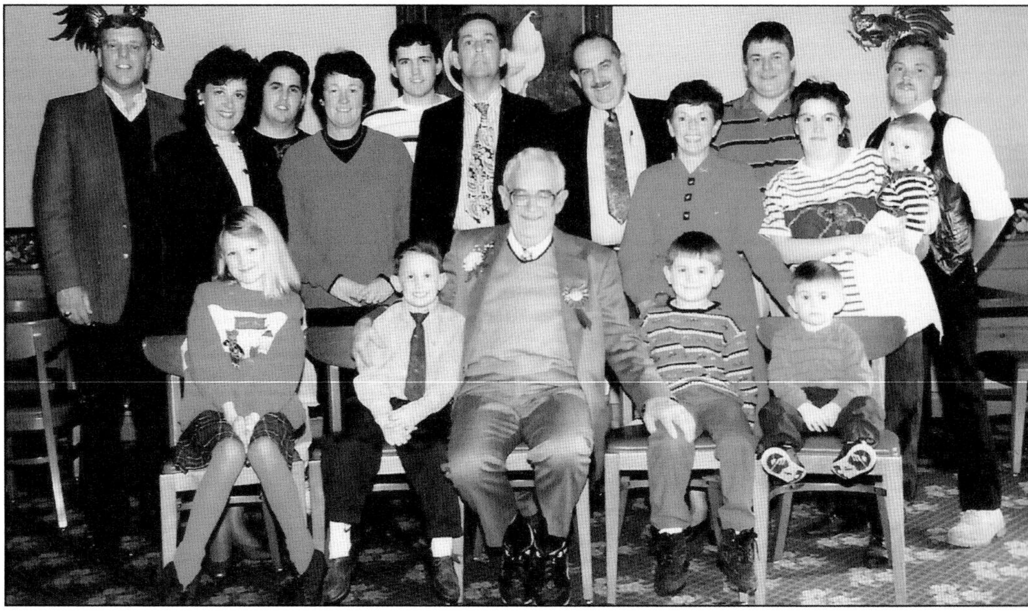

The family of Joseph Baniukiewicz celebrates his 75th birthday in 1994. From left to right are (first row) grandchildren Elizabeth and Matthew Baniukiewicz, Joseph Baniukiewicz, and great-grandsons Richard and Robert Dulude; (second row) son-in-law Dean Stickles, daughter Janice Stickles, grandson Richard Baniukiewicz, daughter-in-law Mary-Jo Baniukiewicz, grandson Robert Baniukiewicz Jr., sons Robert and Joseph Baniukiewicz, daughter-in-law Bernadette Baniukiewicz, Richard Dulude, granddaughter Mindy Dulude holding great-grandson Steven Dulude, and grandson Joseph Baniukiewicz Jr.

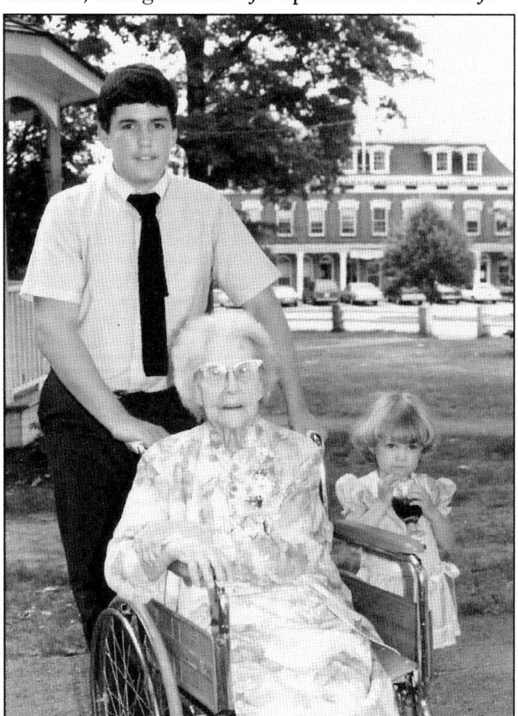

Mary Soliwoda Brodzik is escorted by her great-grandchildren Robert Jr. and Elizabeth Baniukiewicz to the wedding of granddaughter Janice Baniukiewicz to Dean Stickles on July 6, 1985, in Grafton. Born in Lomza in 1890, Mary was married to John Brodzik and had three children, Theresa, Costay, and Jennie. In the early 1950s, Mary Brodzik worked at Cranska Thread Company on McKeon Road, Worcester.

Five

WORK

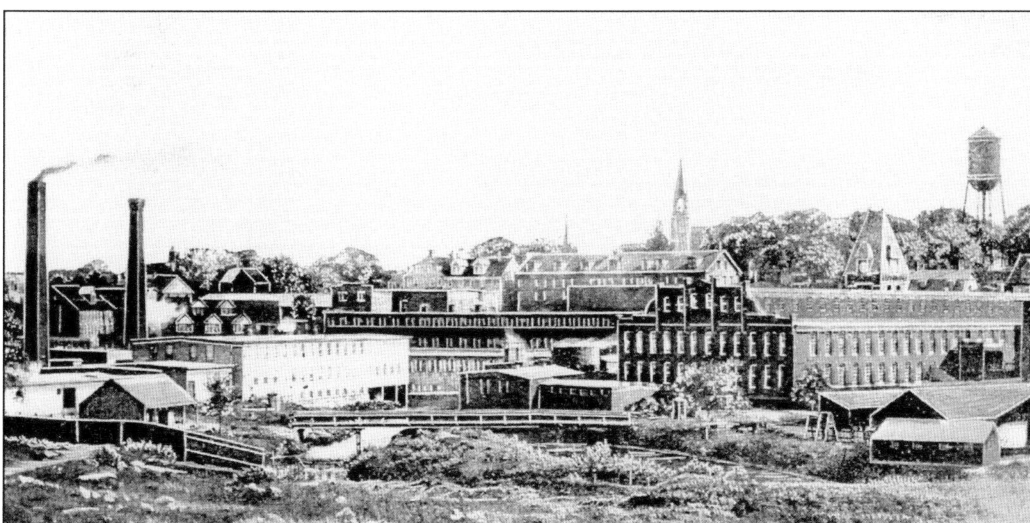

"In 1869 the first contingent of Polish people was brought to town by the agent of Slater's Mills, who had gone to New York for help, and on his return had with him half a dozen of Polish families," reports *History of the Catholic Church in the Diocese of Springfield* (1900). Slater's cotton mill in Webster followed the British system of hiring families instead of individual workers.

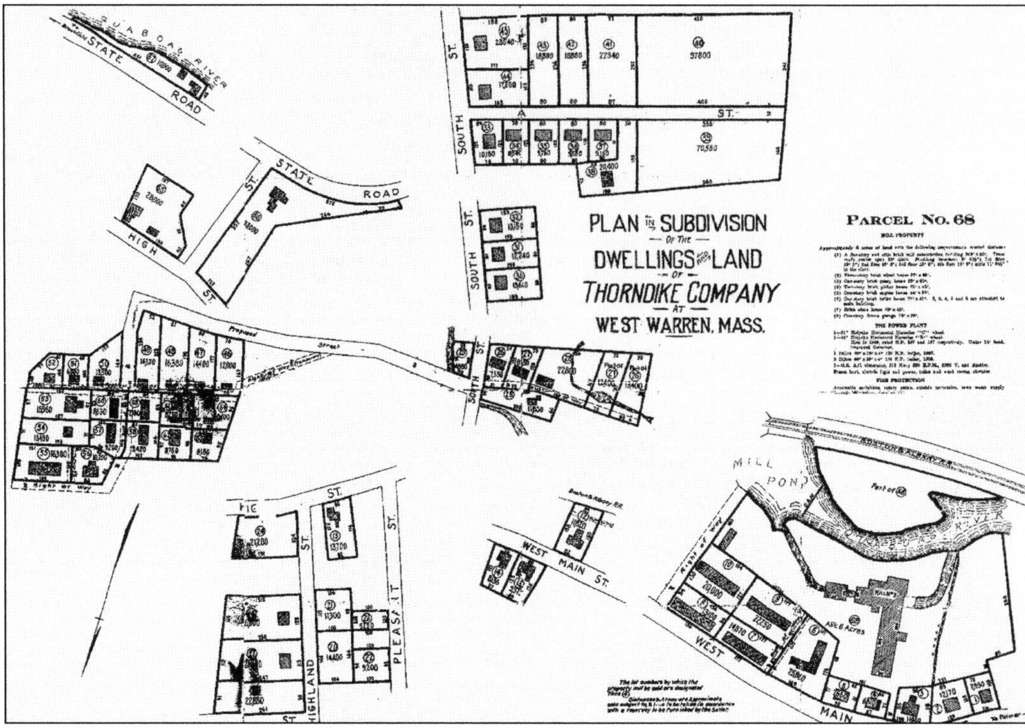

This map describes millworkers' houses for sale in West Warren. South and A Streets offered duplexes with seven rooms per side and "town water, sewer, electric light, toilet and bath." Parcels 46-64, with four rooms per side and limited amenities, are designated "Patch," a location corresponding to Pulaski Street. Patch housing, a model that originated in industrial England, signified rows of houses of a single design, built for workers.

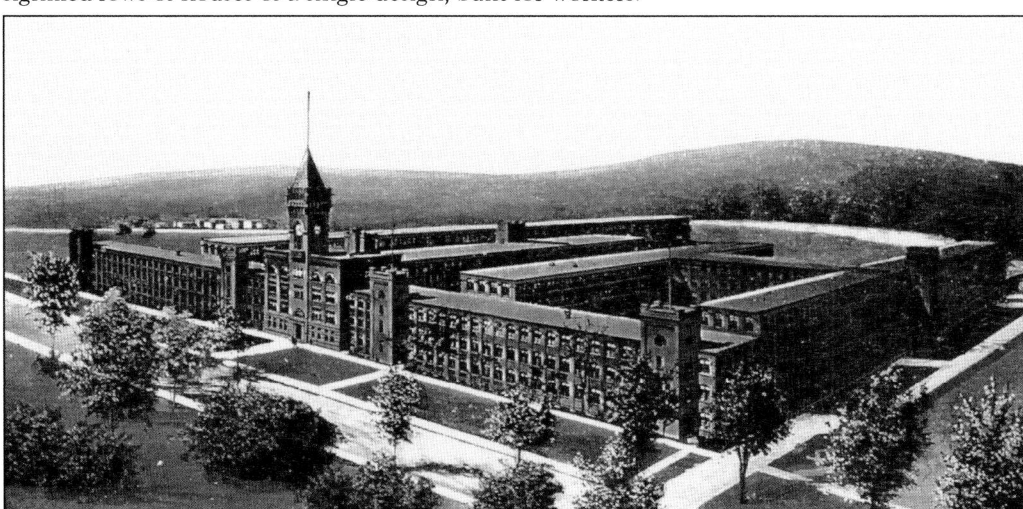

American Optical Company was incorporated in Southbridge in 1869, the outgrowth of a spectacle-making business started in 1833. By 1909, the company was famous for innovations in cutting and fitting lenses and frames. Jobs there and at textile mills attracted thousands of Polish, Irish, French Canadian, and Italian immigrants to "Spectown." Galician Poles settled in Southbridge's Globe Village, while Russian Poles from Bialystok and Suwalki found homes in Sandersdale.

Seen here at New York's Madison Square Garden in 1936, Agnes Czech Shaw of Dudley appeared with the Ringling Brothers, Barnum and Bailey's Combined Circus as a baton-twirling drum major and an aerialist for several seasons. She had earlier been a champion drum major at Bartlett High School, Webster, and performed and competed throughout New England. Today she is one of the region's leading authorities on circuses.

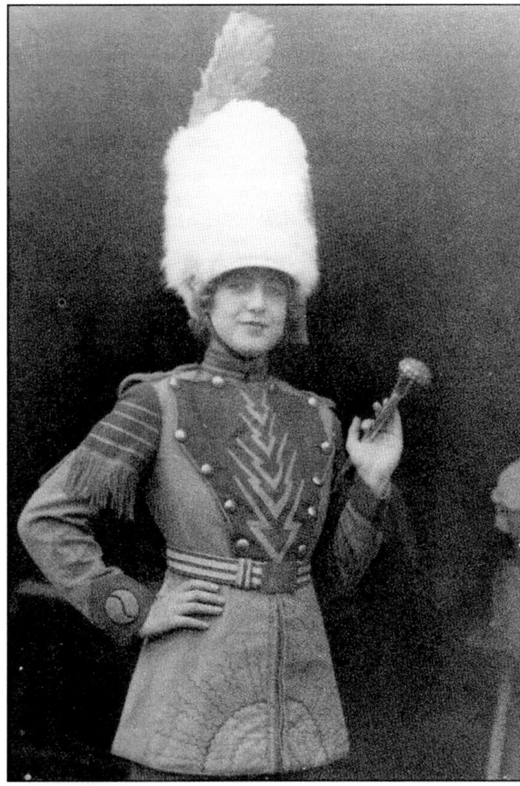

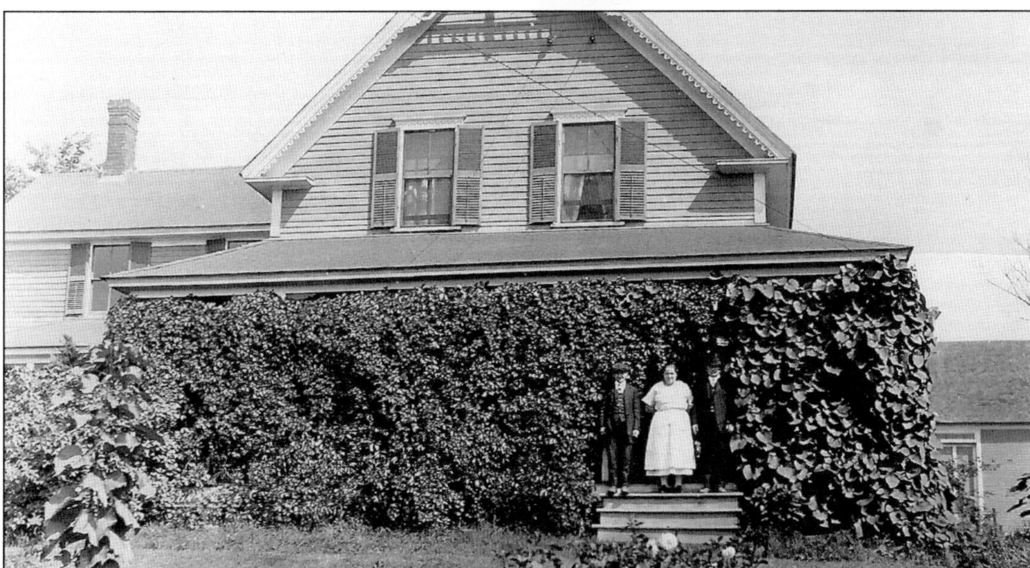

Vines enclose the porch of the Klondike Inn on Providence Road, South Grafton. Antoni Szajna, owner from the 1920s to 1946, was among an informal network of Polish business proprietors in central Massachusetts. His suppliers included Koliss Bakery, Grafton, and Brockert Brewing Company, Worcester. Intermarriages and friendships made these links more than business connections. Szajna served as Brockert's vice president; brewery president Matt Stacey was godparent to Szajna's daughter, Halina.

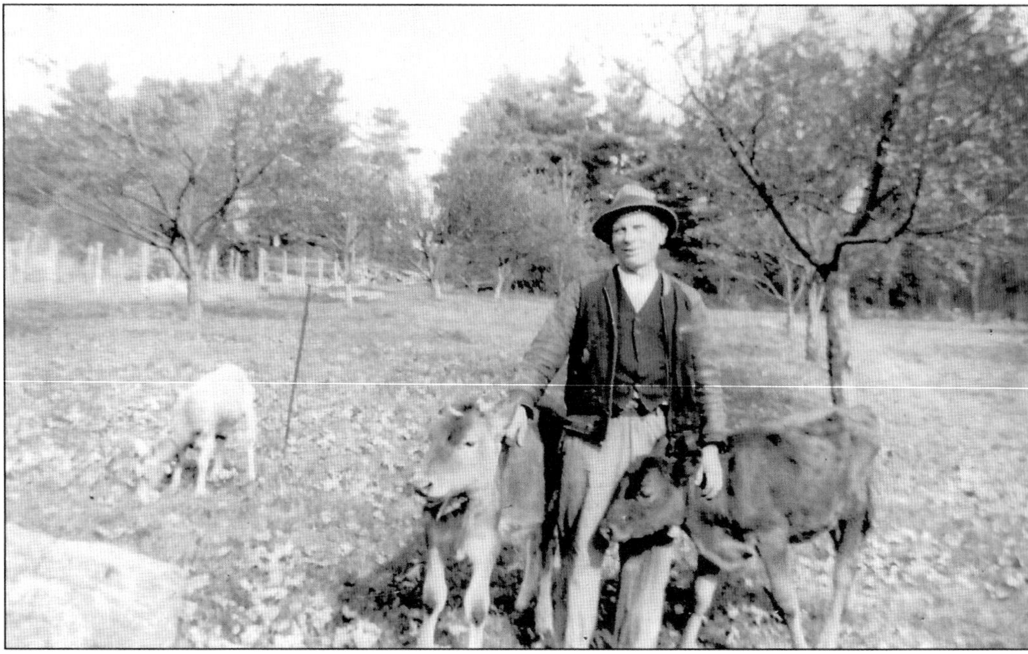

Konstanty Mosczynski smiles as he holds two calves securely at his side. After living in Worcester for about 25 years, the Ostrowie, Bialystok, native bought 200 acres of land in Douglas in 1936. He named it *Oko* ("Eye") Farm, saying it extended "as far as the eye can see." Besides tending a dairy herd, the Mosczynski family raised produce that was sold at Brockelman Brothers markets in Worcester.

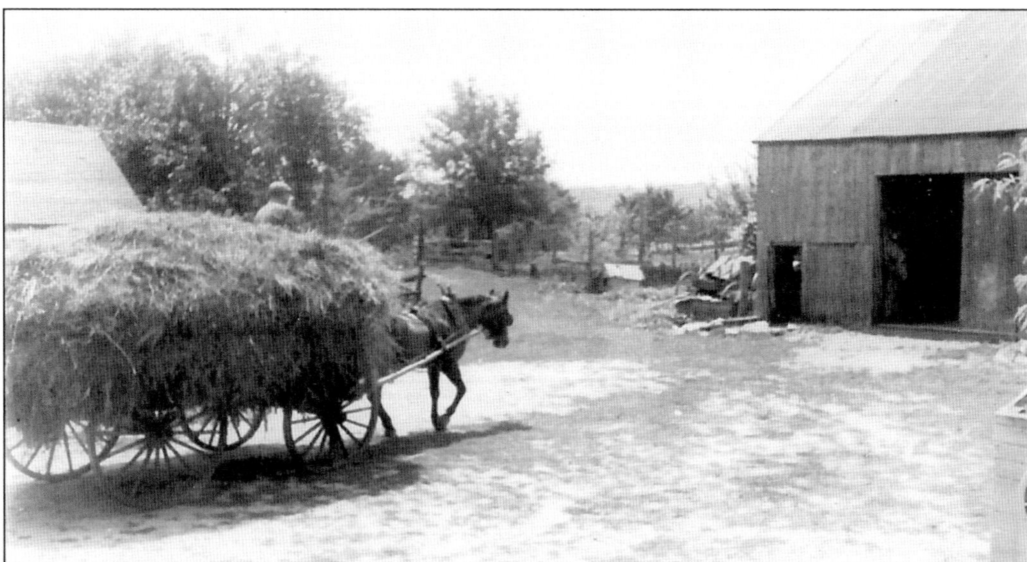

John Makowski heads to the barn on his hay wagon. The Makowski farm was situated off Douglas-Providence Pike (Southeast Main Street) in Douglas. John and Alexandra Makowski bought their 50-acre farm in 1918 and raised cows, pigs, chickens, and crops. Their 10 children grew up there, and the first 3 of 38 grandchildren were born there as well. Makowski also worked at Hayward-Schuster Woolen Mills until his retirement in 1953.

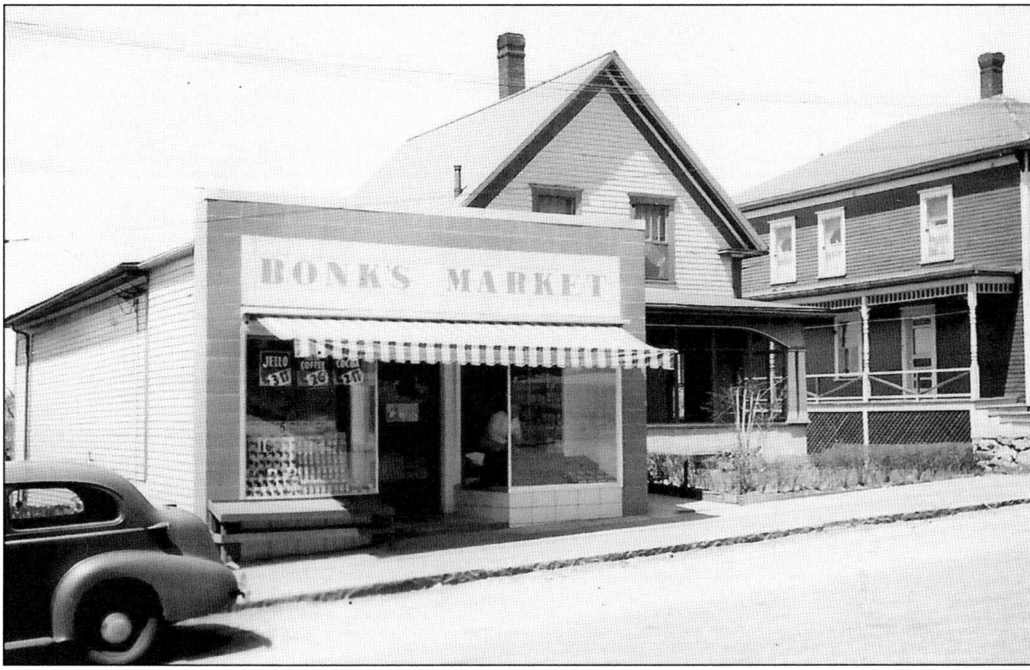

John and Catherine Rampala Bonk opened Bonk's Market at 293 Pine Street, Gardner, about 1916. Their five sons—John, Stanley, Peter, Joseph, and Stephen—all worked there over the decades until ownership changed in 1980. Still in business, Bonk's Market is the oldest continuously operated neighborhood grocery store in Gardner. When this photograph was taken sometime in the 1930s, a shopper could buy three packages of Jell-O for 17¢.

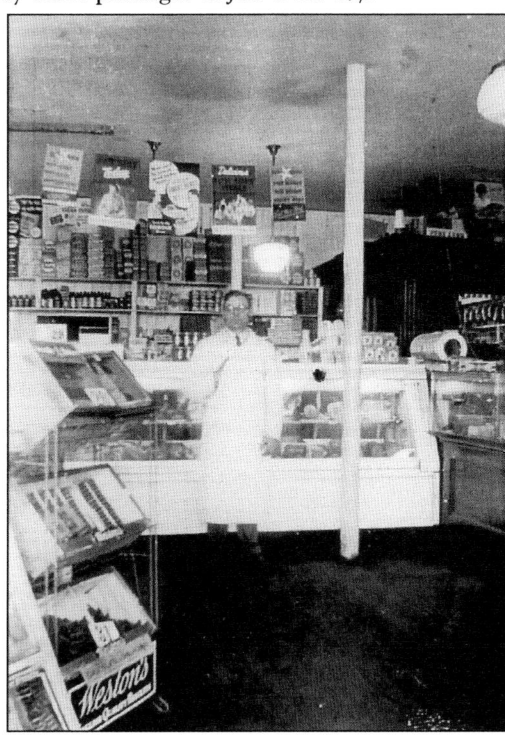

Proprietor Stephen Szlyk stands in front of the meat counter inside Suffield Market, which he operated from the late 1920s until his retirement in 1972. Located on the corner of Perry Avenue and Suffield Street, Szlyk's was one of the many small neighborhood groceries that served the Vernon Hill and Island districts of Worcester. Typical of Polish grocers, Szlyk specialized in homemade kielbasa.

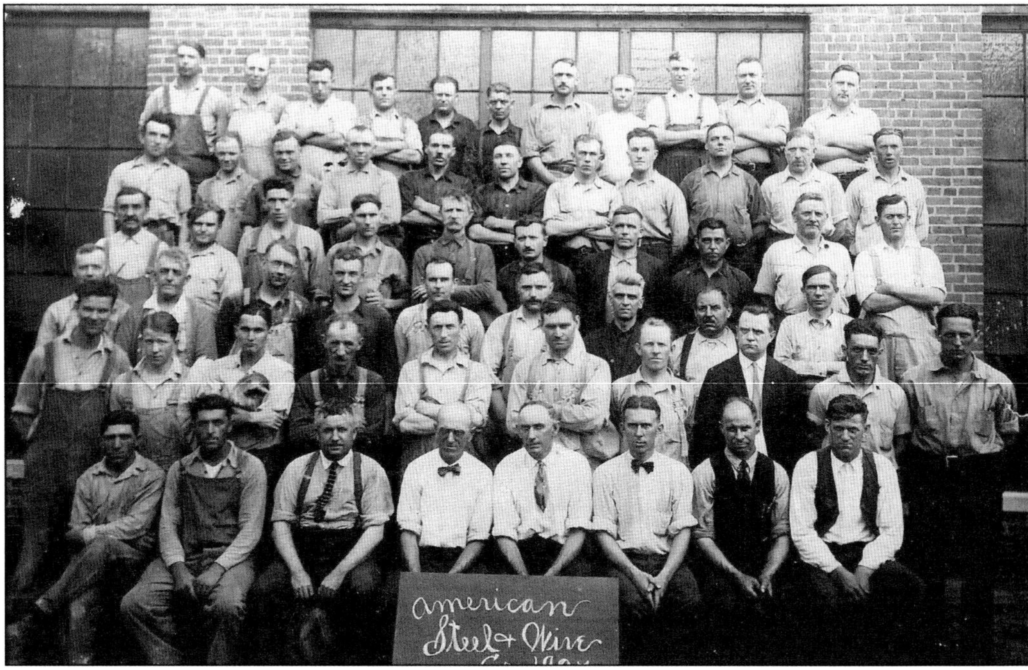

In the first half of the 20th century, American Steel and Wire Company's South Works was the single biggest employer of Polish immigrants in Worcester. Census returns throughout the decades list "wire drawer" as their most common occupation. This 1927 photograph of the mechanical department includes Waclaw (John) Karbowski (fifth row, fifth from left), John Starczewski (fifth row, sixth from left), and Stanley Stoklosa (sixth row, far right).

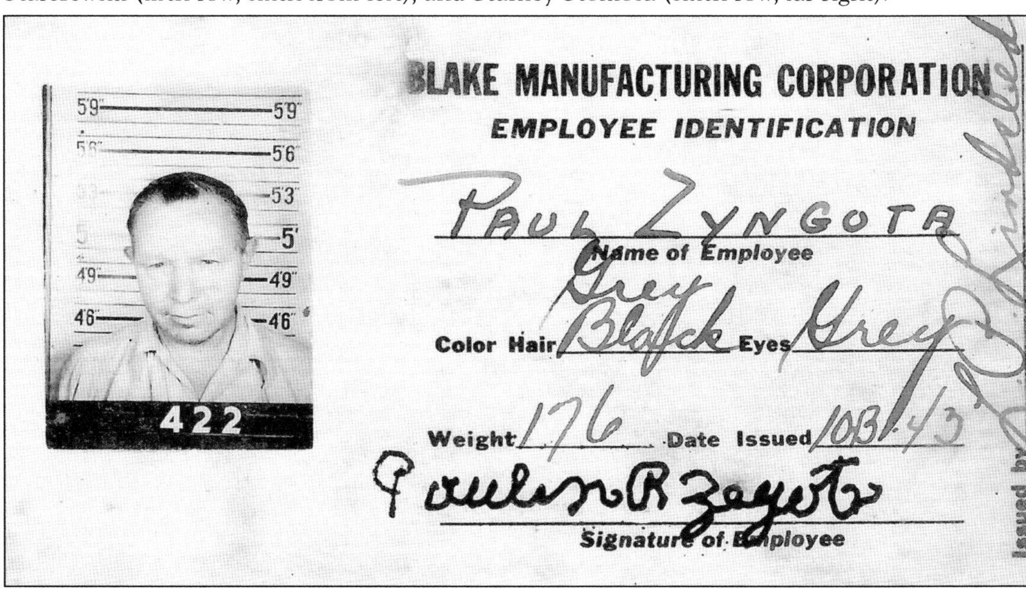

An employee identification badge illustrates how the spelling of Polish surnames was changed, inadvertently or intentionally, through adaptation to American life. Paul Rzegota used his authentic surname spelling in signing this 1943 Blake Manufacturing Corporation badge, but company personnel altered it to Zyngota. Located on Green Street in Clinton, Blake made flashlights for the war effort.

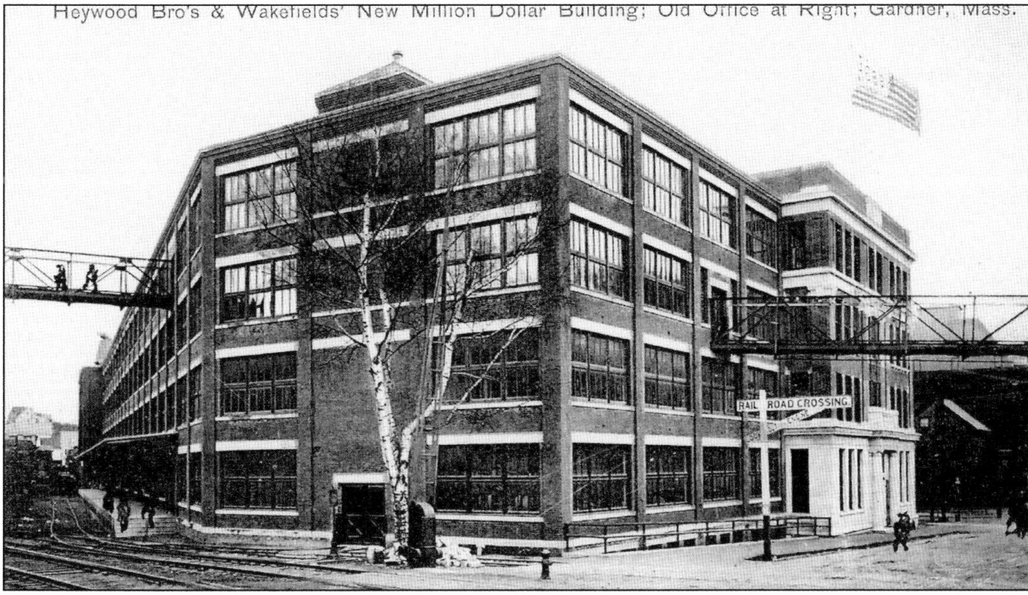

Heywood Brothers and Wakefield Company was preeminent among about 20 manufacturers responsible for Gardner's renown as "Chair City of the World" and "Furniture Capital of New England." In 1900, a third of Gardner's 10,813 residents were foreign born; the population swelled to 14,699 by 1910, largely the result of immigration. Poles, many from the Lomza area of Russian Poland, found jobs in the furniture factories and on railroad construction projects.

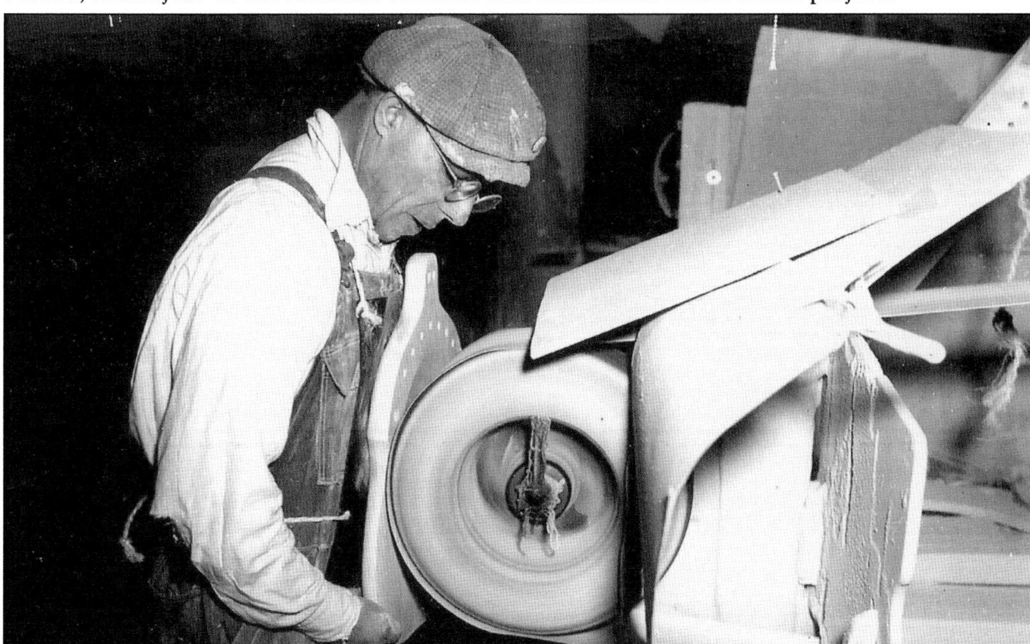

Bronislaw Wagner operates a belt sander on a wooden dining chair seat at Heywood-Wakefield Furniture Company around 1949. Wagner was Heywood's lead chair sander for 18 years until his retirement in 1965. Born in Kraska, Lomza, he emigrated in 1912, served in the U.S. Army during 1914–1917 and in the Polish Army in France during 1917–1920 and returned to Lomza to marry his childhood sweetheart. The Wagners settled in Gardner in 1921.

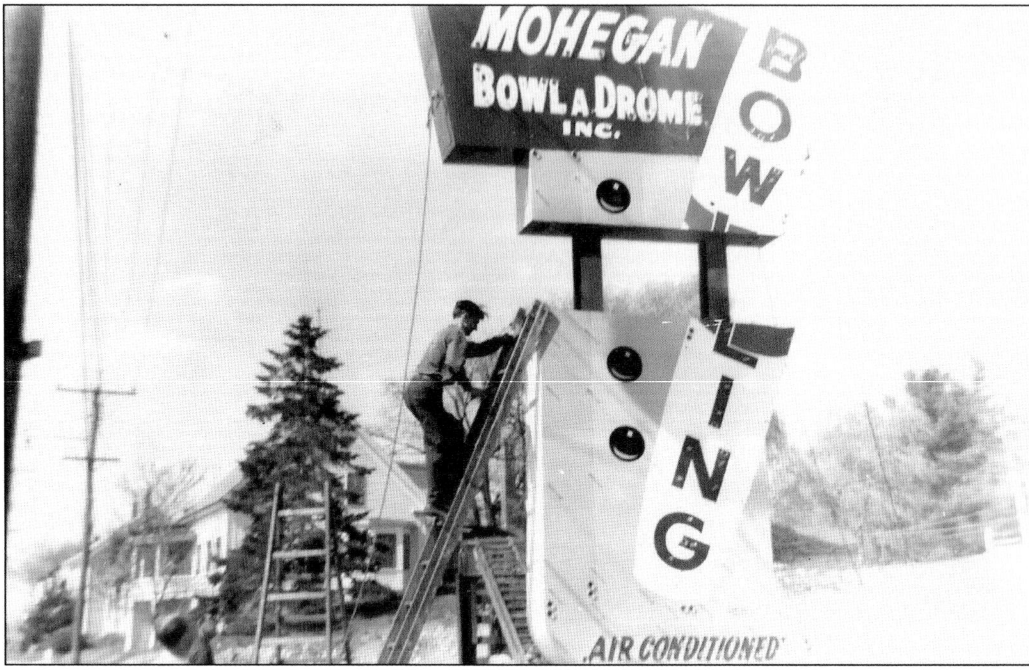

Leader Sign Company founder Anthony Hmura works from a ladder while installing a sign for the Mohegan Bowl-a-Drome on Thompson Road in Webster around 1960. In business since 1946, Hmura is best known for creative neon designs, such as a pulsating rocket ship sign for the now-defunct Flying Yankee Restaurant in Auburn. His work was featured in the 2003 New England Neon exhibition at the National Heritage Museum in Lexington.

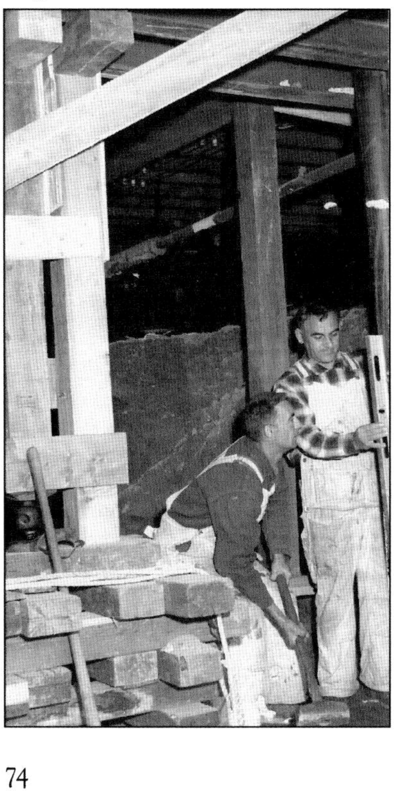

Francis Vigeant (left) and Henry Recko check their work with a level during construction of basement meeting rooms and kitchen facilities at Our Lady of Czestochowa Church in 1959–1960. A self-employed building contractor for more than 45 years, Recko was a member of the White Eagle Association, a president of the Polish National Alliance, and a president of St. Mary's Boosters. He was married to Phyllis Linga.

Walter Banach uses a trawler on a cement floor at a Worcester company in 1960. Before owning and operating B&W Waterproofing Company for 40 years, he worked for E. J. Cross Company, Worcester, as a cement finisher and bricklayer. For 47 years, Banach was a member of the Worcester Chapter of the Bricklayers and Allied Craft Workers Union.

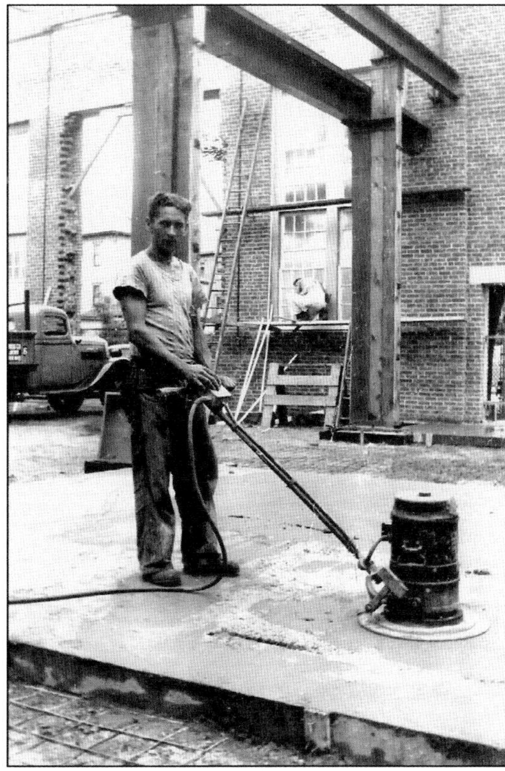

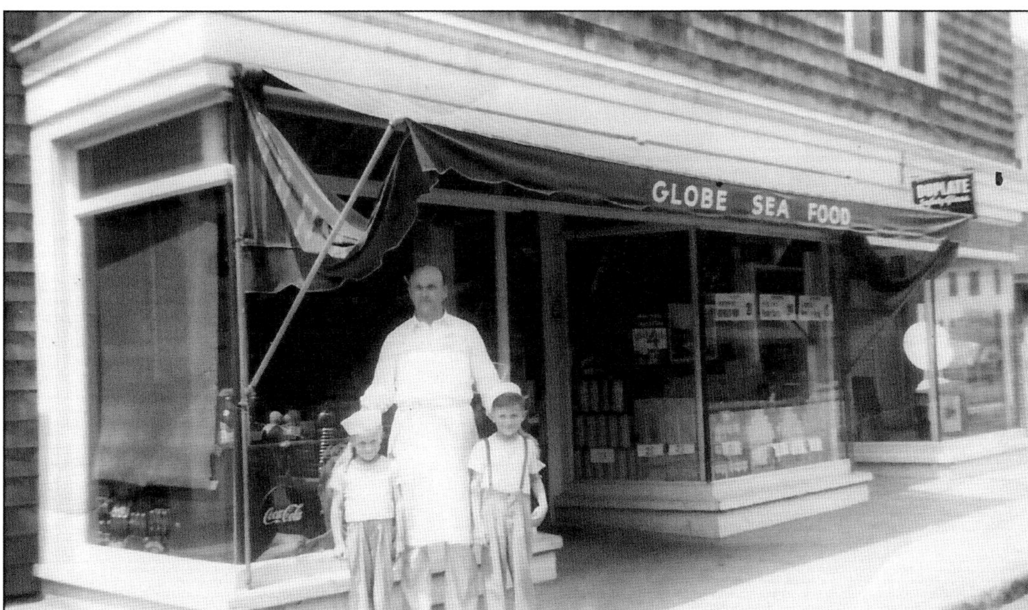

Joseph Swiacki operated Globe Seafood in Southbridge but was perhaps better known as the organist at St. Hedwig's Church from 1932 until his death in 1982. In his memory, a carillon was installed in the church. Swiacki also worked as a district manager for Cumberland Farms Stores, served on several town committees, and was a member of St. Stanislaus Society, the Knights of Columbus, and the American Guild of Organists.

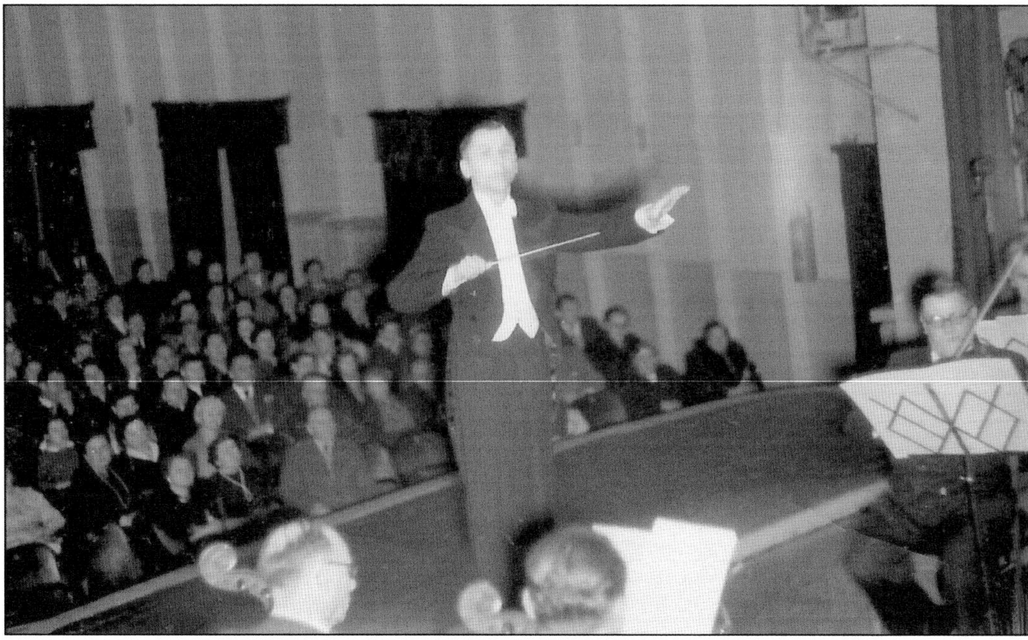

Needing no musical score, director/composer Aleksander Marczewski conducts the Radom Symphony Orchestra in Poland in the 1960s. Born in Irzadze, Kielce, he earned degrees at the Krakow and Warsaw music conservatories. His published works include symphonies, orchestral and chamber music, and an opera. Marczewski immigrated to the United States in 1965 and served as organist at Our Lady of Czestochowa Parish, Worcester, from 1968 until his death in 1981.

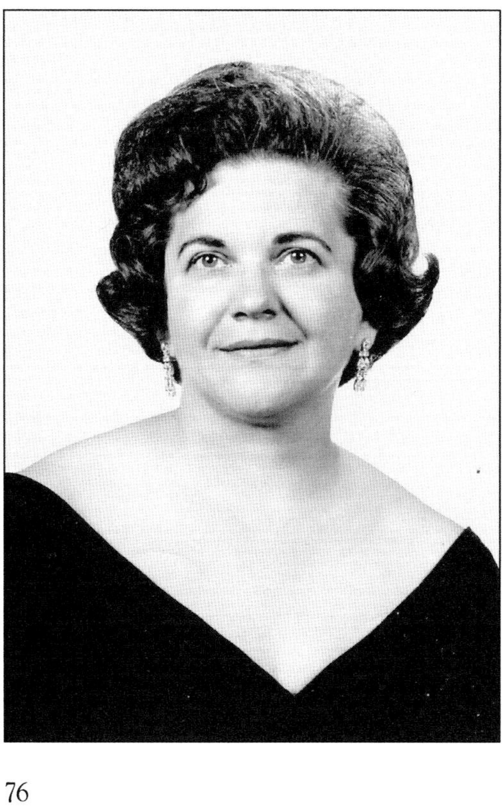

Hedwig Swiacki Kay grew up in Southbridge, where her musical career was influenced by the church. For more than 50 years, she was the organist and soprano soloist for St. Anne's Shrine, Fiskdale. Kay performed in radio and stage productions and at concert halls that included New York City's Metropolitan Opera House and Carnegie Hall. She sang at a 1958 event in Sturbridge where Eleanor Roosevelt was a guest speaker.

In October 1961, the *Worcester Sunday Telegram*'s "Feature Parade" spotlighted Elizabeth Chapowicki, a navy nurse chosen to attend Pres. John F. Kennedy and his family. The daughter of Stanley and Mary Chapowicki, she was educated at Boston College School of Nursing and worked at St. Vincent's and City Hospitals, Worcester, before joining the Navy Nurse Corps in 1959. Secret service and cabinet members were also among her White House charges.

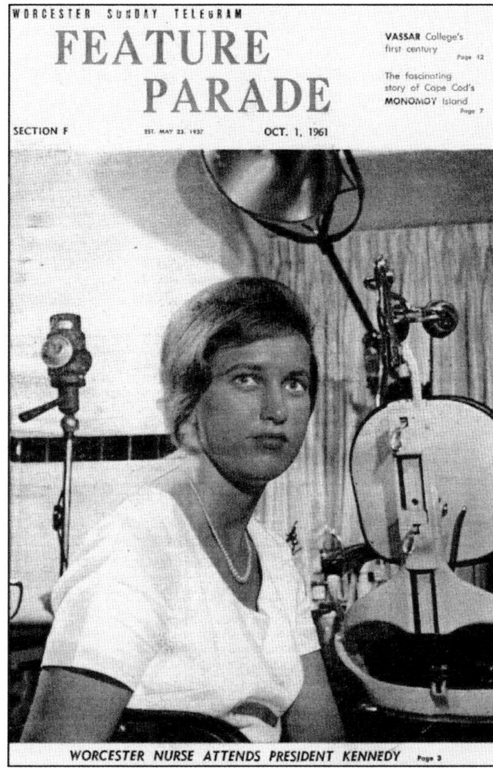
WORCESTER SUNDAY TELEGRAM
FEATURE PARADE
VASSAR College's first century Page 12
The fascinating story of Cape Cod's MONOMOY Island Page 7
SECTION F
EST. MAY 23, 1937
OCT. 1, 1961
WORCESTER NURSE ATTENDS PRESIDENT KENNEDY Page 3

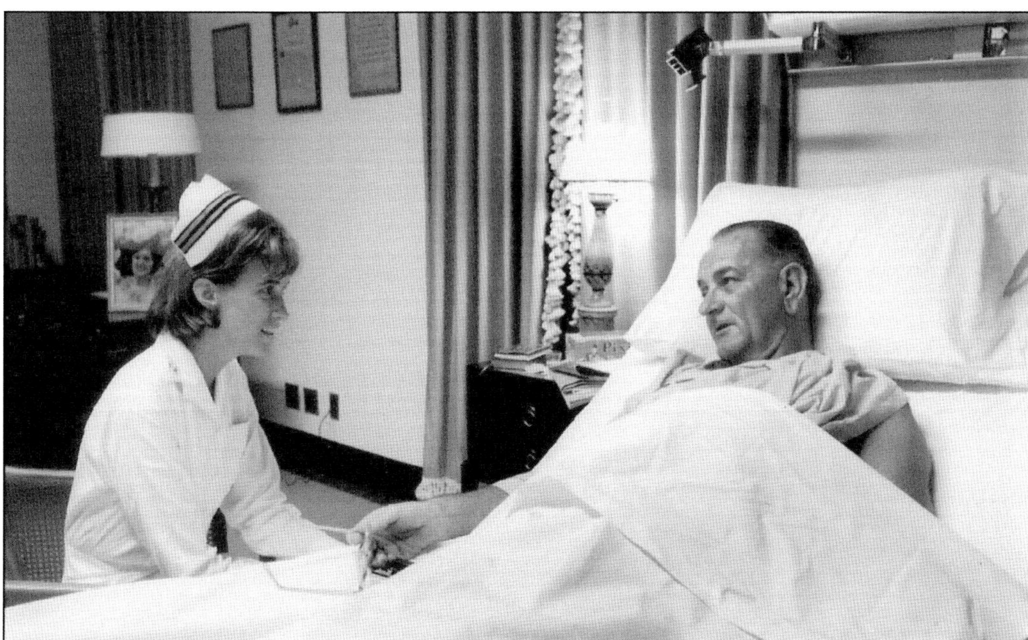

White House nurse Elizabeth Chapowicki, a Worcester native, sits at the bedside of Pres. Lyndon B. Johnson in 1966. Johnson had throat and abdomen surgery that November, the latter to repair an incision made during gall bladder surgery a year before. Chapowicki served two Democratic presidents in the White House.

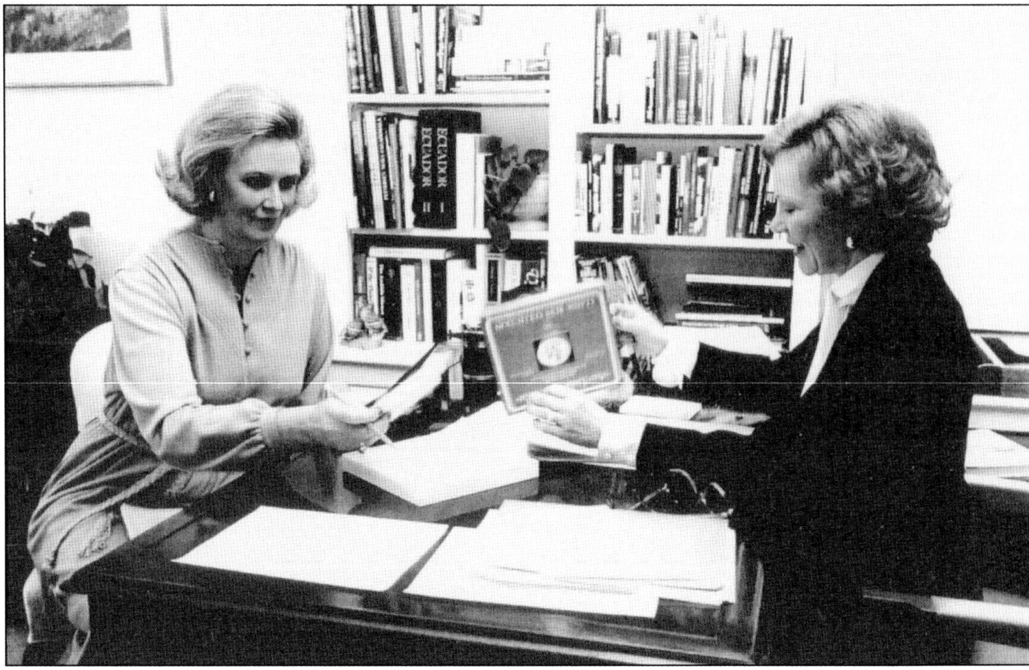

Rita Chadwick Merthan prepares to log in a foreign dignitary's gift displayed by First Lady Rosalynn Carter in her White House office in 1979. One of nine children of Stanley and Mary Chapowicki of Worcester, Merthan served as Carter's personal secretary from 1977 to 1981. The Boston University graduate's first government job was with the Central Intelligence Agency in West Germany in 1953. She was president of the Georgetown Club from 1966 to 1976.

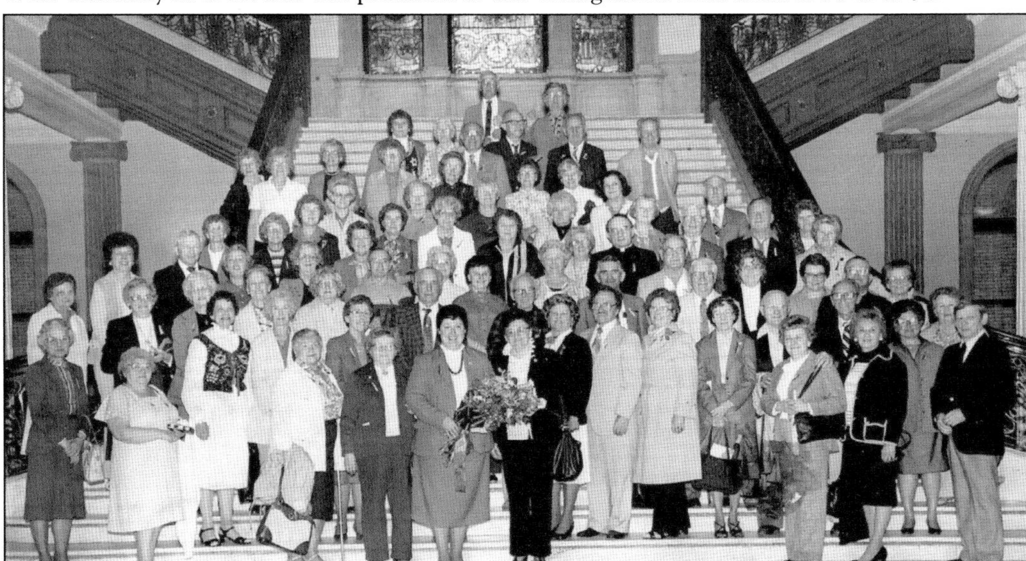

State representative Marilyn Travinski, holding a bouquet, was the first woman of Polish descent to serve in the Massachusetts legislature, the first woman to represent her district, and the first woman to chair the state Committee on Commerce and Labor. The crowd comprises some of Travinski's constituents from Southbridge, Dudley, and Webster, celebrating Polish Constitution Day at the statehouse, Boston, on May 3, 1983.

Six

EDUCATION

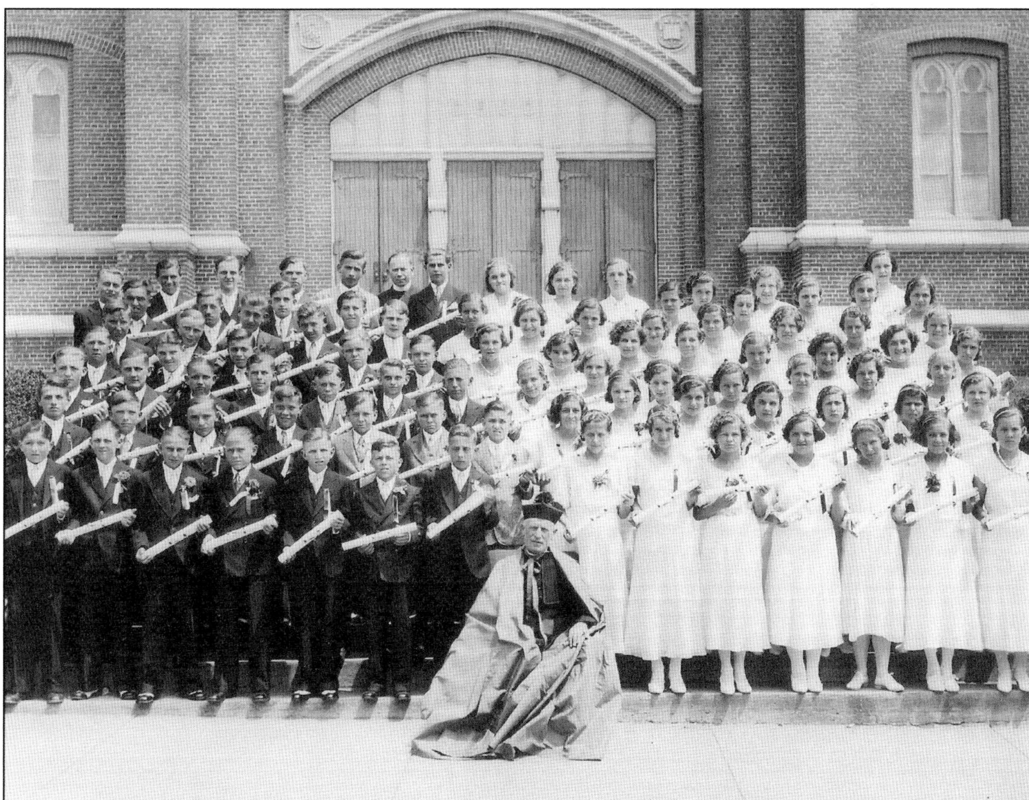

About 80 graduates of St. Joseph's School, Webster, display their eighth-grade diplomas in front of the parish church in the early 1930s. With them is Msgr. Anthony Cyran. The first Polish school in New England, St. Joseph's opened in 1892 with 90 students and four Felician Sisters as teachers. After fire destroyed the facility, it was replaced in 1924 with a 20-classroom brick school. Enrollment peaked at 1,105 in 1928.

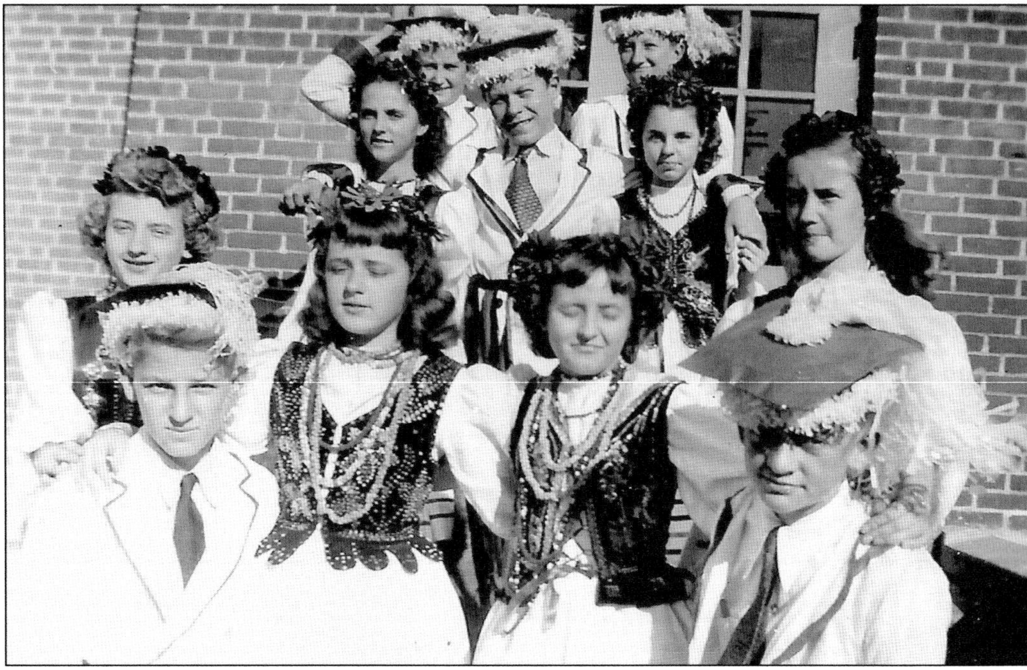

These eighth-grade students at St. Joseph's School, Webster, are dressed in traditional *Krakowiak* costumes for a performance in the 1950s. Pictured from left to right are (first row) Edwin Lebudzinski, Maryann Gorski, unidentified, and ? Stapor; (second row) Rose Cejmer at far left and unidentified at far right; (third row) Sally Madura, Robert Standrowicz, William Strzelewicz, Henry Sroczynski, and unidentified.

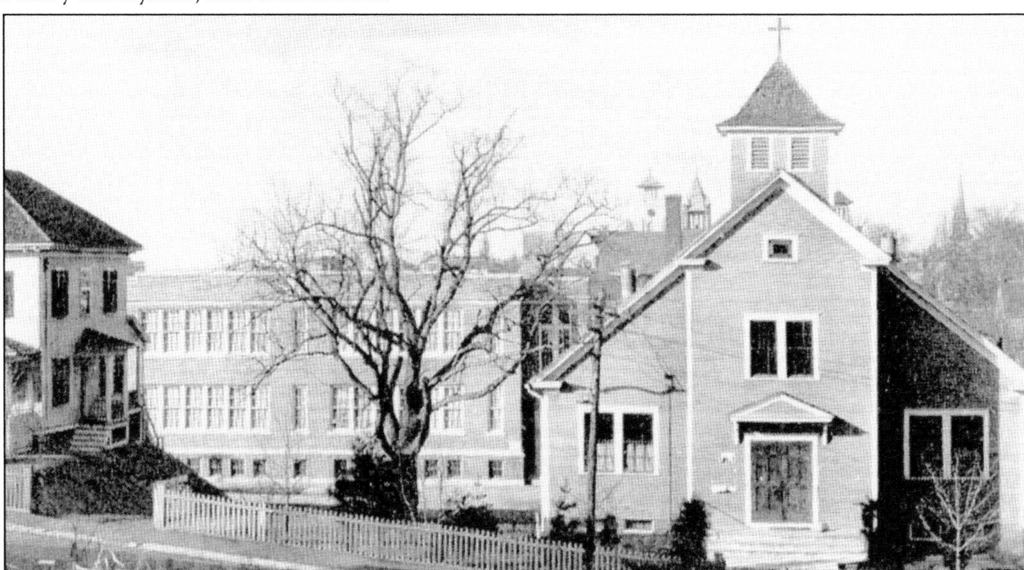

At rear between the rectory and church of Clinton's Polish parish is St. Mary's School, completed in 1926. With Bernardine Sisters of St. Francis as teachers, the school offered grades 1–6 until the Great Depression, when Lancaster Mills closed and many families of jobless Poles left Clifton. St. Mary's reopened in September 1936 with Felician Sisters as teachers, and in 1938, it had a full complement of eight elementary grades.

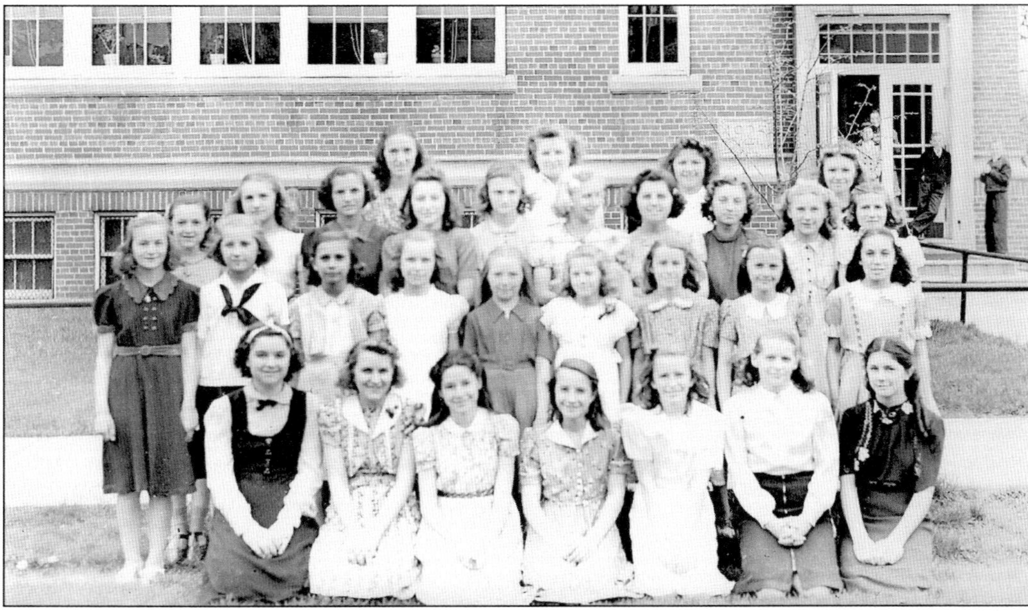

Graduating eighth-grade girls pose in front of St. Mary's School, Clinton, in 1940. Pictured from left to right are (first row) Helen Milewski, Statia Nadolny, Bernice Nicewicz, two unidentified people, Helen Kulis, and Antoinette Andriski; (second row) Gladys Kosiewski, unidentified, Theresa Pianowski, and six unidentified people; (third row) unidentified, Antoinette Kaminski, Agnes Burzenski, Rose Marcik, unidentified, Mary Bastek, Matilda Cermak, and three unidentified people; (fourth row) three unidentified people and Josephine Serewicz.

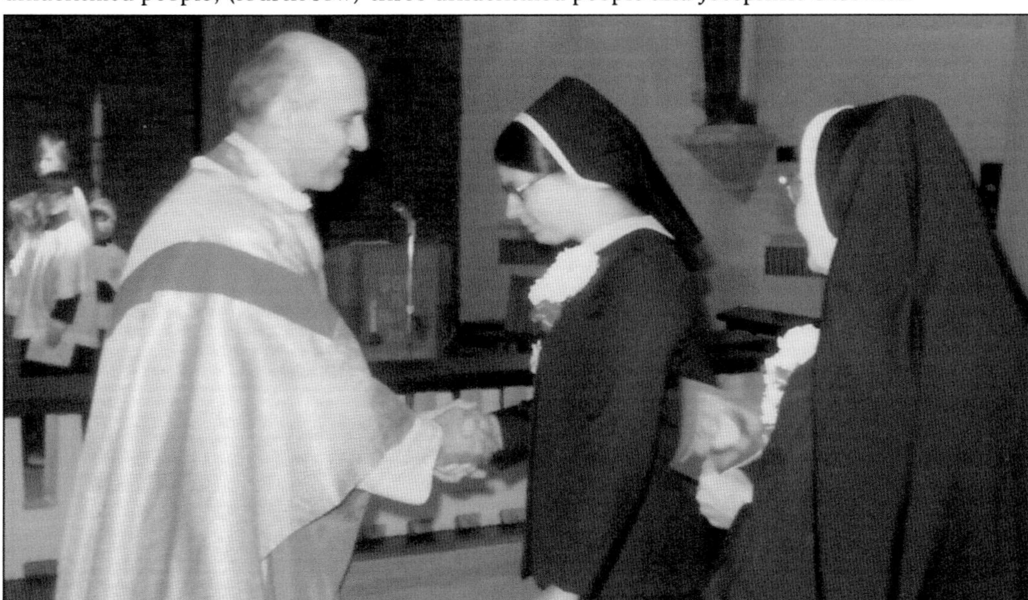

Rev. Joseph Szwach congratulates Clinton native Sr. Antonia Popielarczyk (center) during a parish celebration of the Felician Order's centennial in November 1974. Among the 14 Polish religious communities of women teaching in Polish parochial schools in the United States, the Felicians were the most numerous, followed by the Sisters of the Holy Family of Nazareth. In Massachusetts, Felicians taught in Clinton, Webster, Boston, Lowell, Salem, Adams, and Indian Orchard.

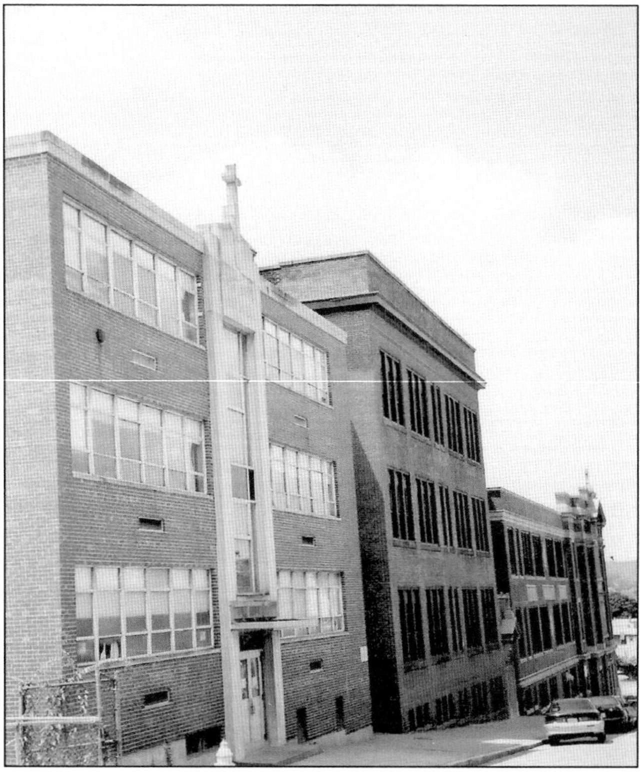

The Richland Street hill shapes the contours of St. Mary's Schools in Worcester. Descending from left to right are the current high school, which opened in 1965; the original 1915 elementary school; the 1920 elementary addition, later used as the high school; and the 1928 addition, which provided Our Lady of Czestochowa Parish with an auditorium, gymnasium, cafeteria, meeting rooms, and related facilities. Kosciuszko Auditorium, complete with balcony, seats 1,000.

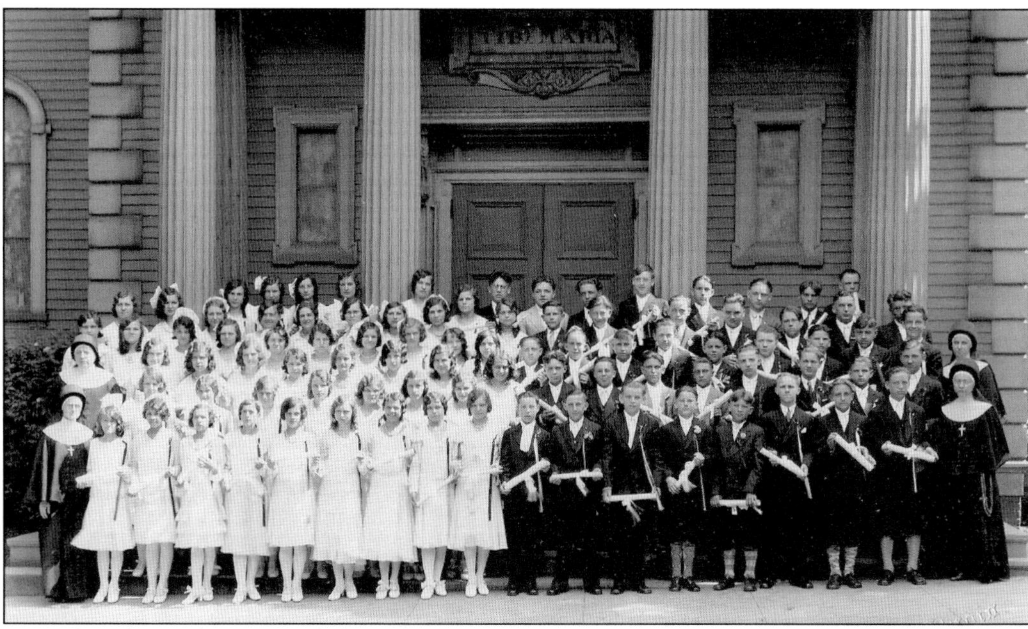

Records indicate that 125 eighth graders graduated from St. Mary's School, Worcester, in 1930. About 90 holding their diplomas stand before Our Lady of Czestochowa Church. Standing with them are four members of the Sisters of the Holy Family of Nazareth, the Polish order that taught at St. Mary's from 1915 to 2005. St. Mary's School graduated 2,763 eighth graders between 1918 and 1950, according to a commemorative school history.

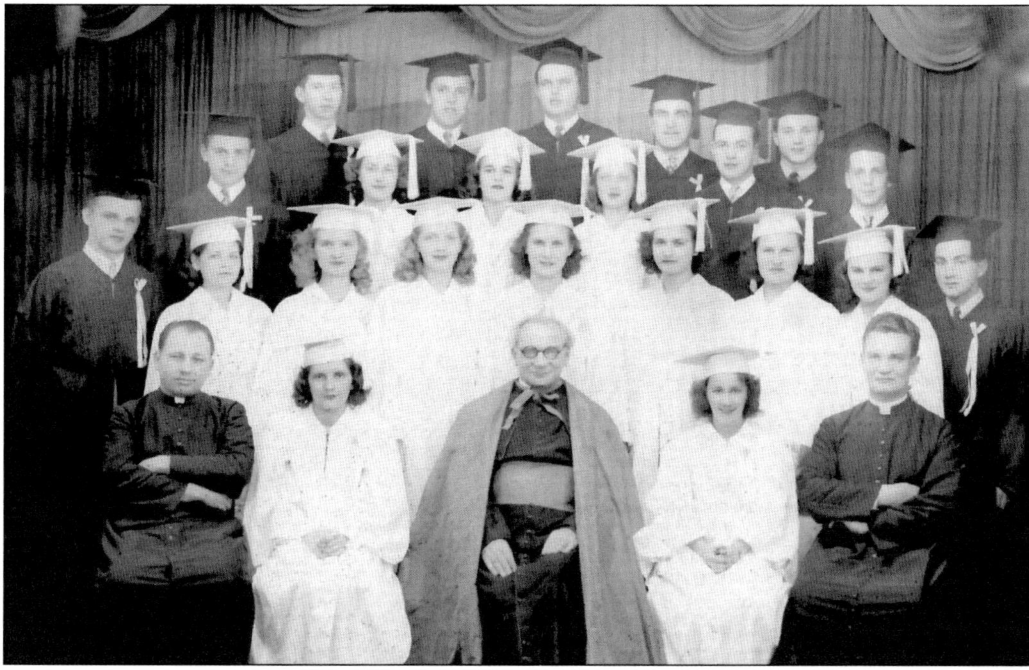

The class of 1942 was the third to graduate from St. Mary's High School, Worcester. From left to right are (first row) Rev. Ladislaus Radzik, Elizabeth Samborski, Msgr. Boleslaw Bojanowski, Regina Romaszko, and Rev. John Mieczkowski; (second row) Charles Jocz, Jessie Gierczak, Wanda Butrym, Theresa Karbowska, Stasia Sasnowska, Florentina Krajewska, Gertrude Sadowska, Halina Zurawinska, and Chester Mysliwiec; (third row) Raymond Zaleski, Hedwig Rydzel, Regina Labenska, Regina Golas, Charles Sliwoski, and Edward Skonieczny; (fourth row) Raymond Oniszko, Walter Kackiela, John Swalec, Edward Grudzinski, and Frank Glinski.

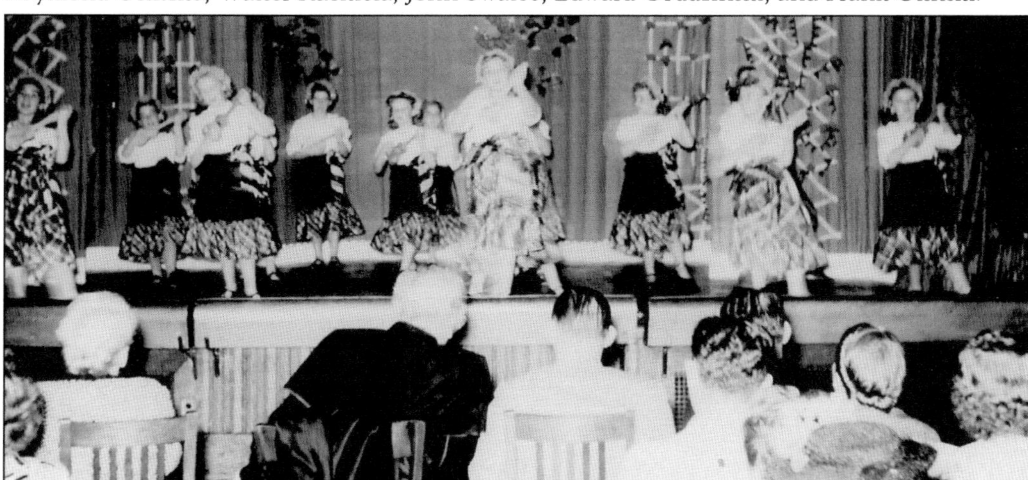

Girls perform at Kosciuszko Auditorium in St. Mary's School's 1949 June Play, an annual musical and dramatic revue with acts presented by each homeroom from kindergarten through seventh grade. It was the younger students' tribute to the eighth-grade graduates who were moving on to St. Mary's High School. Seated second from left in the audience is Msgr. Boleslaw Bojanowski, who developed the school's curriculum with a strong emphasis on Polish language, culture, and history.

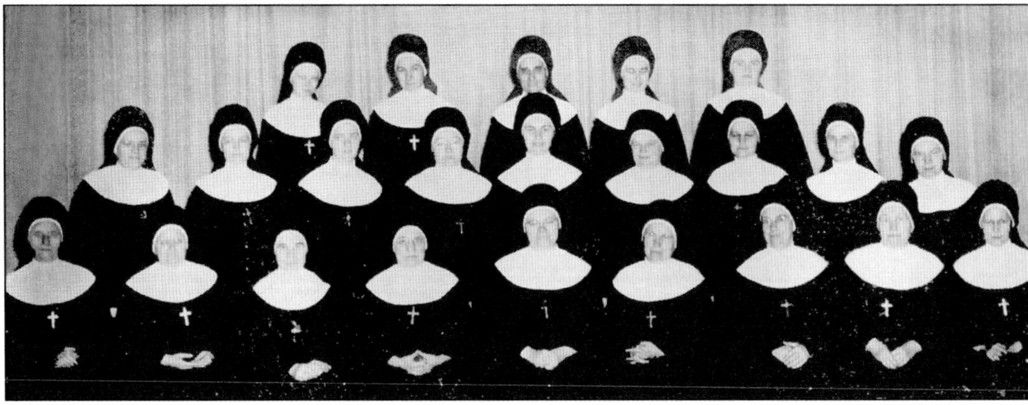

The Sisters of the Holy Family of Nazareth who staffed St. Mary's Elementary and High Schools in 1958 are, from left to right, (first row) Sister Felixilla, unidentified, Sister Philomena, unidentified, Mother Assumpta, Sister Erica, Sister Victorette, Sister Remigina, and unidentified; (second row) Sister Gloria, Sister Scholastica, Sister Roselita, Sister Antonine, unidentified, Sister Catherine, Sister Stephen, Sister Benedict, and unidentified; (third row) unidentified, Sister Sylvine, two unidentified people, and Sister Marilyn.

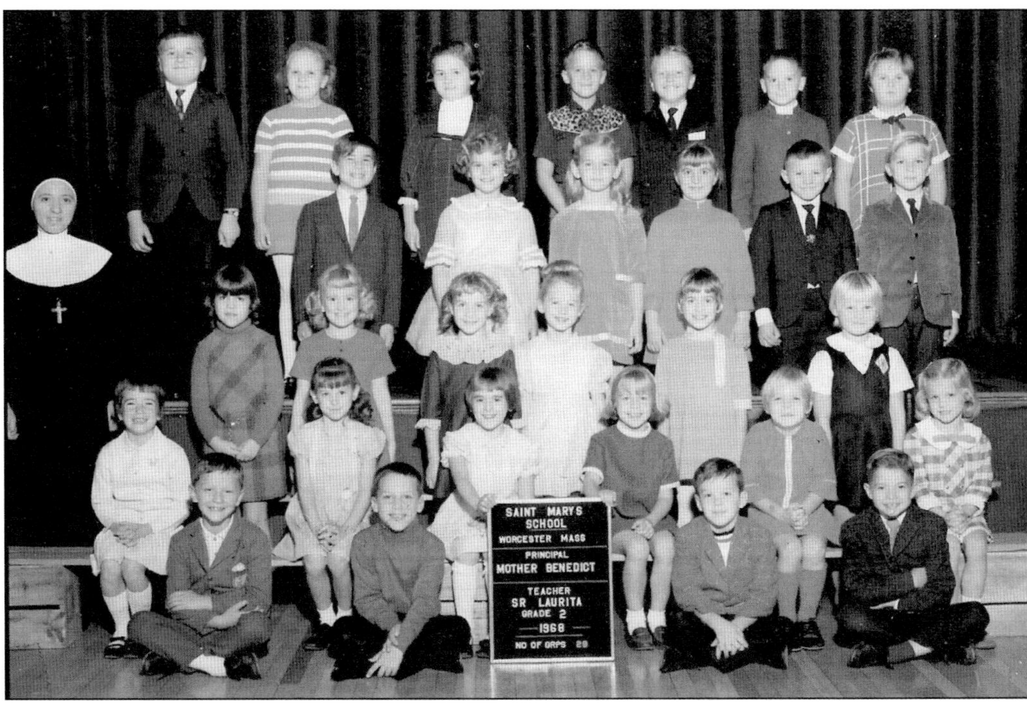

Sr. Mary Laurita and her second graders pose for a class photograph at St. Mary's, Worcester, in 1968. From left to right are (first row) Bogdan Lucic, Michal Bonder, William Grimaldo, and Charles Rogacz; (second row) Mora Canary, Debbie Narel, Genevieve Laconto, Deborah Radzinski, Patricia Winkiewicz, and Deidre Carol; (third row) Robin Jozefowski, Kathy Barry, Lori Meduski, Christine Szymczak, Kathy ?, and Wanda Gotswoski; (fourth row) Christopher White, Cheryl Oslowski, Mary Kisiel, Christine Kaczorowski, Slavomir Parzych, and Mark Karolkiewicz; (fifth row) Albert Banach, Sally ?, Kathy ?, John Dufresne, Larry Midura, Christopher Murphy, and Karen Kubasiak.

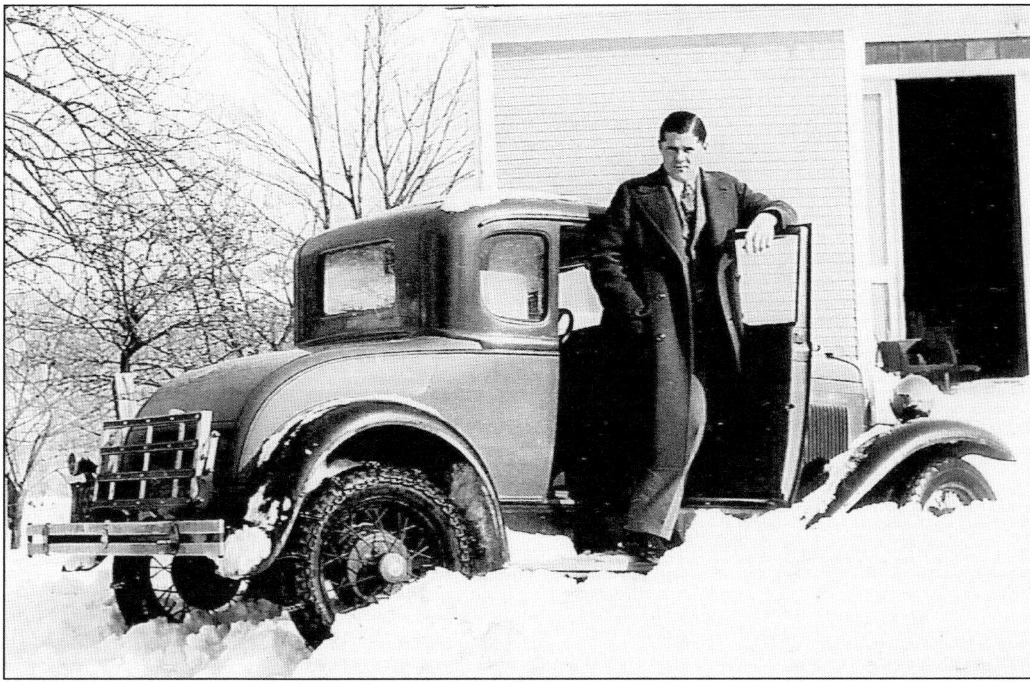

Stanley Szajna of South Grafton attended St. Bonaventure and earned a business degree at Alliance College. He was a salesman for Brockert Brewing Company, a member of the Polish American Citizens Club and Polish Tigers Athletic Club, and a director of the Polish National Home Association and Polish National Alliance. Alliance College was founded in Pennsylvania by the Polish National Alliance to encourage the study of Polish culture and language.

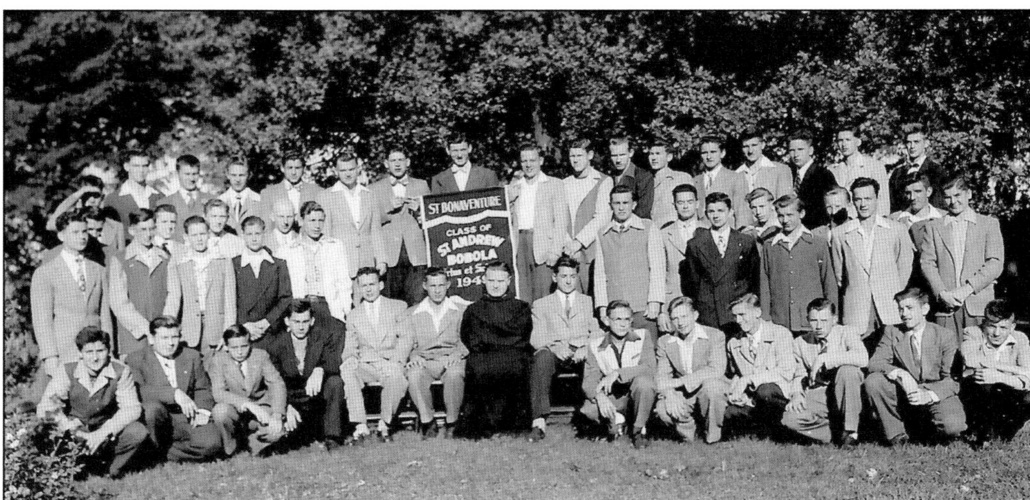

For immigrants whose opportunities for schooling had been limited, their children's chance to be well educated loomed large. The son of such immigrants, Leon Mosczynski of Douglas graduated from St. Bonaventure High School in Wisconsin in 1949. He earned a bachelor's degree at Providence College and a master's degree in education at Worcester State College. Mosczynski taught general science and earth sciences at Northbridge Junior-Senior High School for 32 years.

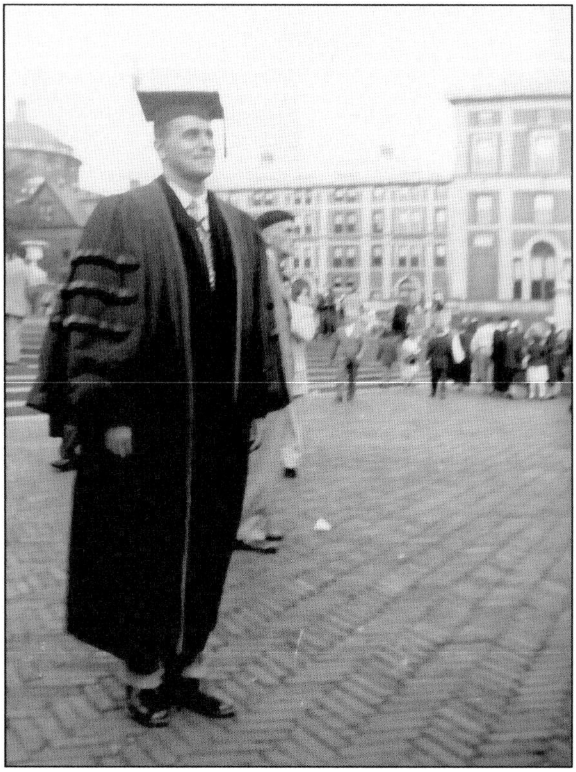

Francis Swiacki of Southbridge graduated from Columbia University Medical School in New York in 1953. During World War II, he served in the U.S. Navy aboard a hospital ship. Swiacki became an ophthalmologic surgeon in New York. He was the son of Francis and Helen Kosakowska Swiacki of Southbridge. The doctor's sister Sophie also worked in the medical field as a nurse at Harrington Memorial Hospital, Southbridge.

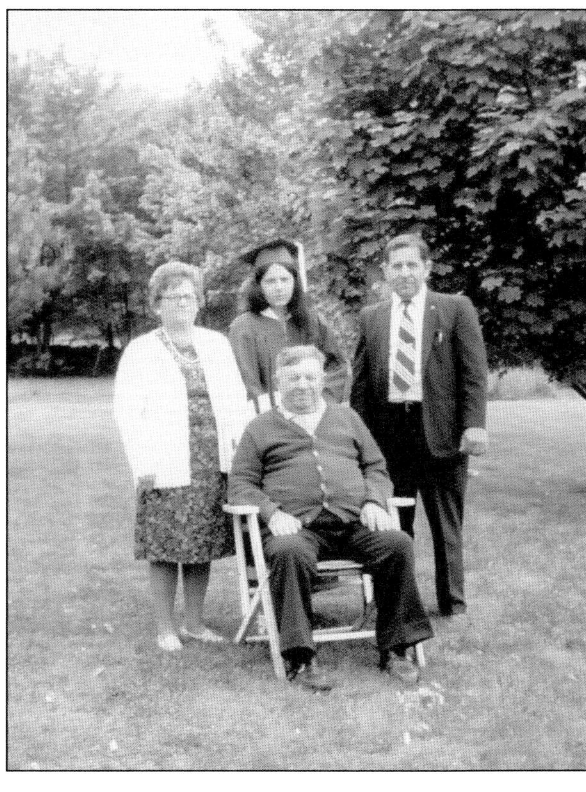

Alice and Joseph Makowski stand in their backyard on Franklin Street, Douglas, during a celebration for their college graduate daughter Janice in June 1974. John Makowski (seated) had 38 grandchildren, and Janice was the first to graduate from a four-year college. Janice earned a bachelor's degree at Worcester State College and pursued a career in education.

Seven

SPORTS

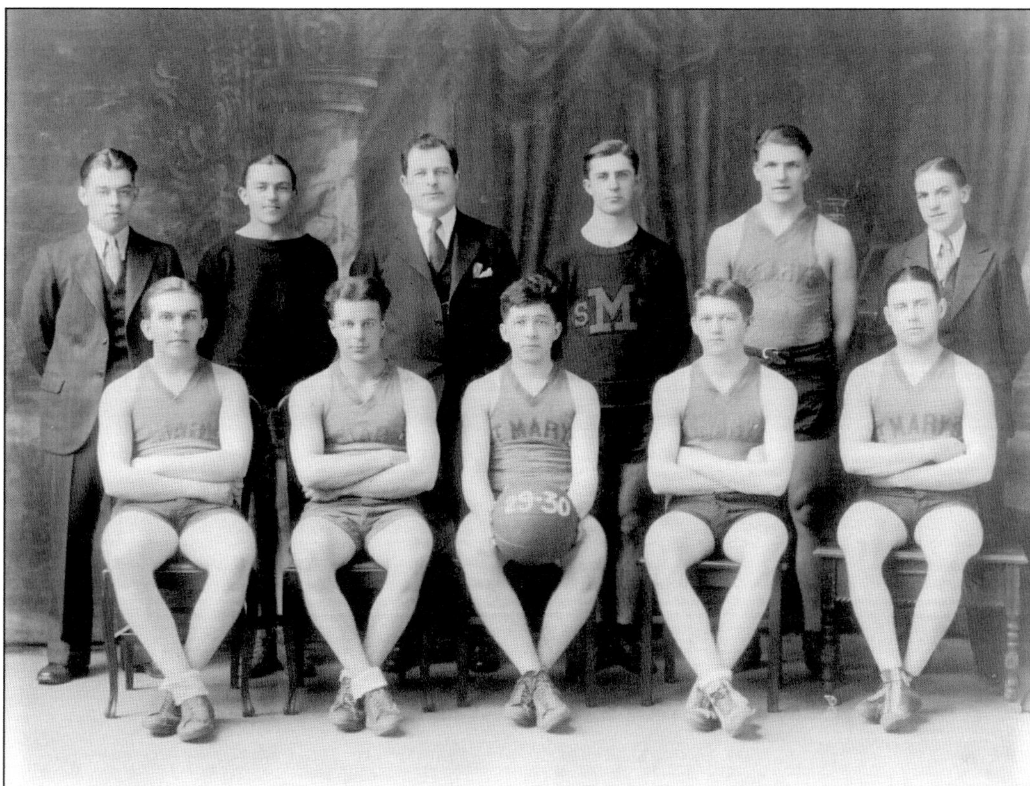

Lauded by Knute Rockne as "a wonderful type of athlete," Archie Golembeski (standing third from left) became physical education director for Worcester's Polish parish in 1927. He had earlier coached Holy Cross and Providence College football teams and cofounded the professional football team Providence Steamrollers. He also enjoyed success as a Millbury Street retailer at Archie's Men's Shop. Golembeski's 1929–1930 St. Mary's team included Joseph Targonski Benedict (seated second from right).

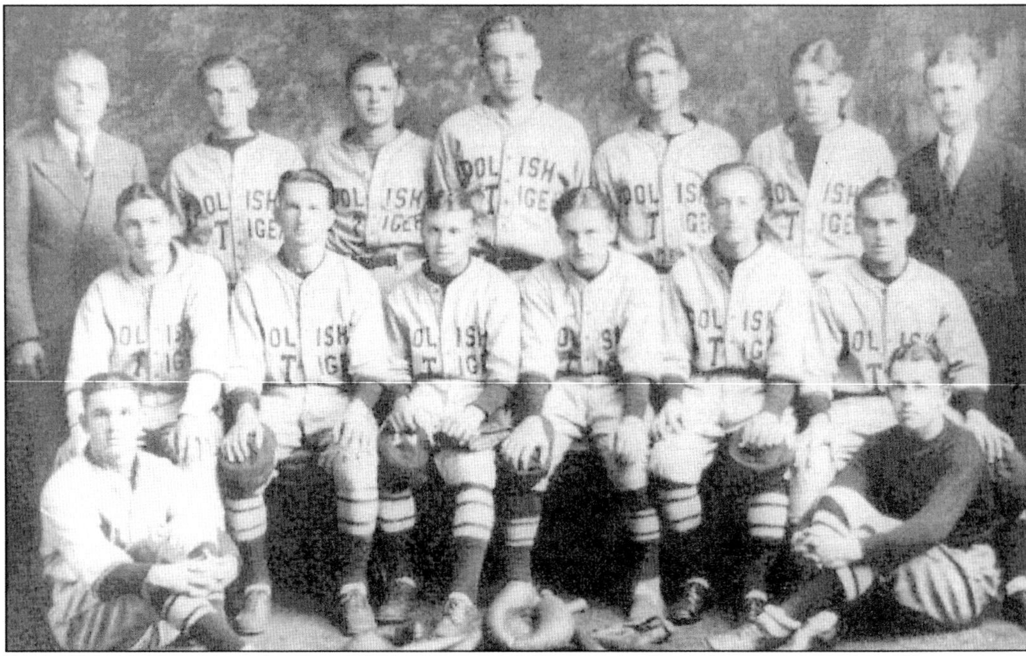

The Fisherville Polish Tigers are shown here in their 1929 season. Seated on the floor are Walter "Pat" Baran (left) and Vincent Wenc. From left to right are (second row) C. Kroll, Walter Baran, Henry Such, Stanley Zastawny, Walter Obara, and Ted Klosek; (third row) J. Pelczarski, Stanley Matuszek, Henry Podsiadlo, P. Pelczarski, H. Zionc, Louis Nadolink, and Walter Such.

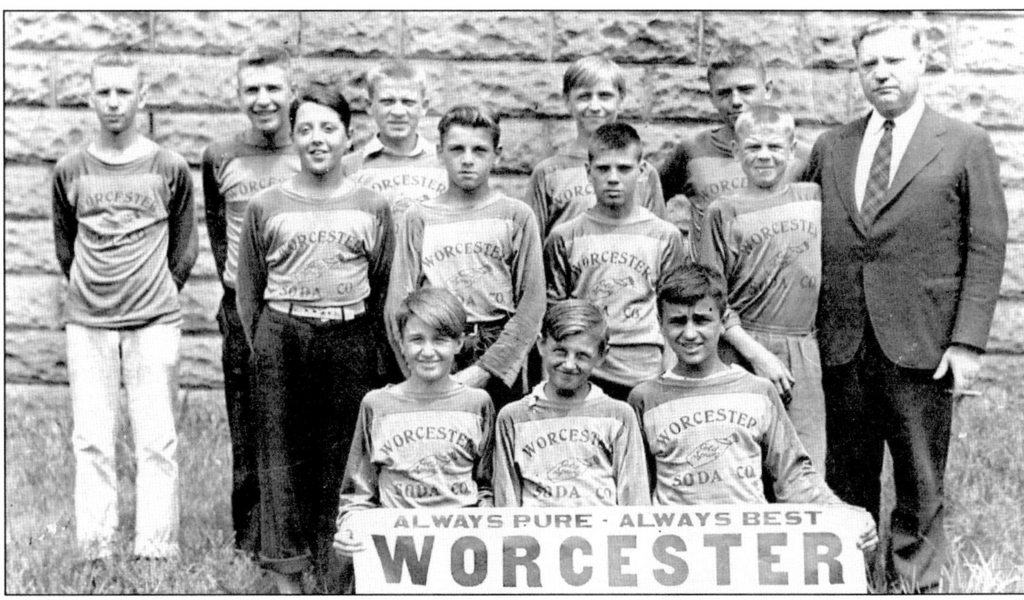

Sporting their team jerseys are Worcester Soda Company's young baseball players around 1937, from left to right, (first row) Chester Skrocki, Henry Skrocki, and Joseph Rossick; (second row) Henry Gutkowski, Edward Piasecki, Bernard Prusaczyk, and Joseph Logan; (third row) George Parzych, John Jablonski, Joseph Sulkowski, Peter Kruczynski, and Raymond Zaleski. With them is team manager and company cofounder Stefan Jadziewicz. Worcester Soda operated on Perry Avenue from about 1930 to 1968.

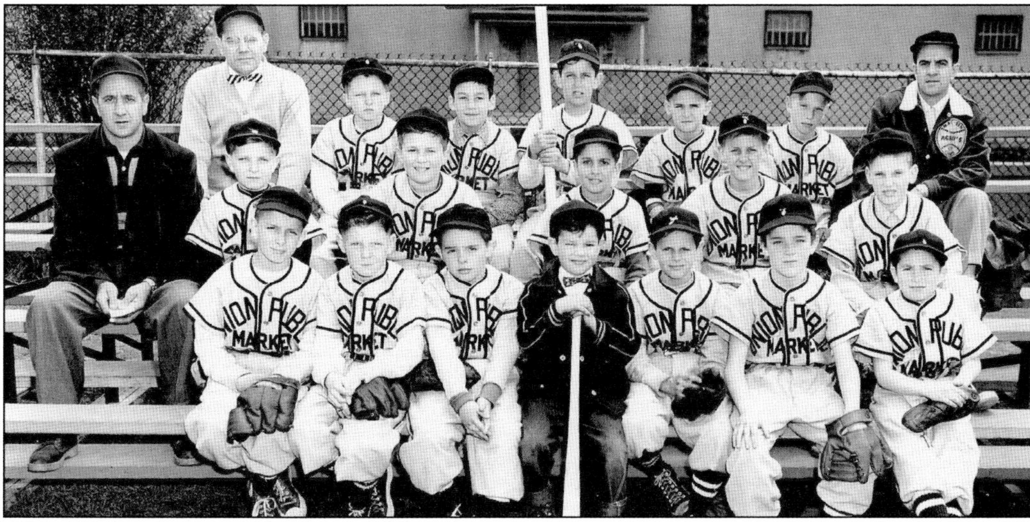

Union Public Market's Maranville Little League players are pictured around 1953 at Maloney's Field, Cambridge Street, Worcester. From left to right are (first row) Daniel Sloane, unidentified, Dennis Flannery, batboy Paul Salek, Peter Salek, Thomas Quinn, and unidentified; (second row) an unidentified assistant, two unidentified players, Richard Beland, Henry Kaymack, and unidentified; (third row) coach Peter Salek, two unidentified players, Robert Baniukiewicz, Robert Giacobbi, Jack Burch, and an unidentified assistant.

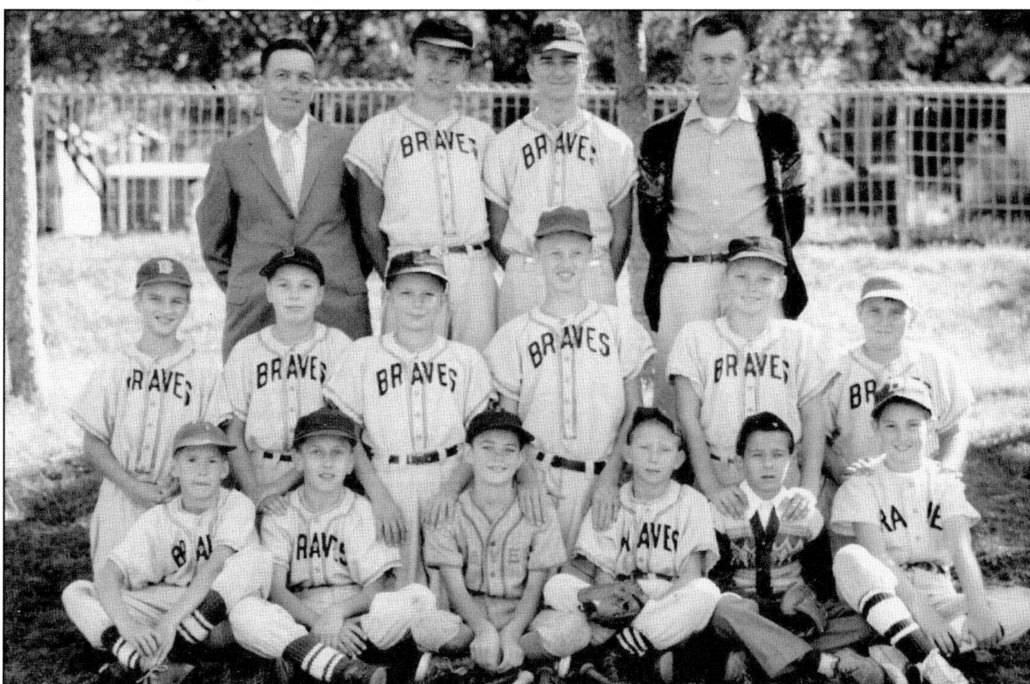

The Gilbertville Braves, sponsored by the Pilsudski Club, were 1959 Junior Baseball League champions. Team members from left to right are (first row) Chester Kurr, Edward Kowynia, Michael Gareau, Robert Rucki, Ronald Rucki, and Dwight Bramble Jr.; (second row) Ronald Skowyra, Thomas Swiatlowski, Roland Kosla, David Campbell, Raymond Mitus, and Donald Ward; (third row) coach Julian Miarecki, Richard Pluta, James Skowyra, and coach Matthew Czabaj.

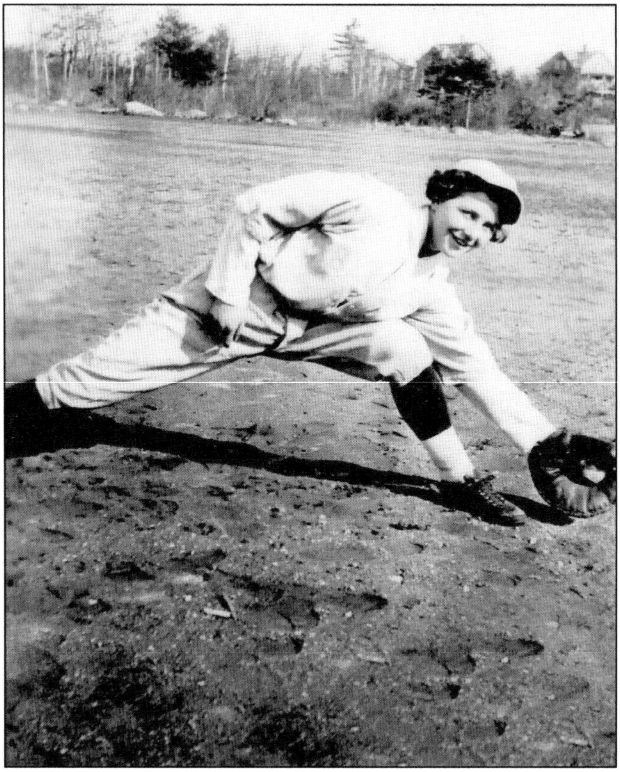

Nellie Twardzik of Dudley gained national recognition in 1935 as the first American girl to start on a high school boys' baseball team. She played first base for Bartlett High School, 1935–1937, and later had her own semiprofessional team, Nellie's All Stars. Twardzik Thompson was assistant director at Crawford Field Playground and coached the Dudley Lassie League. Her memorabilia is on permanent display at the National Baseball Hall of Fame.

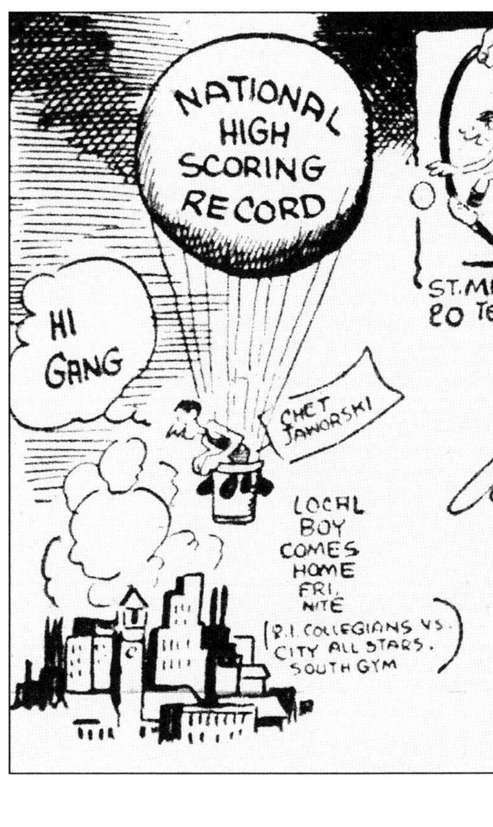

Evening Gazette cartoonist Al Banx anticipates Chet Jaworski's "descent" upon Worcester for a basketball game pitting his Rhode Island Independents against the City All Stars in March 1939. Jaworski, a Taylor Street "Islander," had just set a collegiate record as the nation's all-time highest scorer with 477 points for the 1938–1939 season and 1,428 points in his 76 games at Rhode Island State College. (Worcester Telegram and Gazette.)

This Al Banx cartoon announces a March 1942 testimonial basketball game featuring Stanley "Stutz" Modzelewski, record-breaking U.S. collegiate scorer, and his Rhode Islanders in action against Ziggy Strzelecki and the Worcester All-Stars. Modzelewski scored 1,714 points at Rhode Island State. As "Stan Stutz," the Worcester native was in the starting lineup for the New York Knicks and Baltimore Bullets, then refereed for the National Basketball Association. (Worcester Telegram and Gazette.)

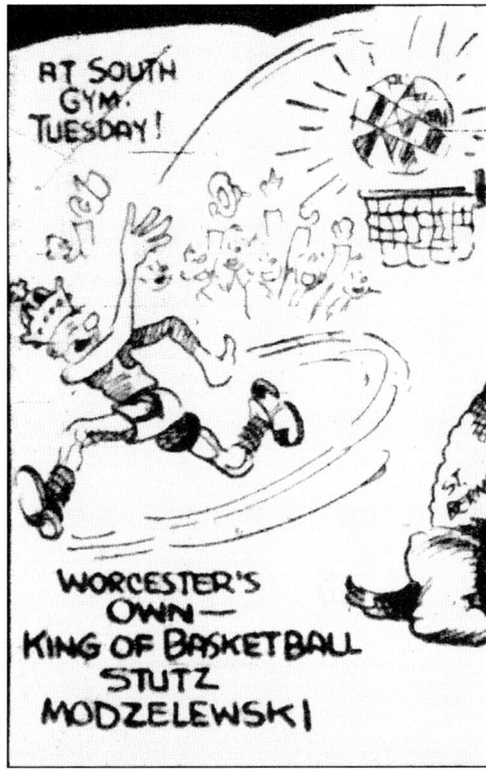

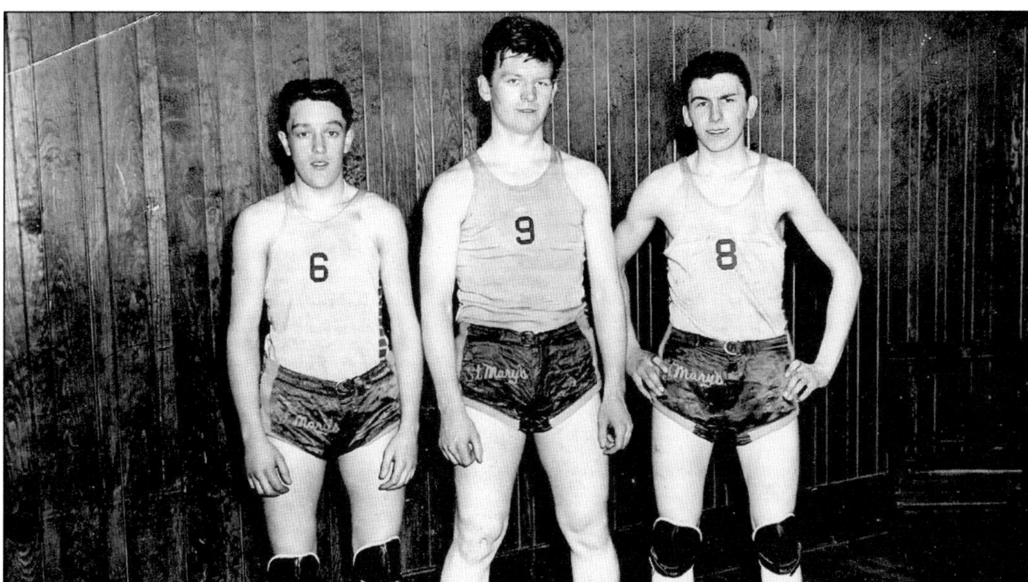

Eugene Szklarz (left), Chester Siniawski (center), and Edward Babinski (right) were starters for St. Mary's High School's 1942–1943 Eagles, who played against Assumption, St. John's, St. Peter's, Commerce, North, and South High Schools of Worcester; St. Bernard's of Fitchburg; St. Louis of Webster; and St. Mary's of Milford. Szklarz later attended Catholic University; Siniawski served as a corpsman in the U.S. Navy; and Babinski pursued a religious vocation as a Jesuit.

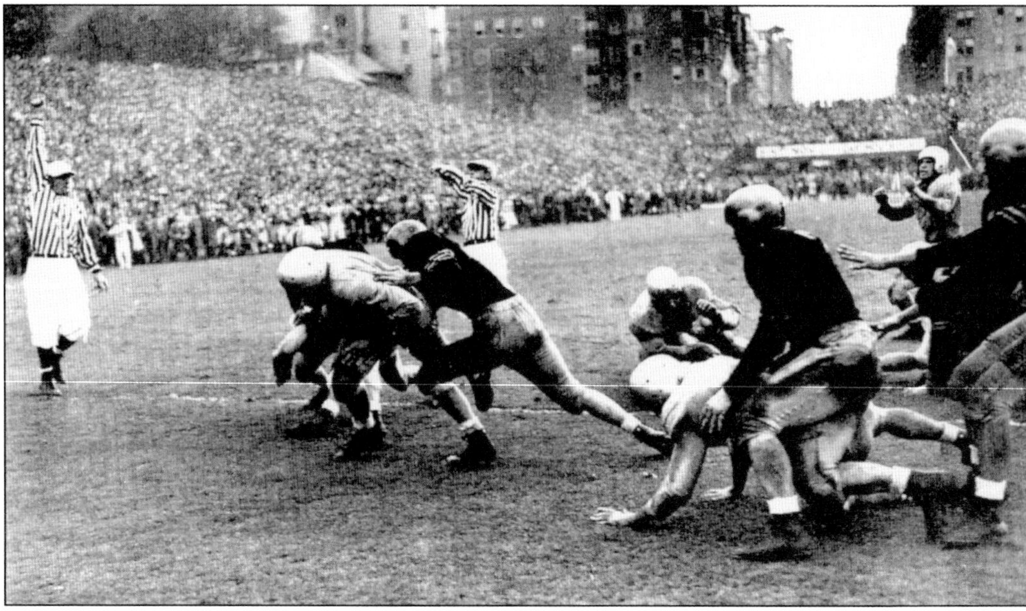

Columbia University split end Bill Swiacki of Southbridge (far right rear) has his hands poised to catch a pass during the 1947 Columbia-Army game that ended the Cadets' 32-game winning streak. During that game, Swiacki caught a pass that sportswriters nationally dubbed the greatest catch in college football history. Named to 16 All-America teams, he was inducted into the College Football Hall of Fame and Columbia Athletics Hall of Fame.

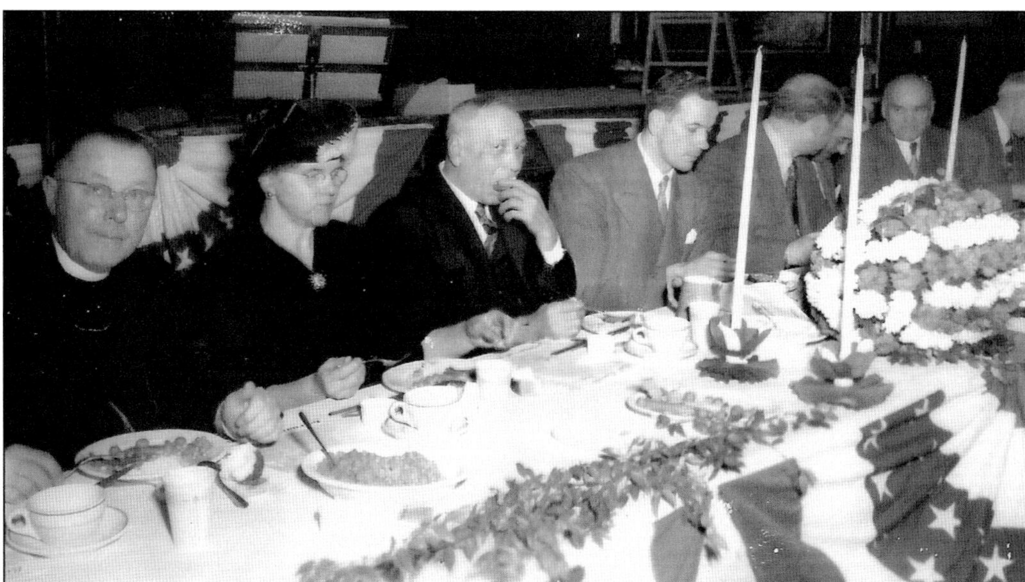

In 1948, Southbridge hosted Bill Swiacki Day for its hometown football hero. Enjoying the banquet are, from left to right, Rev. Martin Hanyz of St. Hedwig's Church, parents Helen and Francis Swiacki, Bill Swiacki, and others unidentified. Swiacki played professional football for the New York Giants (1948–1950) and Detroit Lions (1951–1952) and was an assistant coach for the Giants and Los Angeles Rams and head coach for the Toronto Argonauts.

In only 33 games, sophomore Robert Szklarz, in January 1967, became the first basketball player to score 1,000 points at Becker Junior College, Worcester. In 2006, he was inducted into Becker's inaugural hall of fame class. Szklarz was inducted in the New England Basketball Hall of Fame twice: in 2002 for his Becker efforts, and in 2003 as a member of St. Mary's High School's 1964 New England championship team.

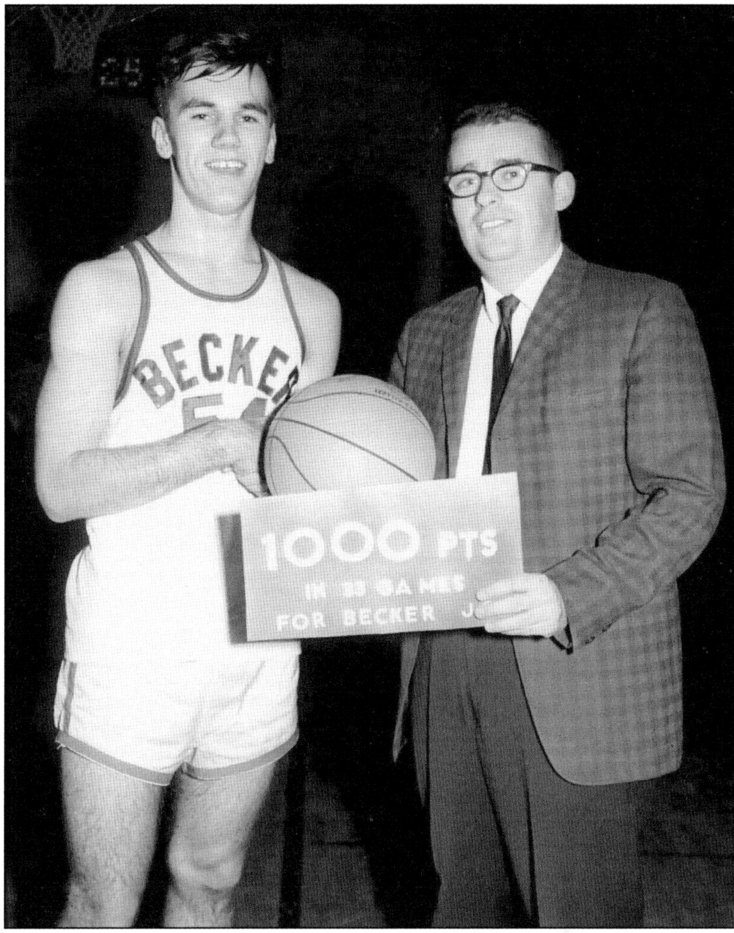

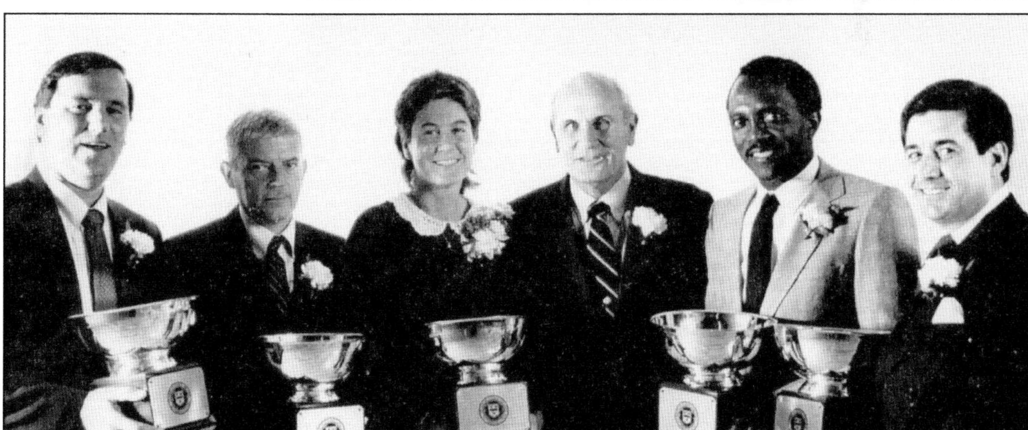

Robert Szklarz (far left) was inducted into the inaugural class of Franklin Pierce College's Hall of Fame in 1987 for his basketball achievements. He scored 1,000 points as a senior, averaging more than 53 points per game and once scoring 85 points in a single game. *Sports Illustrated* featured him in "Faces in the Crowd," and *Converse Magazine* ranked him as the fourth-leading scorer in the nation in 1968.

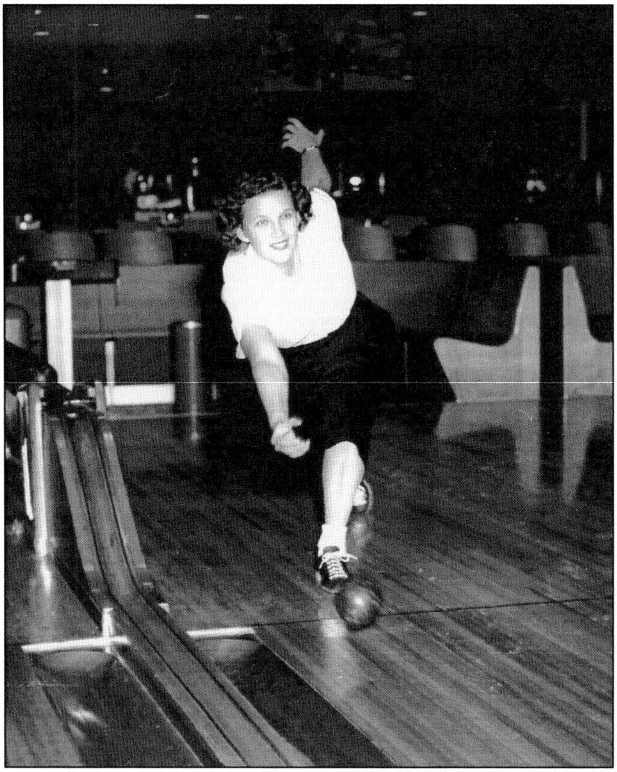

Stasia Milas Czernicki, a lifelong resident of Webster, shows her winning candlepin bowling form in 1960. She competed regularly and won frequently on a local popular television show *Candlepins for Cash*. Czernicki holds the world record score of 1,388 for 10 strings of candlepin bowling. In 1999, the *Boston Globe* named Czernicki as one of New England's top 100 century's best sports figures.

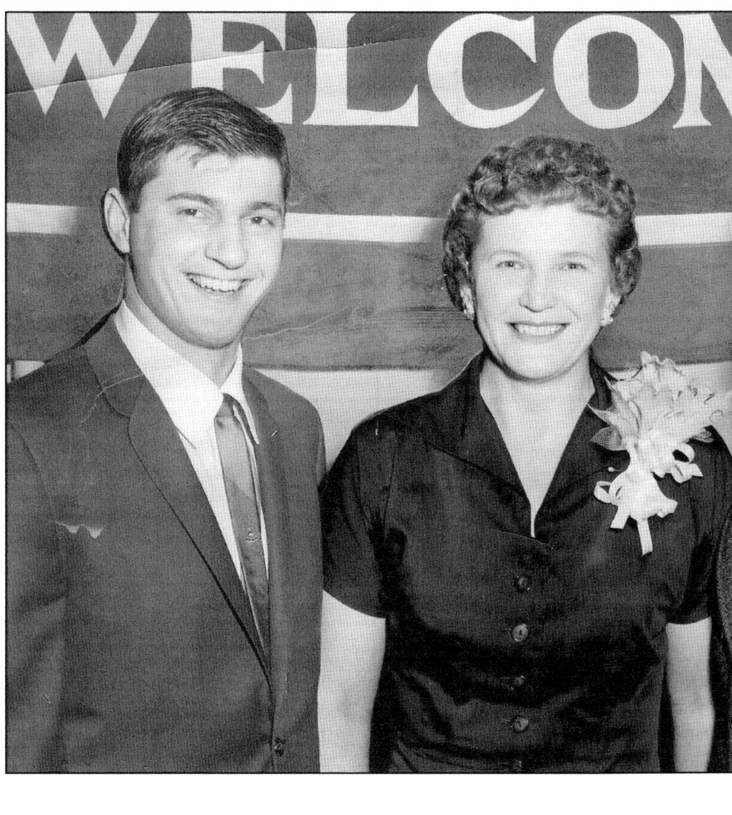

Czernicki, eight-time world champion candlepin bowler and an inductee of the International Candlepin Bowling Hall of Fame, is pictured in 1964 with Carl Yastrzemski, left fielder for the Boston Red Sox and an inductee of the National Baseball Hall of Fame. Along with other members of the Red Sox and New York Yankees, they were being honored by Webster's American Legion for their athletic achievements.

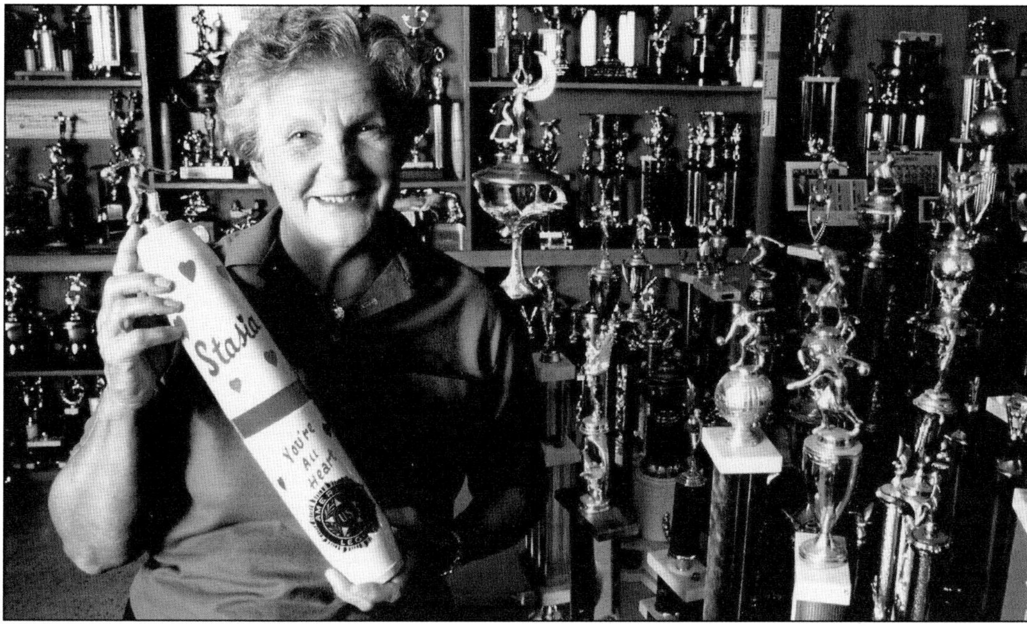

Czernicki is surrounded by more than 300 trophies she earned in her winning career as a candlepin bowler. She displays the bowling pin the Webster American Legion presented her around 1970. The pin's inscription, "You're All Heart," recognized her for being a friendly, down-to-earth person. Other career awards included six-time world singles champion and 12-time Massachusetts state champion.

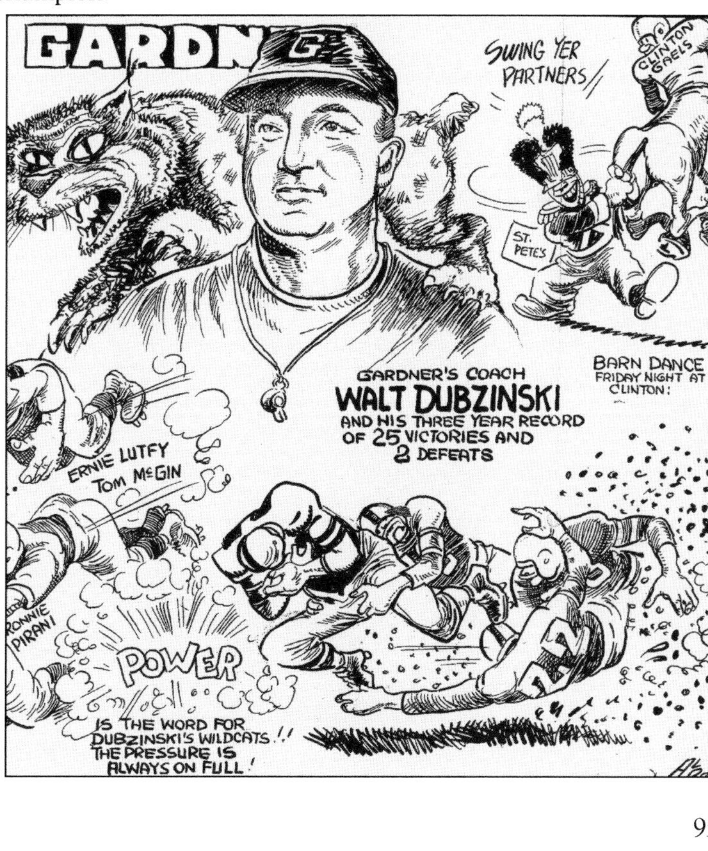

Al Banx saluted Walter Dubzinski Sr.'s coaching success in 1958. Dubzinski cocaptained the 1936 Gardner High School football squad; played for Boston College in Cotton and Sugar Bowl games, and for the New York Giants and Boston Yanks; and coached the Gardner High School Wildcats, 1946–1965. Dubzinski founded a dynasty: sons Walter Jr. and John and grandchildren John, Michael, Steven, and Kathryn have all coached high school sports. (Worcester Telegram and Gazette.)

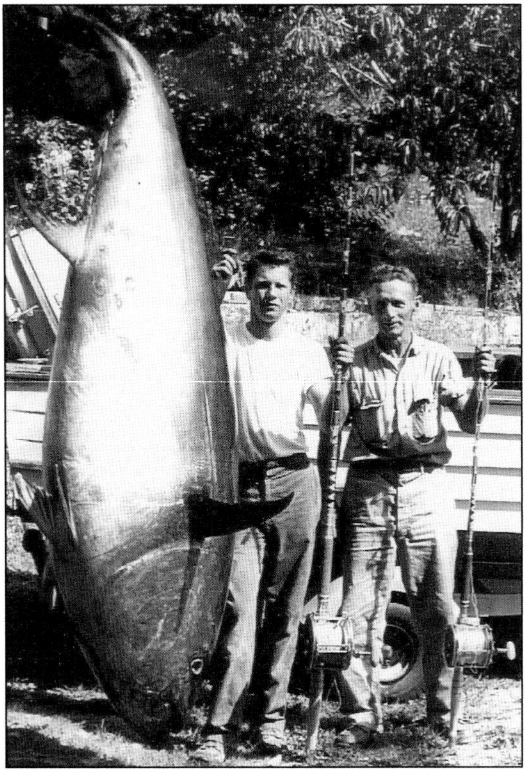

Walter S. (left) and father Walter G. Banach display an 815-pound tuna they caught off Pleasant Bay, Cape Cod, from their 17-foot boat in 1966. The senior Banach was a longtime member of the Singletary Rod and Gun Club, a president of the Worcester Striper Club, and a founder and president of the South Grafton Sportsmen's Club.

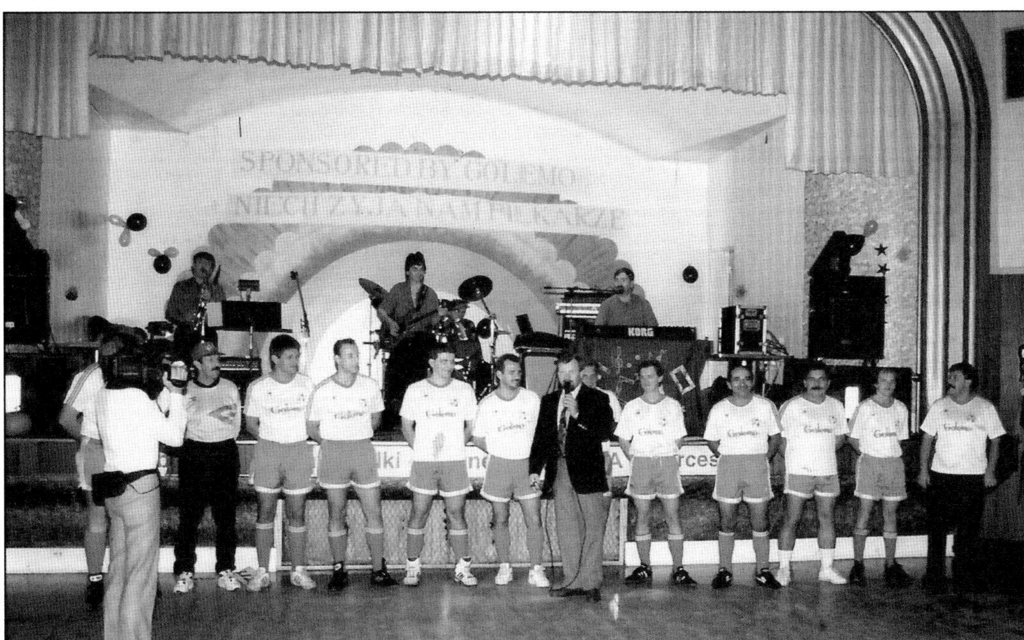

A Polish soccer team sponsored by Golemo's businesses on Millbury Street lines up for media coverage in the Arcadia Ballroom of the White Eagle Hall on Green Street, Worcester, in 1993. They competed with about a dozen teams based in Oxford, Millbury, and other communities and played in tournaments in Massachusetts and Connecticut.

Eight

SERVICE

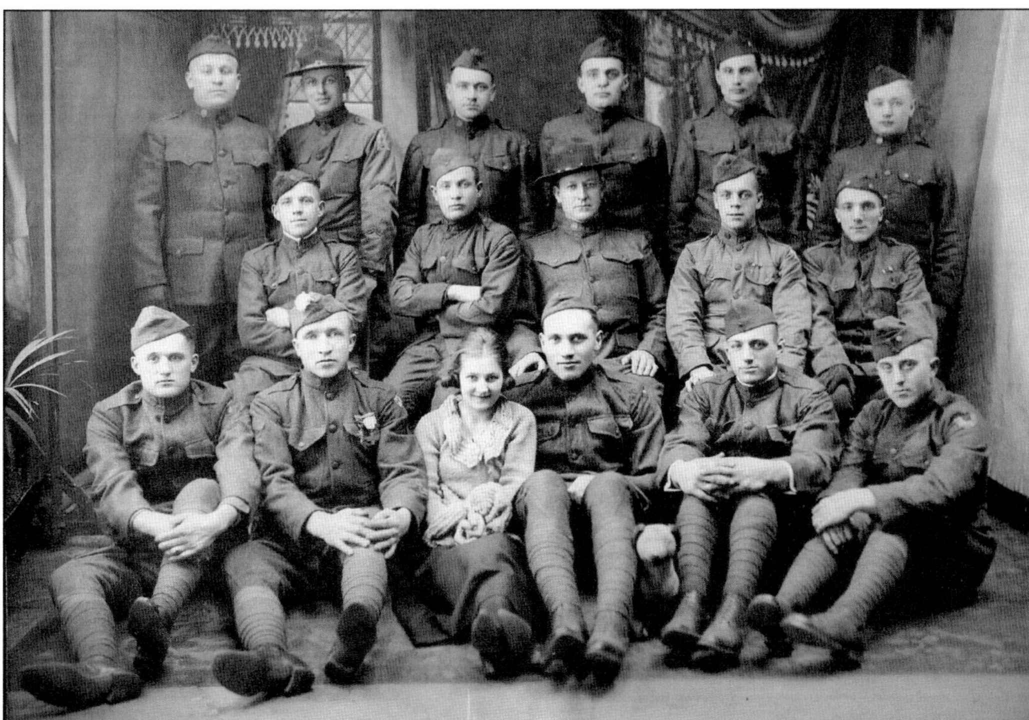

A group of World War I veterans from Worcester's Polish neighborhood had a portrait made at Kosciuszko Photo Studio on Millbury Street, in conjunction with a 1920 reunion. Identified in the third row, second from left, is Stanley Chrapowicki. According to information provided on his draft registration card, Chrapowicki was born in Szczuczyn, Lomza, Russian Poland. He later worked as a wire drawer at American Steel and Wire.

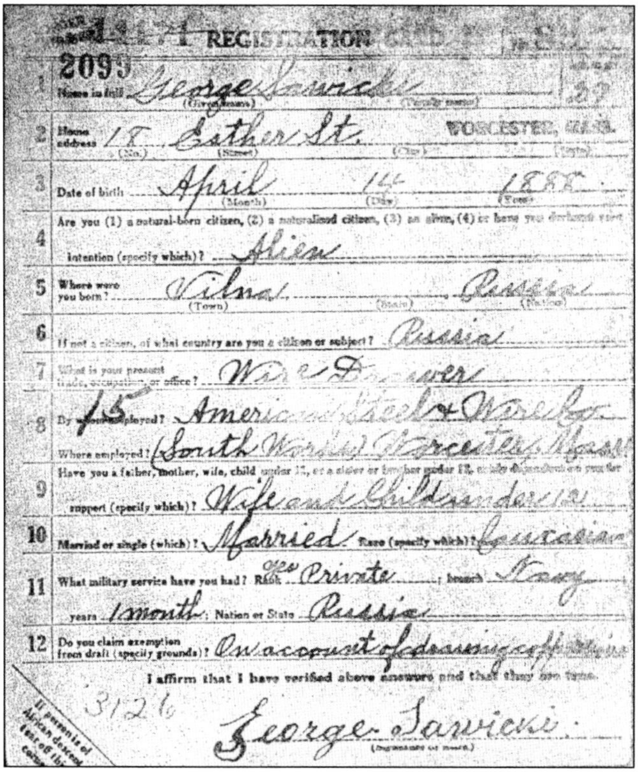

REGISTRATION CARD

2093

1 Name in full George Sawicki (Given name) (Family name)

2 Home address 18 Esther St. WORCESTER, MASS. (No.) (Street) (City) (State)

3 Date of birth April 14 1888 (Month) (Day) (Year)

4 Are you (1) a natural-born citizen, (2) a naturalized citizen, (3) an alien, (4) or have you declared your intention (specify which)? Alien

5 Where were you born? Vilna Russia (Town) (State) (Nation)

6 If not a citizen, of what country are you a citizen or subject? Russia

7 What is your present trade, occupation, or office? Wire Drawer

8 By whom employed? American Steel & Wire Co. Where employed? (South Works) Worcester, Mass

9 Have you a father, mother, wife, child under 12, or a sister or brother under 12, solely dependent on you for support (specify which)? Wife and Child under 12

10 Married or single (which)? Married Race (specify which)? Caucasian

11 What military service have you had? Rank Private; branch Navy; years 1 month; Nation or State Russia

12 Do you claim exemption from draft (specify grounds)? On account of dependency

I affirm that I have verified above answers and that they are true.

3126

George Sawicki (Signature or mark)

Regardless of their citizenship status, immigrants were required to register for the draft in World War I. The cards offer rich data: George Sawicki of 18 Esther Street, Worcester, reported he was born April 14, 1888, in Wilno, Russian Poland; worked as a wire drawer at American Steel and Wire; was married and had a child; and had previously served one month as a private in the Russian navy.

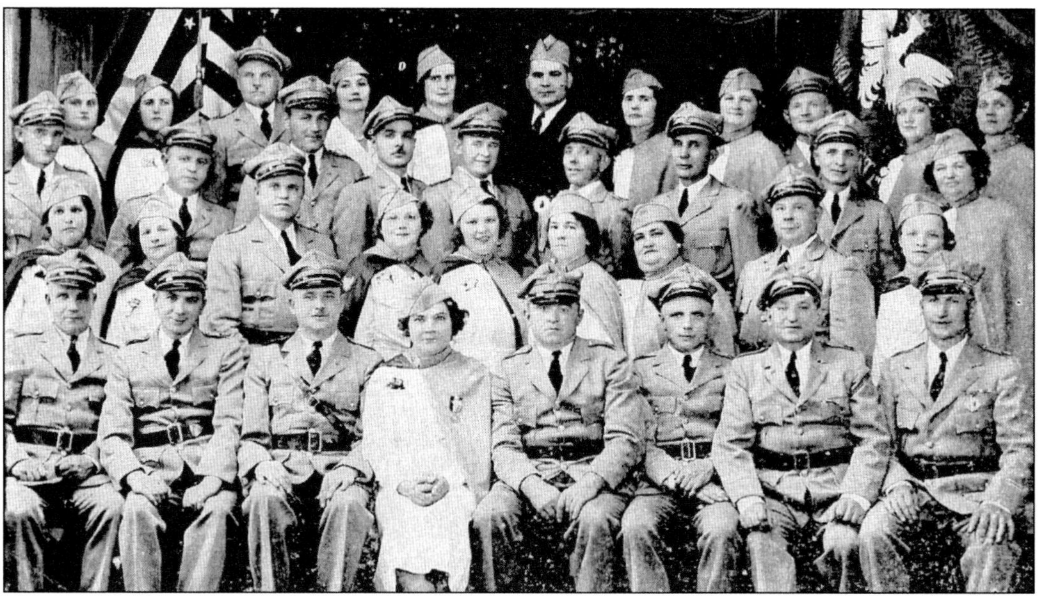

Polish Army World War I Veterans Post 52 and Auxiliary, Worcester, photographed around 1935, are (first row) fourth from left, Agnes Mazurkiewicz; (second row) ? Mis, two unidentified, Helena Piaszczyk, two unidentified people, ? Tomoczko, unidentified, and Frances Radula; (third row) far right, Aniela Prostak; (fourth row) Sophie Krukowska, two unidentified people, ? Fedyk, Apolonia Lejman, unidentified, ? Pawlina, two unidentified people, Jozefa Kozakiewicz, and unidentified. The Polish Army was led by Gen. Jozef Haller.

Konstanty Sobiech, who was in his early 20s when this portrait was made in 1938, was born and raised in Kadzidlo, west of Lomza, Poland. During his service in the Polish Army, he was held by the Germans as a prisoner of war in East Prussia. He and his wife, Alexandra, and children emigrated to the United States in 1962 and settled in Worcester.

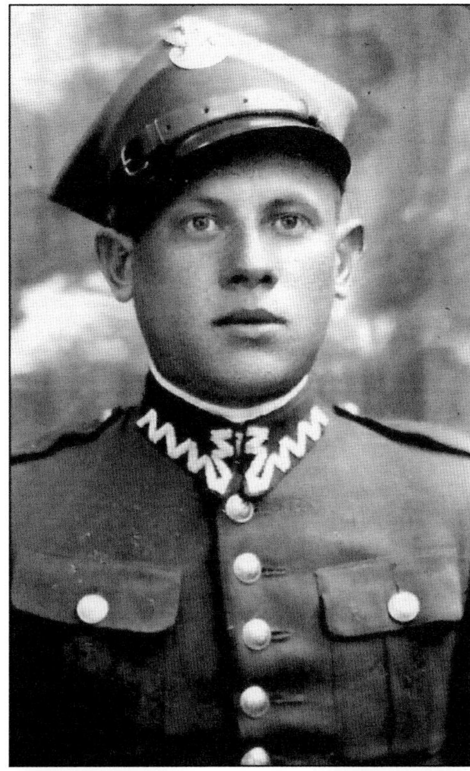

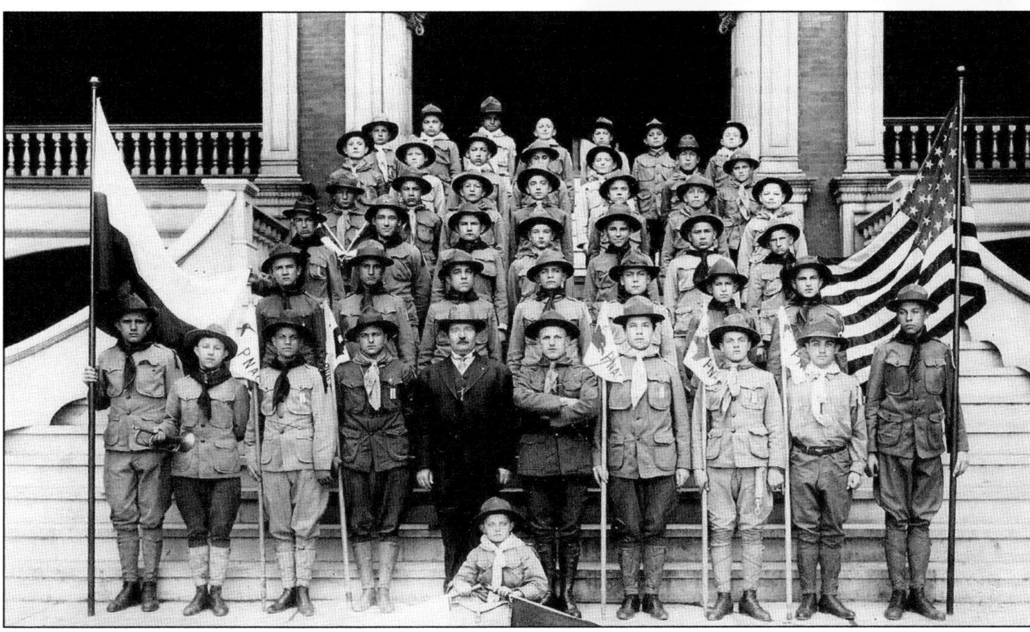

Hoping from afar for Poland's eventual reunification, America's Polonia welcomed the opportunity that arose in 1917 for resident aliens to volunteer for the Polish Army in France (Haller's Army). About 160 Worcester area men signed up at the local Polish Falcons' recruiting center. Some are believed to be among the enlistees pictured here in military training at Polish National Alliance College in Pennsylvania later that year.

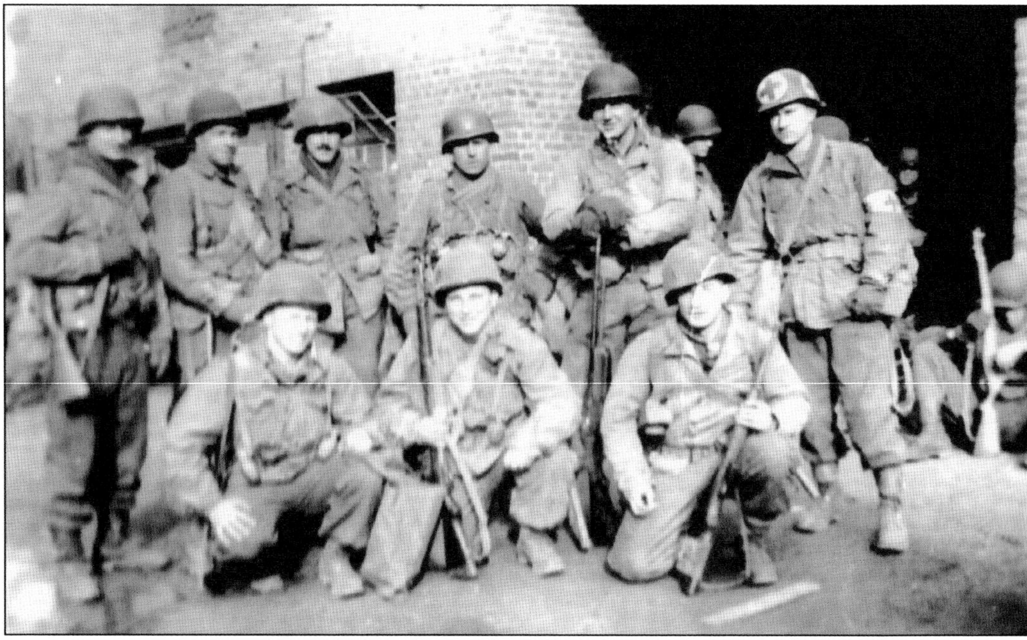

Chester Majewski (back, fourth from left) was a staff sergeant in the U.S. Army in 1944. He saw action in northern France, the Rhineland, the Ardennes, and central Europe and earned a bronze star. When he returned to Worcester after the war, he worked as a molder at Rice Barton and a steelworker at Johnson Steel and Wire. He was a member of the Polish American Veterans of World War II.

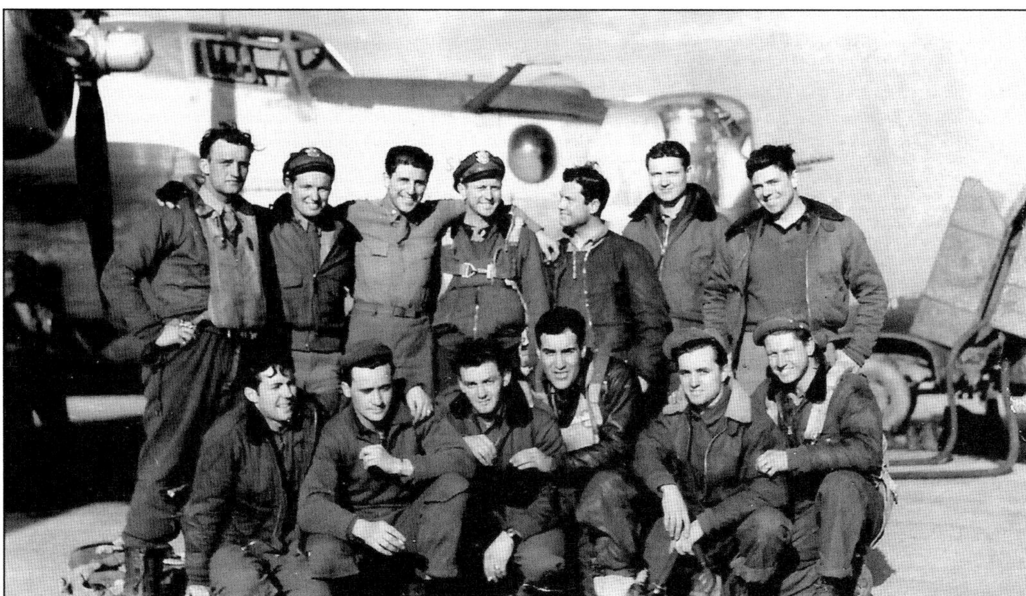

Anthony Hmura, an assistant engineer gunner on a B-24 Liberator bomber, kneels second from right with members of the 445th Bomb Group stationed at Tibenham, England, during World War II. After enlisting in 1943, the Worcester native flew 27 missions for the United States. He participated in the Kassel Mission aerial bombing raid over Germany in September 1944. His unit was awarded two presidential citations.

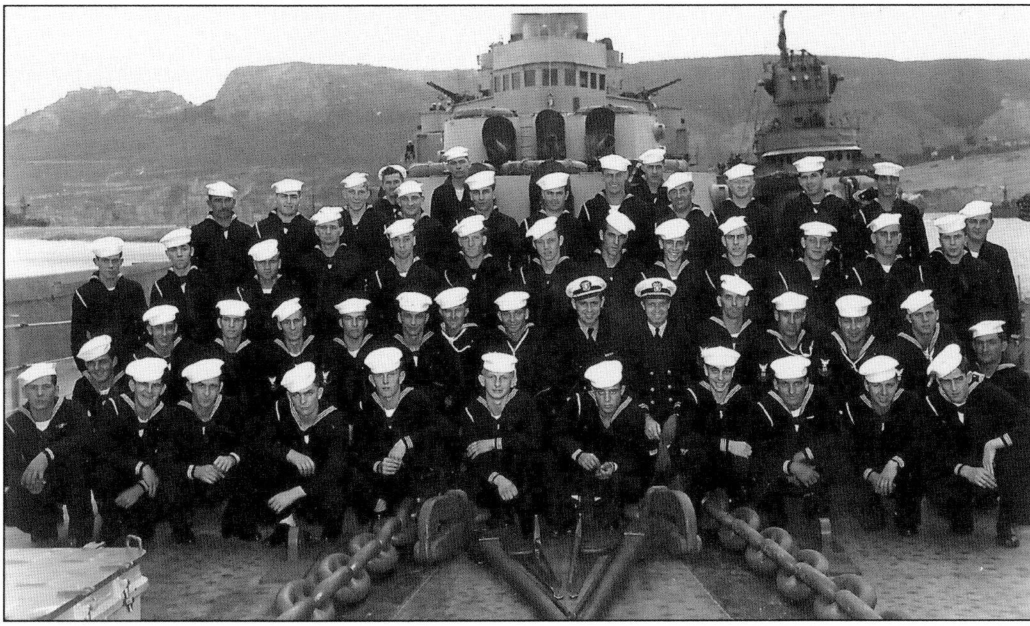

Stephen "Shea" Sablack is pictured in the second row, far right, with his shipmates on the deck of the USS *Brooklyn* off the coast of North Africa. Sablack joined the U.S. Navy in December 1941 soon after Japan bombed Pearl Harbor. He was aboard the *Brooklyn* during the invasion of Italy and remained on the ship for the duration of the war. Sablack lived on Pulaski Street, West Warren.

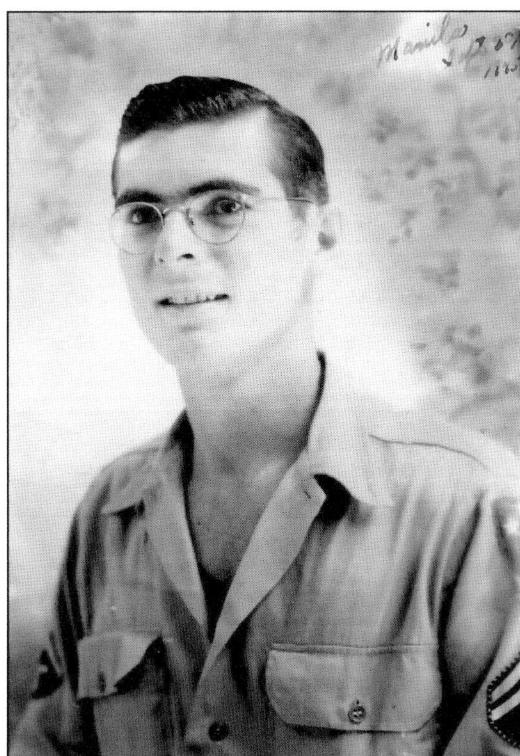

Frank Wojcik served in the U.S. Army's Americal Division, formed on the Pacific island of New Caledonia in 1942 from the 182nd Infantry Regiment of Massachusetts and two other regiments. Wojcik served in the liberation of Manila in 1945 and in the postwar occupation of Japan. Partially visible on his uniform is the Americal Division shoulder patch, with four white stars on a blue background. Wojcik's family resided in Webster-Dudley.

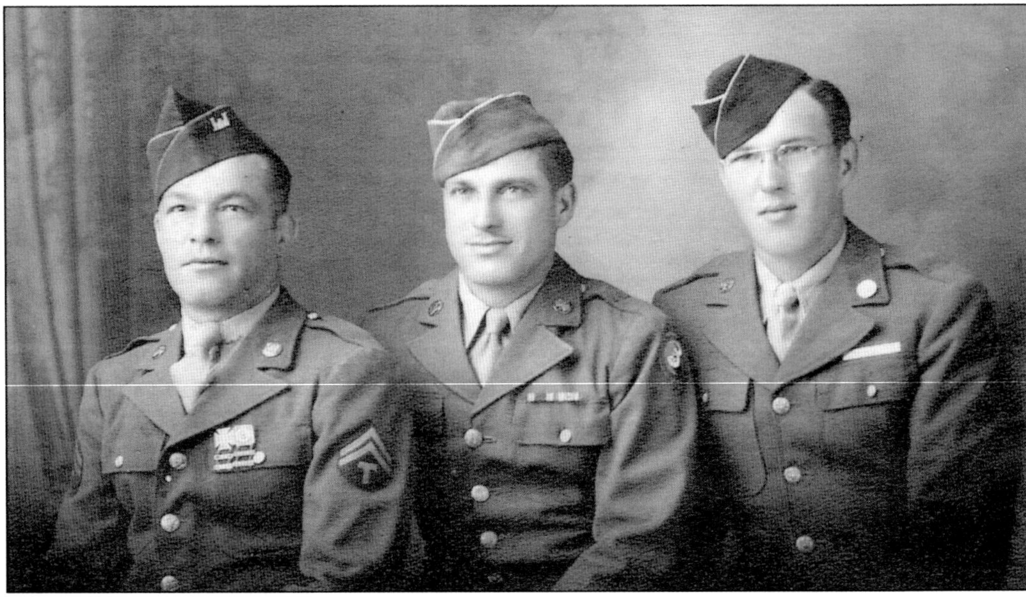

Brothers Ignatius (left), Bruno (center), and Edmund Kozlowski of Dudley all served in the U.S. Army during World War II. Ignatius later served in the Dudley Police Department, retiring after 20 years. Bruno was a tree warden in Dudley, and Edmund worked at Pratt and Whitney in Hartford, Connecticut.

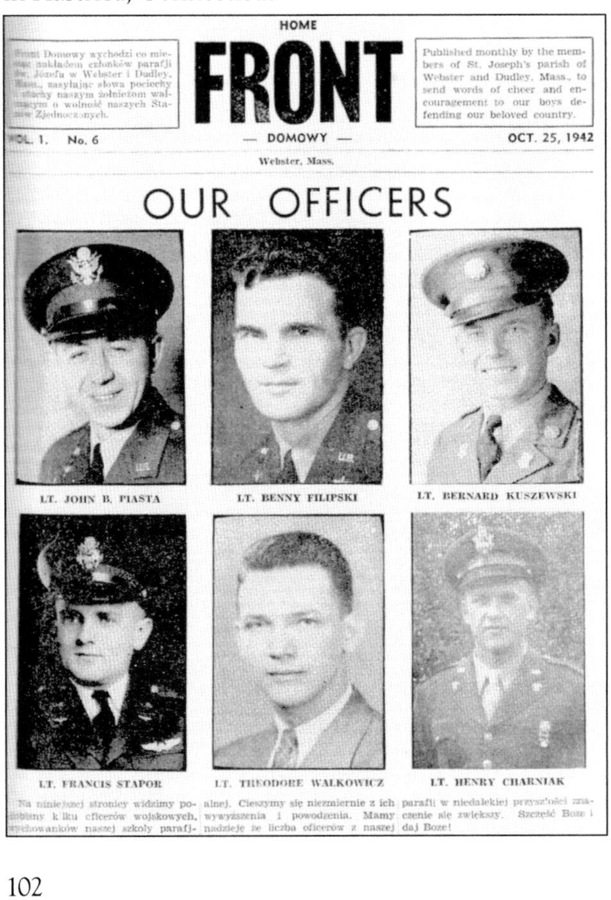

HOME

FRONT

Domowy wychodzi co mie- nakładem członków parafji Józefa w Webster i Dudley, Mass., zasyłając słowa pociechy naszym żołnierzom wal- o wolność naszych Sta- Zjednoczonych.

Published monthly by the members of St. Joseph's parish of Webster and Dudley, Mass., to send words of cheer and encouragement to our boys defending our beloved country.

— DOMOWY —

VOL. 1. No. 6 — OCT. 25, 1942

Webster, Mass.

OUR OFFICERS

LT. JOHN B. PIASTA

LT. BENNY FILIPSKI

LT. BERNARD KUSZEWSKI

LT. FRANCIS STAPOR

LT. THEODORE WALKOWICZ

LT. HENRY CHARNIAK

Na niniejszej stronicy widzimy podobizny kilku oficerów wojskowych, wychowanków naszej szkoły parafjalnej. Cieszymy się niezmiernie z ich wywyższenia i powodzenia. Mamy nadzieję że liczba oficerów z naszej parafii w niedalekiej przyszłości znaczenie się zwiększy. Szczęść Boże i daj Boże!

Established by St. Joseph's Parish in Webster, the *Home Front* began publication in May 1942. The monthly newspaper was mailed free to parishioners in the armed forces and cost locals 10¢. A typical 20-page issue, in English and Polish, offered news, columns, opinion pieces, and stories by Webster and Dudley residents; updates about those promoted, injured, missing, or killed in action; and attention to the war's impact on Poland.

Members of Uxbridge's Polish Service Committee display Christmas packages being mailed to 89 local Polish Americans serving in the U.S. armed forces as well as members of the Polish Army in England and Canada. From left to right are (first row) Tekla Wisniowski, Jennie Marteka, and Mary Gniadek; (second row) committee chair Joseph Jeziorski, Stanley Burnat, and Frank Kogut. Jeziorski was president of the Polish American Citizens Club for 50 years.

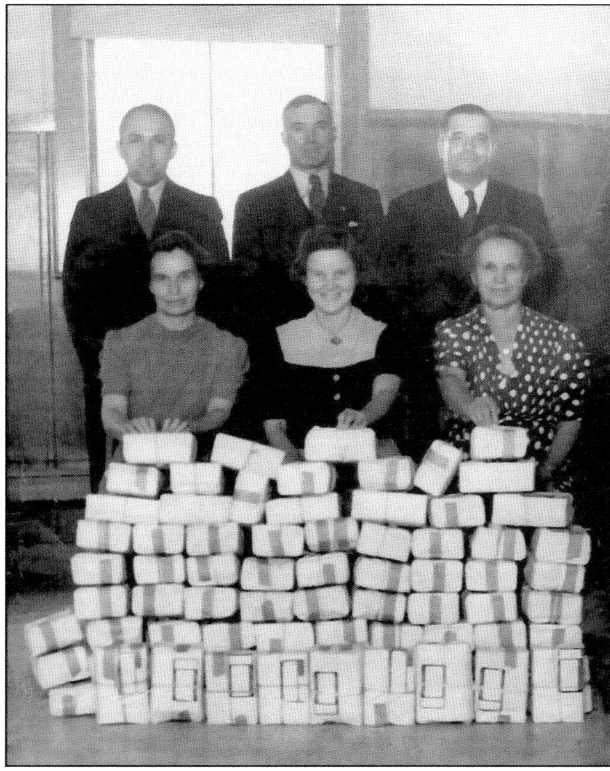

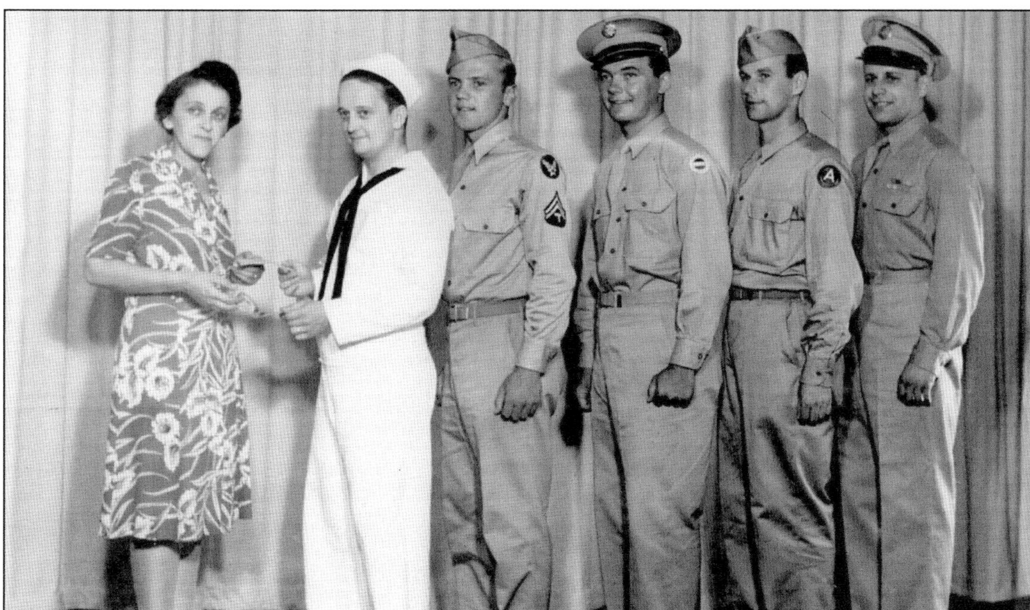

Ida Kupis Augusciak and five local servicemen prepare for a benefit dance at the Polish hall in Uxbridge. The event raised funds to send a case of 1,000 packs of cigarettes to the Polish Army in England. Servicemen standing from left to right are Joseph Kogut of the U.S. Coast Guard, and Cpl. Theodore Podles, Pvt. Chester Jasikowski, Cpl. Frank Pianka, and Sgt. Matthew Novack all of the U.S. Army.

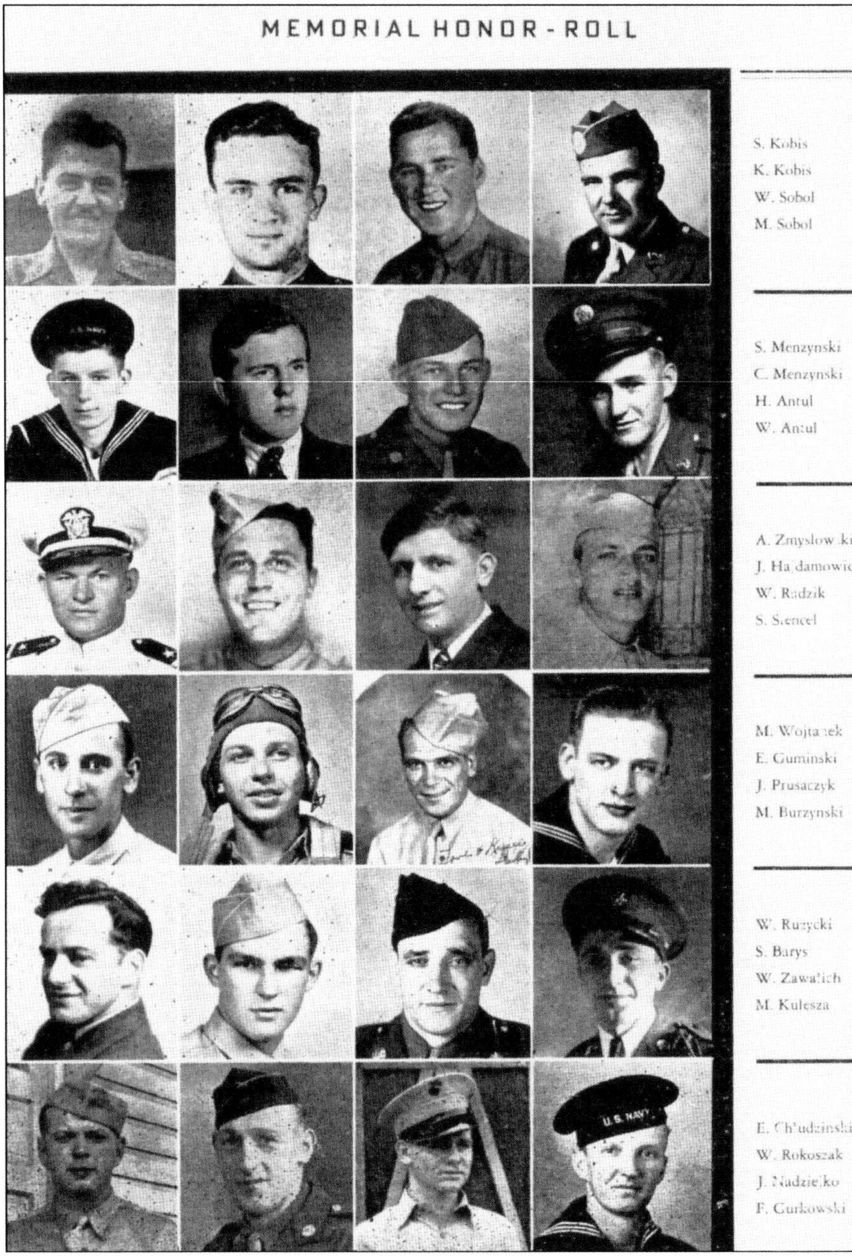
MEMORIAL HONOR-ROLL

S. Kobis
K. Kobis
W. Sobol
M. Sobol

S. Menzynski
C. Menzynski
H. Antul
W. Antul

A. Zmyslowski
J. Hajdamowicz
W. Radzik
S. Siencel

M. Wojtanek
E. Guminski
J. Prusaczyk
M. Burzynski

W. Ruzycki
S. Barys
W. Zawalich
M. Kulesza

E. Chudzinski
W. Rokoszak
J. Nadziejko
F. Gurkowski

When the Worcester post of the Polish American Veterans of World War II was founded in 1946, a primary concern of its 400 members was to commemorate their 52 family members, friends, and neighbors who had lost their lives in service. A memorial honor roll filled two pages of the post's Memorial Day installation program book. This page bears the names and photographs of 24 of Polonia's young heroes. The veterans also worked to have monuments erected in honor of their fallen comrades. Memorial squares on the Island and Vernon Hill pay tribute to Mieczyslaus Burzynski, Edward Guminski, Edward Kimbar, Peter Kosciuszek, Frank Maciejewski, Joseph Mierzejewski, John Prusaczyk, Walter Radzik, Charles Ruszala, Walter Sobol, and Walter Zawalich. Additionally, a World War I monument commemorates Joseph Grabowski, and Casimir Pulaski Square honors the Revolutionary War hero.

The Polish Civic and Social Corporation dedicated a flagpole and U.S. and service flags in front of the Mendon Street Polish Home in 1942. Rita Targonski presents the flags to corporation president Vincent Marteka on behalf of the Polish Service Committee. More than 500 people participated in the day's events, which included a parade and banquet. Uxbridge servicemen of Polish descent numbered well over 100 in World War II.

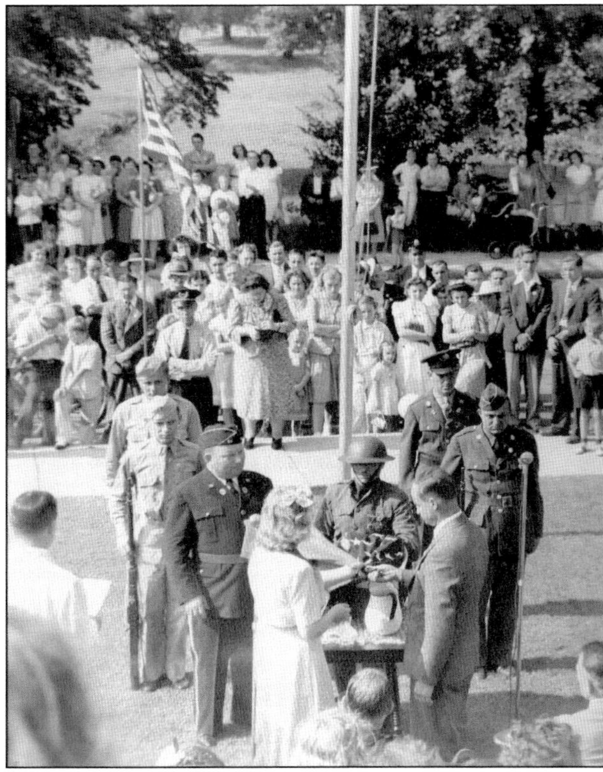

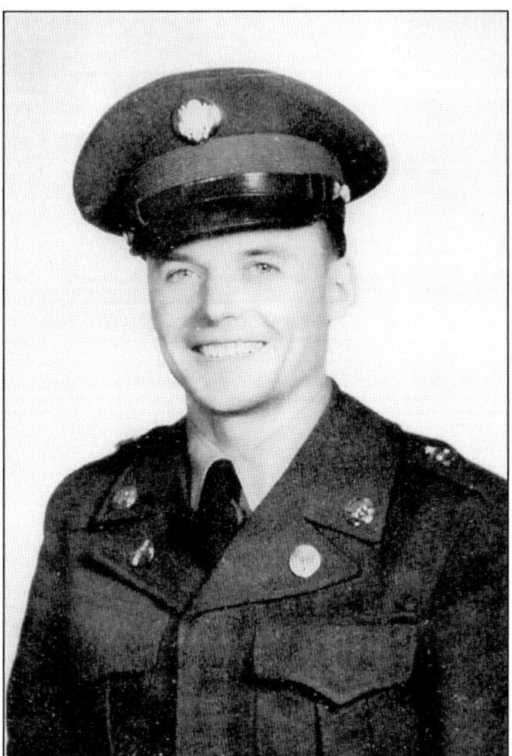

Henry Kaczynski was born in Fall River but raised near Ostrow Mazowiecki, Poland, on a farm his parents bought with Massachusetts mill earnings. During World War II, Kaczynski was seized by the Nazis for forced labor in East Prussia. He was freed when Russian troops overran the area near the end of the war. When he returned to America, he was drafted and served in the U.S. Army in 1948–1949.

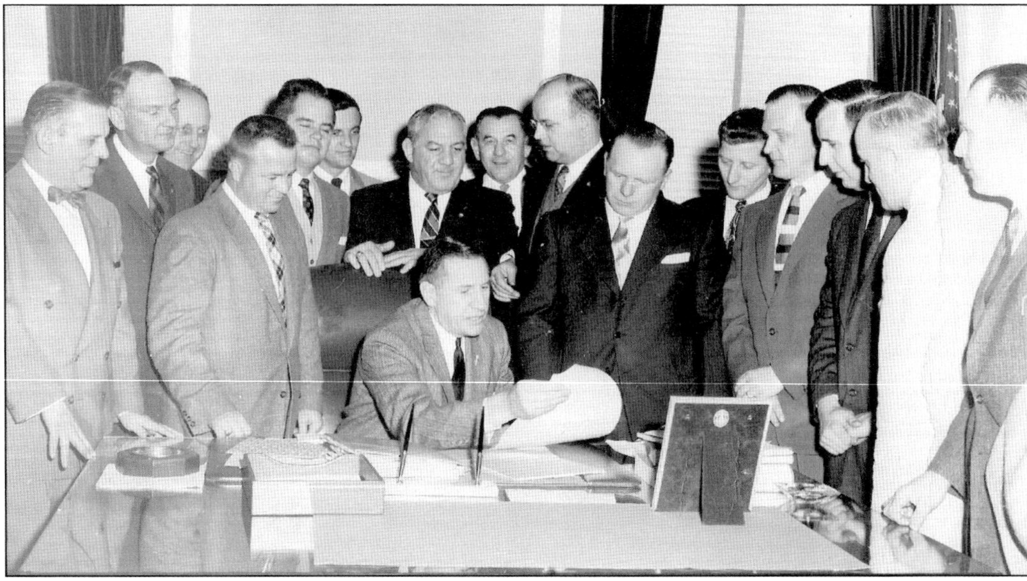

Massachusetts governor Foster Furcolo (seated) congratulates the Southbridge Polish American Veterans (PAV) post on receiving its charter in 1958. From left to right are Charles Samborski, Worcester; Paul Benoit; Thaddeus Kosakowski, Southbridge; PAV State Department commander Edward Lepkowski, Gardner; Walter Rojcewicz, Worcester; Stanley Ciukaj, Southbridge; Michael Favulli; Frank Salek, Southbridge; Stanislaus Wondolowski, Worcester; and post commander Telesphore Libuda, Alexander Kowaleski, Henry Remian, Edward Seremet, Ferdinand Szczypien, and Louis Seremet, all of Southbridge.

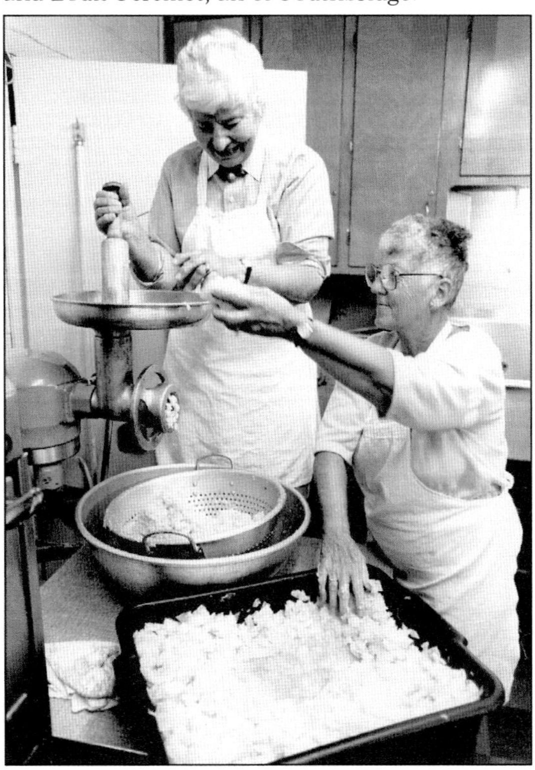

Auxiliary members Nellie Kosakowski and Clara Czyzewski grind cabbage in preparation for the Polish picnic sponsored by the Southbridge PAV post in September 1988. *Golabki*, pierogi, kielbasa, and *kapusta* are traditional fare at Polish picnics, with fresh corn on the cob, a popular summer addition. Homemade food for these events depends on many volunteers spending many hours in the kitchen.

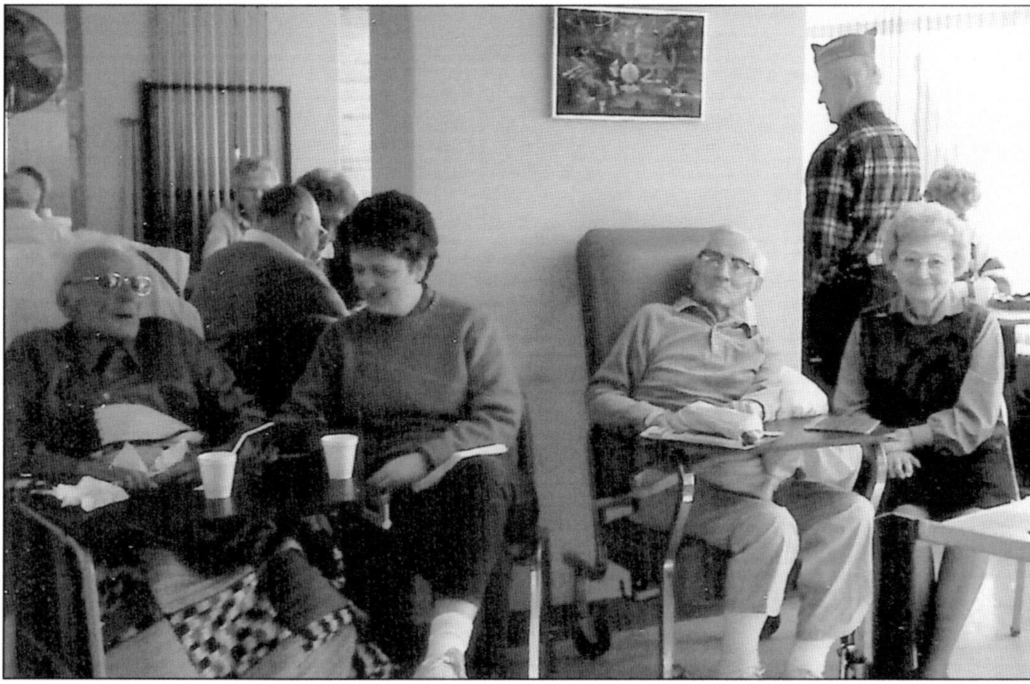

Visiting the Soldiers' Home in Holyoke has been one of the regular activities of the Southbridge PAV post and auxiliary since 1960. Home-cooked lunches, conversation, and games highlight the occasions. The Soldiers' Home provides long-term care, assisted living, and supportive care services for veterans. The post was also involved in March of Dimes fund-raisers in its early years.

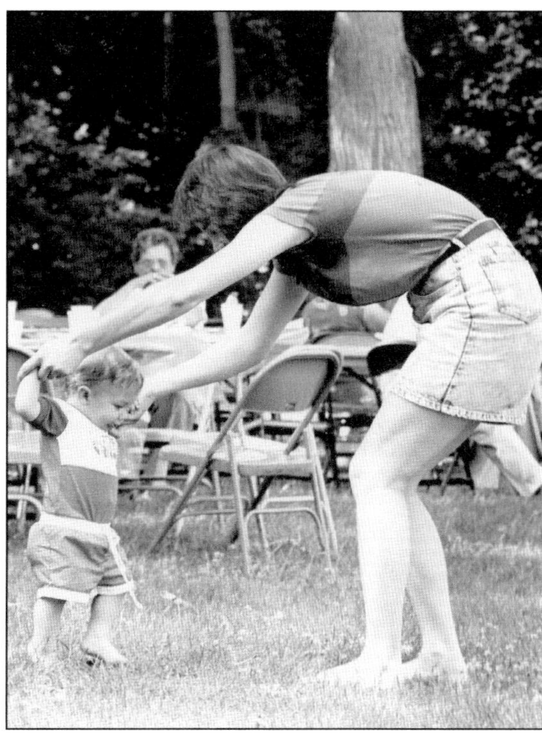

Tamara Athole teaches a toddler how to polka during the Polish picnic sponsored by the Southbridge PAV post in September 1988. Ray Henry's Orchestra provided music for the festivities. Whether a picnic features a live band or a disc jockey, polka music is guaranteed to fill the air and the dance floor. Some picnics begin with a polka Mass.

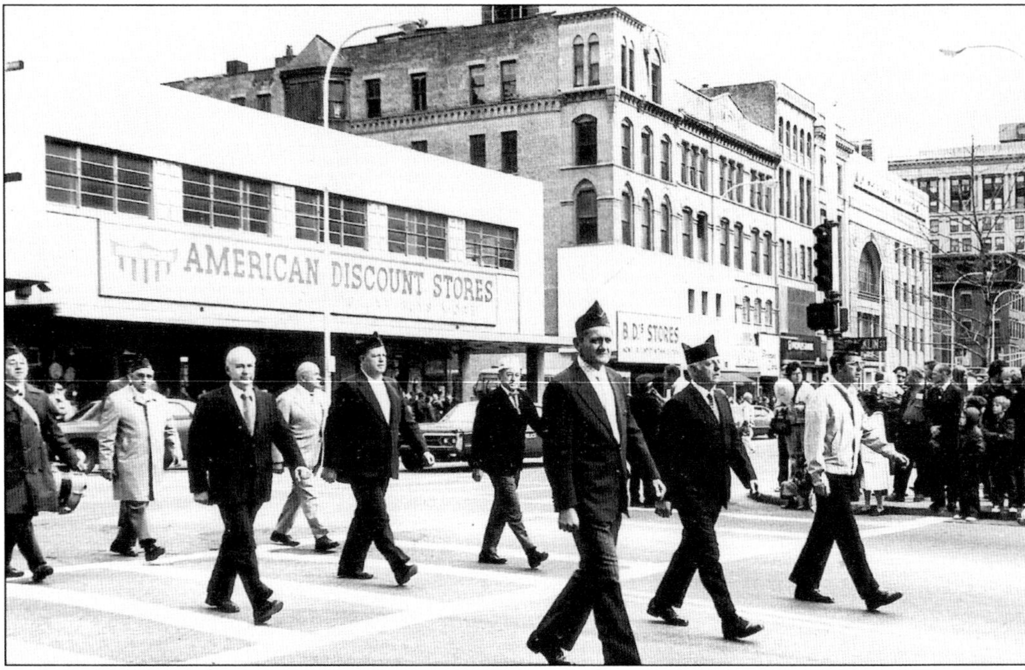

Members of the PAV of World War II post of Worcester march from Main Street onto Franklin Street at City Hall Plaza during a Memorial Day parade in the 1970s. At the May holiday and Veterans Day in November, posts honored their lost comrades and recalled their own service in parades and ceremonies at local monuments.

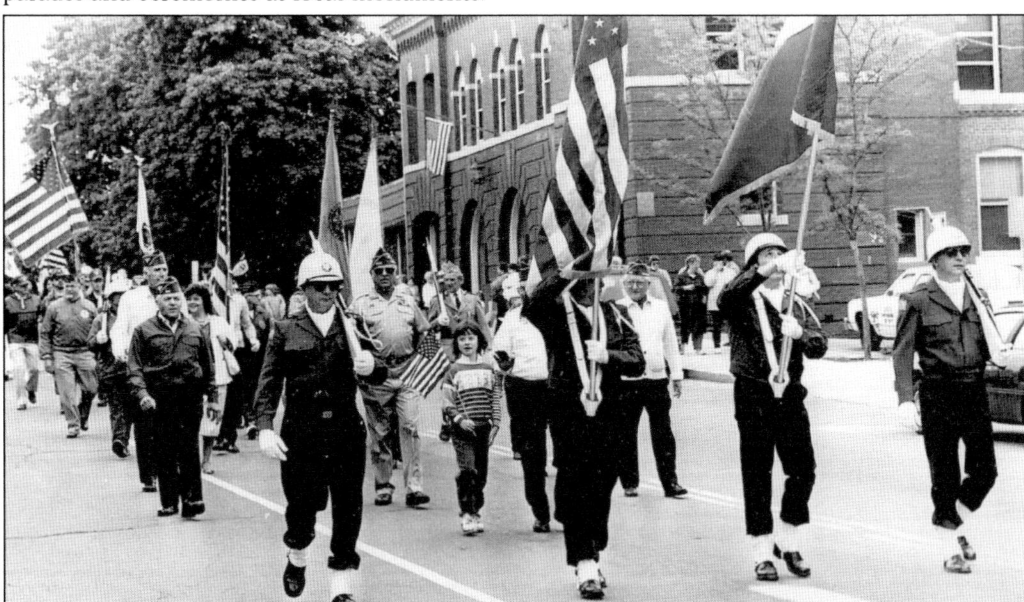

The color guard and members of the Southbridge PAV post march in the 1987 Memorial Day parade honoring those who died in service. About 15 Polish American men from Southbridge died in World War I, World War II, and the Korean War. The post in October 1961 dedicated a monument near the Pilsudski Polish American Club at Ballard Court as a permanent symbol of remembrance.

Gertrude and Raymond Zaleski have achieved the highest honors in the PAV of World War II, having served as Massachusetts state auxiliary president and state commander, respectively. The Massachusetts State Department of the PAV comprises about 20 posts, Worcester, Clinton, Gardner, Uxbridge, Southbridge, and Webster among them. To date, the Worcester chapter has produced eight state commanders and 12 state auxiliary presidents.

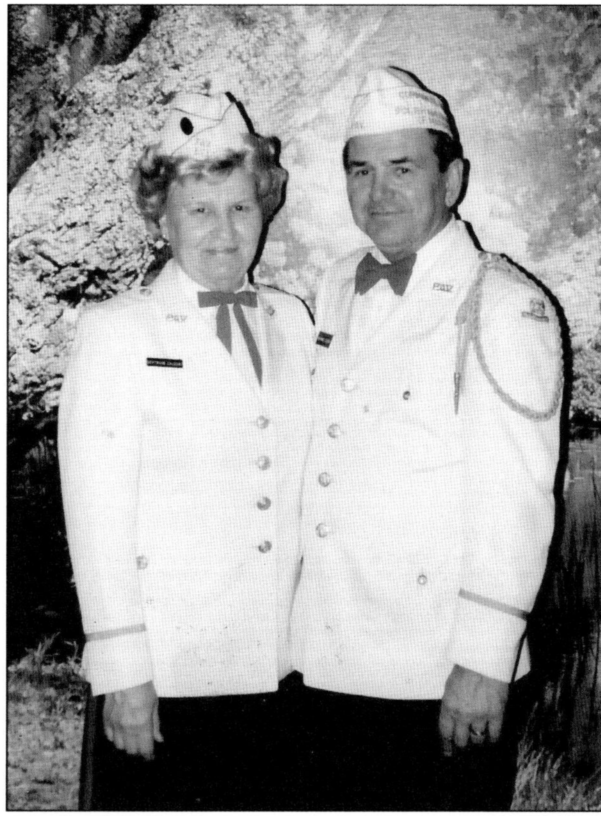

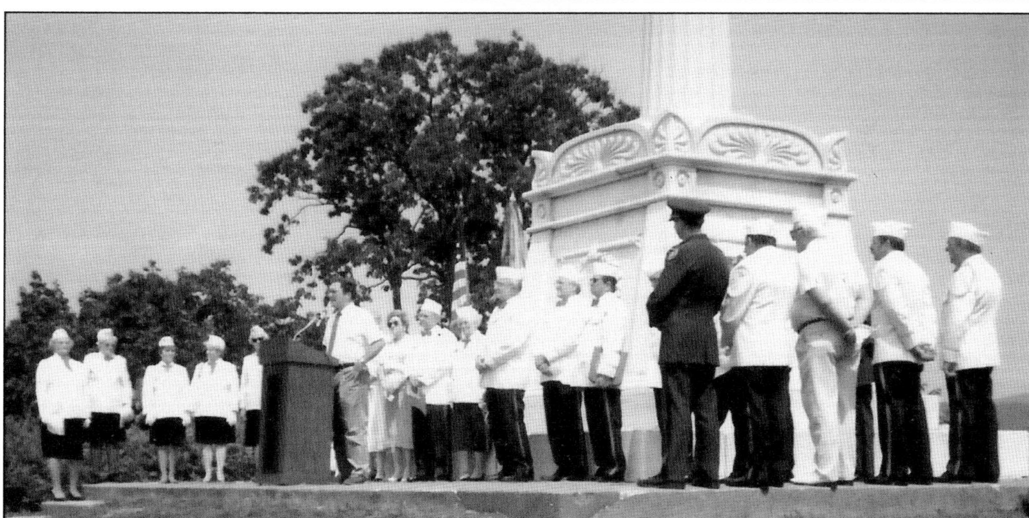

The Massachusetts State Department of the PAV participates in a ceremony at Kosciuszko Monument at the United States Military Academy at West Point around 1990. The department provides financial support for the maintenance of Kosciuszko's Garden, which the Revolutionary War hero personally constructed in 1778. Acclaimed for his outstanding battle site fortifications, Thaddeus Kosciuszko served as chief engineer of West Point and was later appointed a brigadier general.

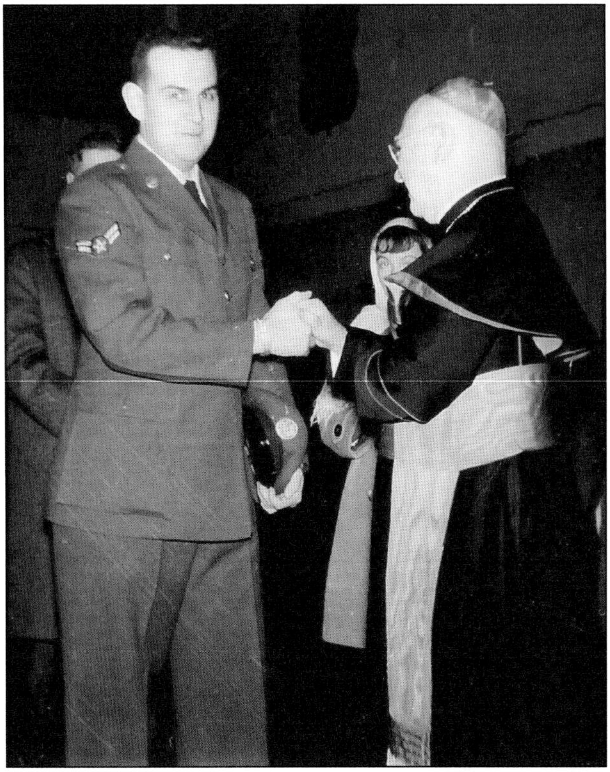

Airman 2nd Class Joseph Baniukiewicz of Worcester is pictured with Francis Cardinal Spellman, archbishop of New York, in Frankfurt, Germany, in December 1961. During the Berlin Crisis, Baniukiewicz was among 148,000 guardsmen and reservists called up to active duty by Pres. John F. Kennedy to prevent the Soviet Union from cutting off Allied access to West Berlin. He was a radar operator for the air force.

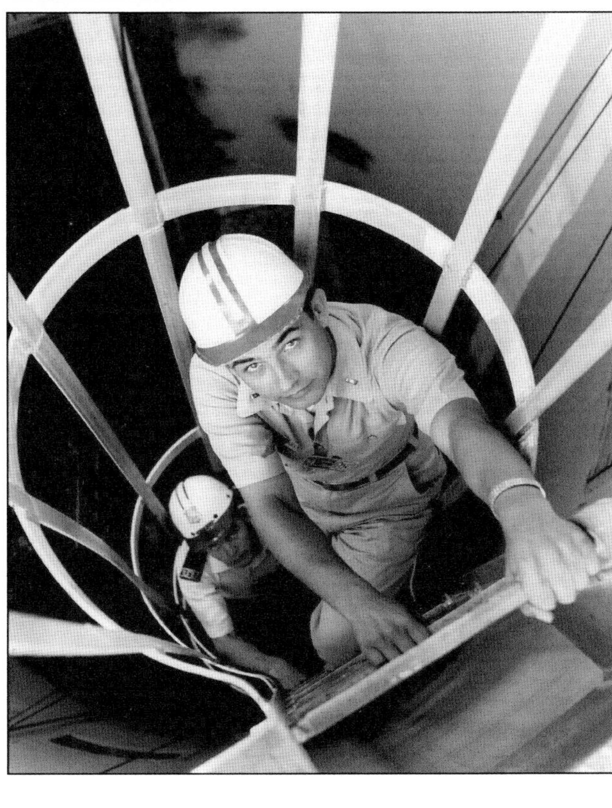

Thomas Mark Sieminski served in the U.S. Air Force for over 30 years and retired as a full colonel. Literally a rocket scientist, he worked on many defense-related projects involving Minuteman missiles, the space shuttle, the MX missile, and Star Wars missile defense system. Born in Augustow, Poland, and raised in Clinton and Gardner, Sieminski was the son of a Polish Army officer who perished in the 1940 Katyn massacre.

Nine

HERITAGE

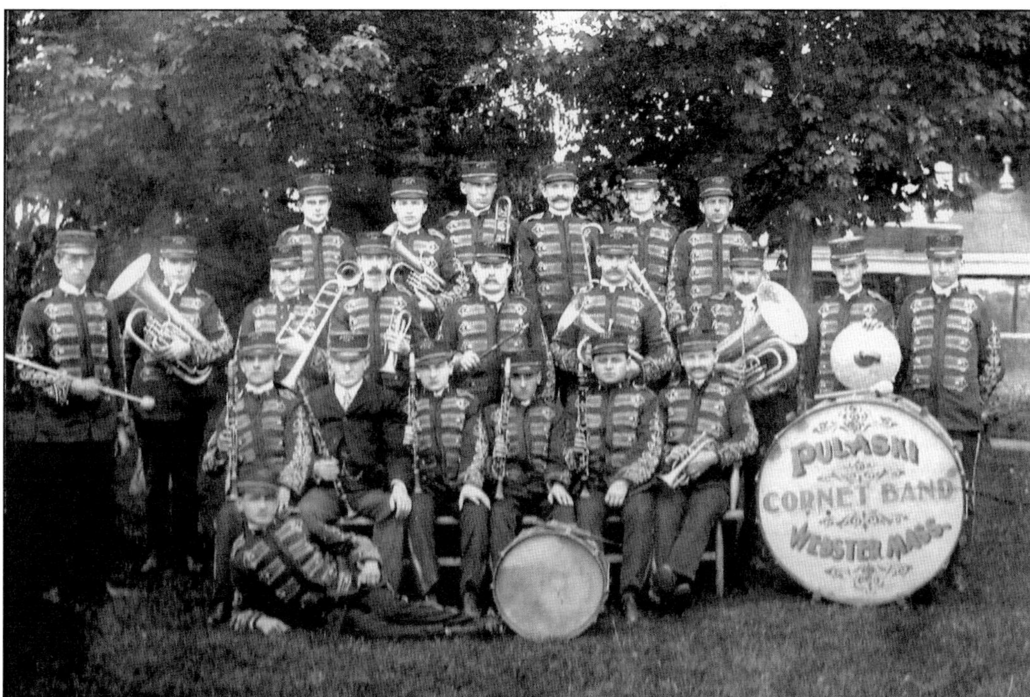

The Pulaski Cornet Band of Webster, founded in 1889, played regularly at Beacon Park, where this photograph was taken around 1907. In the second row are drum major John Czech Shaw (far left) and cofounder Valerian Kreft with baton (fifth from left). Shaw was drum major for the subsequent Pulaski Brass Band and performed with two drum corps. A well-known baton twirler, he participated in competitions throughout New England.

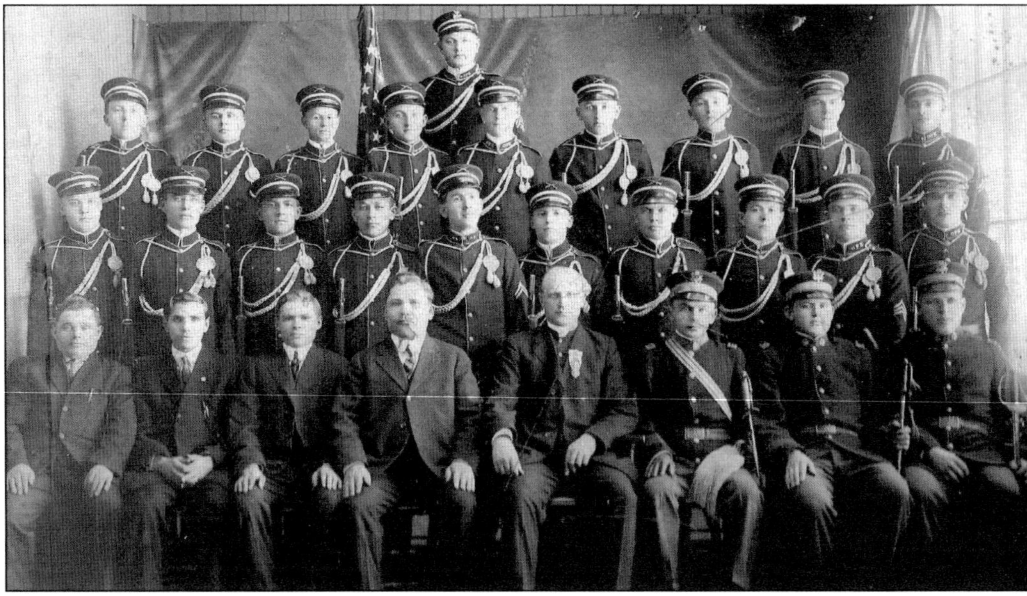

The Polish Cadets of Webster were organized in 1910. The pastor of St. Joseph's Parish, Rev. Anthony Cyran (first row, fifth from left) served as their chaplain. Also identified in this photograph is Adam Repik (second row, third from left), who served as the group's president for 25 years. Organizations with a military theme were popular among Poles who felt poised to fight for their homeland's freedom.

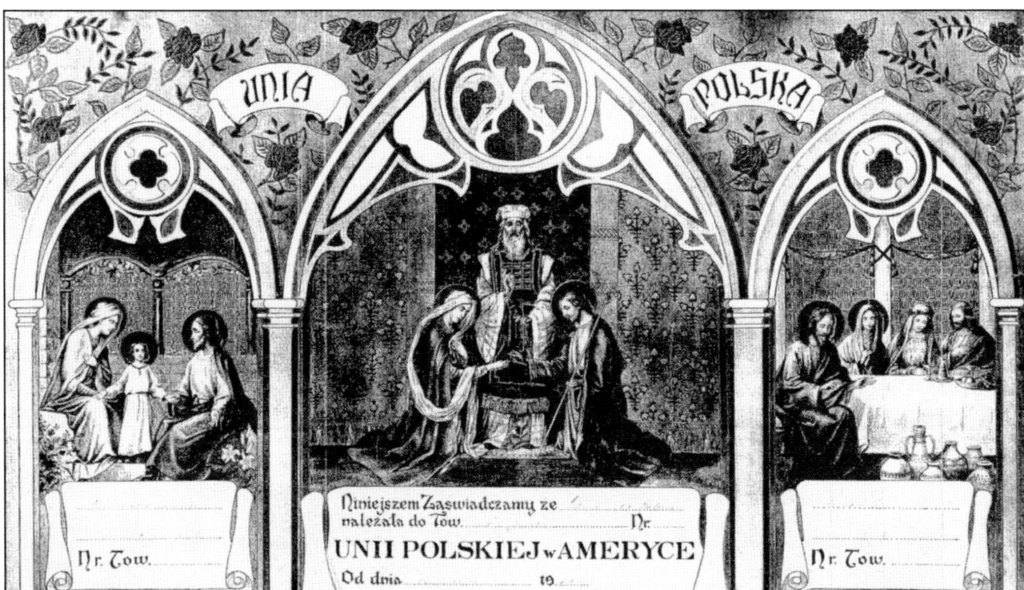

An oversize certificate, embellished with gilt-printed Bible scenes, confirms that Gabryela Gluchowska joined Worcester's St. Joseph Society of the Polish Union of America (Unia Polska w Ameryce) on September 16, 1914, and married Konstanty Mosczynski on August 10, 1916. The Polish Union was a fraternal benefit society, akin to the Polish National Alliance and Polish Roman Catholic Union. A member's dues assured receipt of a death benefit to cover burial expenses.

Members Adolf Witkowski (left) and Joseph Pietrzak wear the distinctive uniforms of the Krakusy (Krakow Guards) of the St. Francis of Assisi Society. Believed to be Worcester's earliest Polish organization, this mutual benefit society incorporated in 1896 with 28 members and helped fund church and school construction at Our Lady of Czestochowa Parish. The Krakow Guards, along with Worcester's Pulaski Guards, conducted military drills and participated in parades.

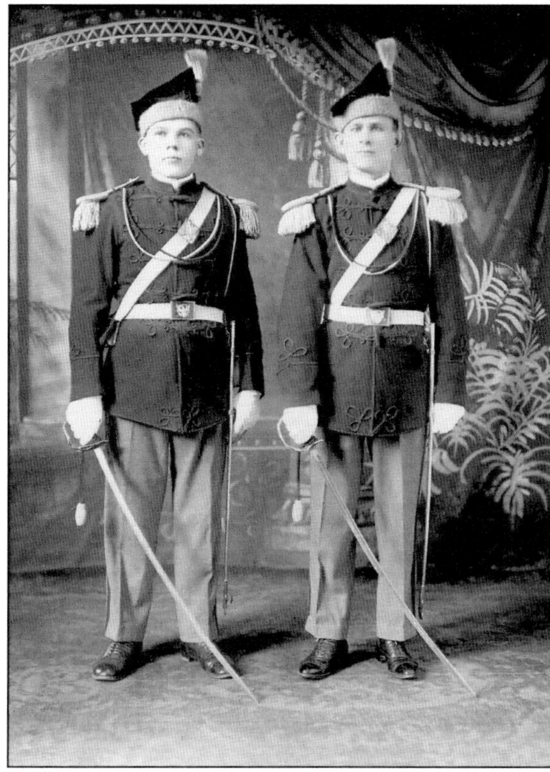

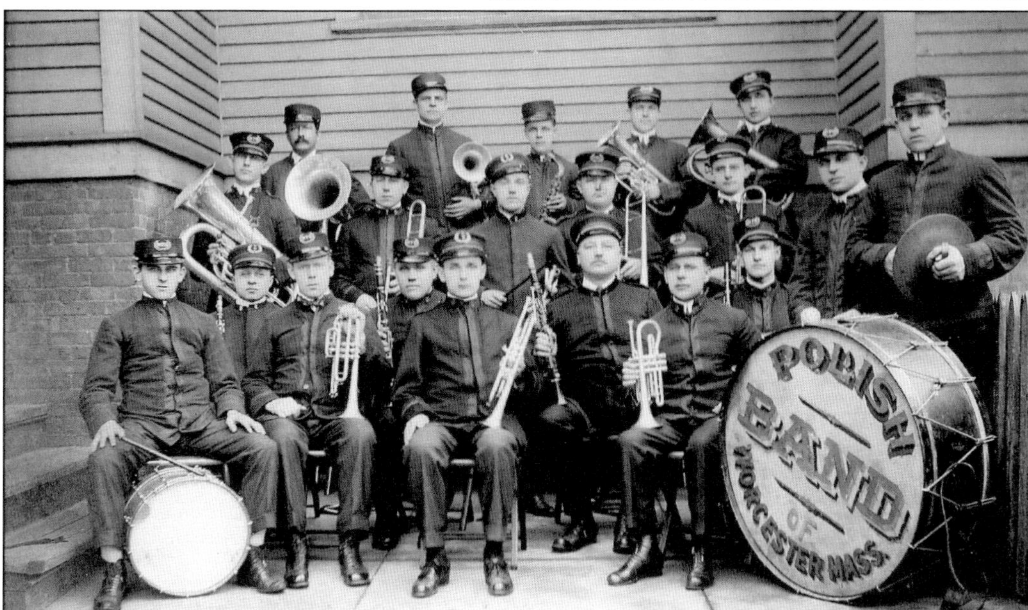

The Polish Band of Worcester, shown here around 1914, formed in the early 1900s and played in civic parades and ethnic celebrations. A notable appearance was the November 29, 1906, dedication of Our Lady of Czestochowa Church, when the band headed a contingent of Worcester and Webster societies that attended the ceremonies en masse. In the second row, third from left, is George Prusko, who built a home on Burncoat Street after residing briefly on Vernon Hill.

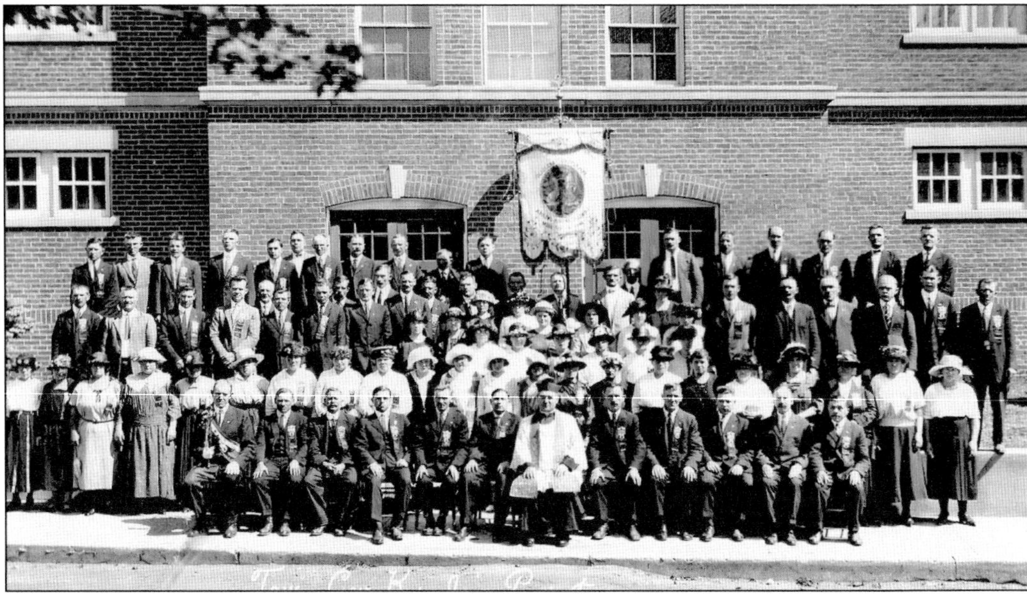

Members of Our Lady of Czestochowa Society, Polish Roman Catholic Union Chapter 830, gather in 1923 in front of St. Joseph's Church, Gardner. Seated at front center is their pastor and chaplain, Rev. Stanislaus Chlapowski. The local group was formed in 1914 with 15 members and grew steadily. The founding president was Jozef Figon, with vice president Aleksander Walendziak, financial secretary Stanislaw Sendrowski, recording secretary Aleksander Muszynski, and treasurer Romuald Kulczyk.

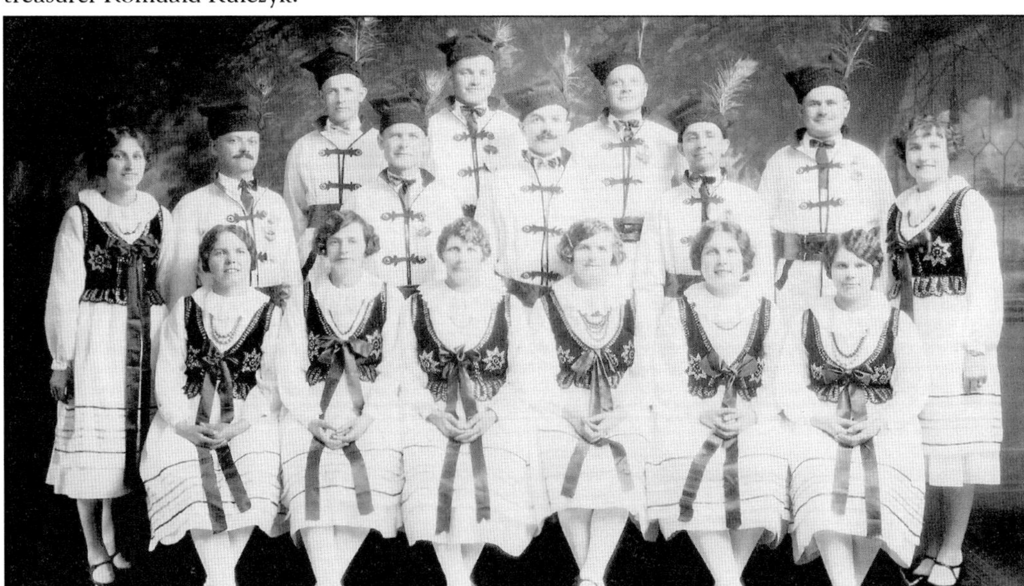

When Uxbridge celebrated its bicentennial in 1927, Poles were among the ethnic groups sponsoring a parade float. Traditionally dressed for their appearance are, from left to right, (first row) Anna Jasikowski, Stasia Lamanski, Jadwiga Novack, ? Paszkiewicz, Stella Rak Gniadek, and Josephine Galas; (second row) Helen Burnat Binkowski, John Rozak, Joseph Kieronski, Stanley Lemiech, Stanley Kosciak, Andrew Kusiak, and Anna Mayka; (third row) Stefan Augusciak, John Novack, and Stanley Lamanski.

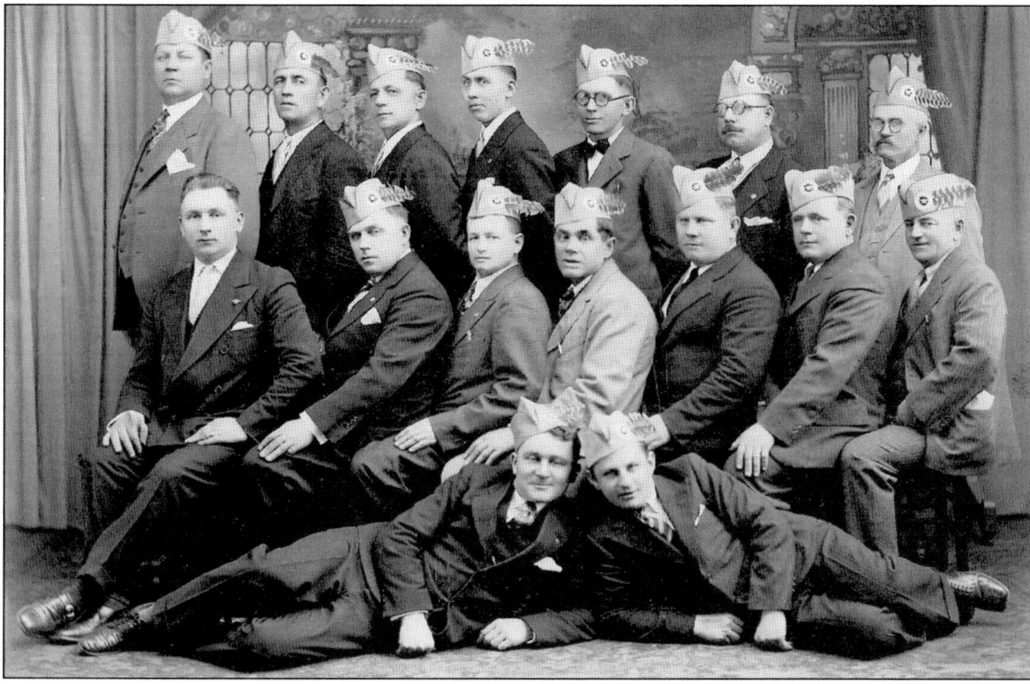

The Polish Falcons of Webster sport distinctive caps with pins and feathers in this 1920s photograph. Members include George Pluta (left) on the floor; seated, "nest" president Frank Grzyb (far left), and ? Grzyb (fourth from left); standing, ? Moczadlo, ? Wiatr, Adam Repik, three unidentified people, and ? Moskwa. The Falcons were based at a hall on Frederick Street. Between 1907 and 1936, Falcons nests were also founded in Worcester, Gardner, Farnumsville (Grafton), Gilbertville, Warren, Clinton, and Milford.

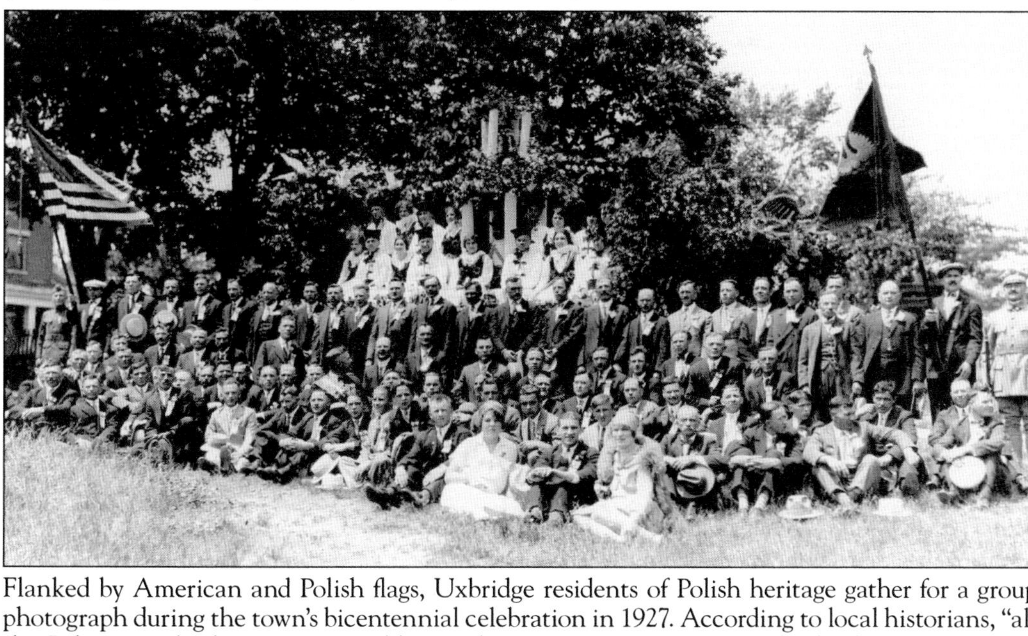

Flanked by American and Polish flags, Uxbridge residents of Polish heritage gather for a group photograph during the town's bicentennial celebration in 1927. According to local historians, "all the Poles in Uxbridge" are pictured here. The 1920 U.S. census for Uxbridge lists 105 heads of household as born in Poland and six in Galicia; they were a mix of Russian and Austrian Poles.

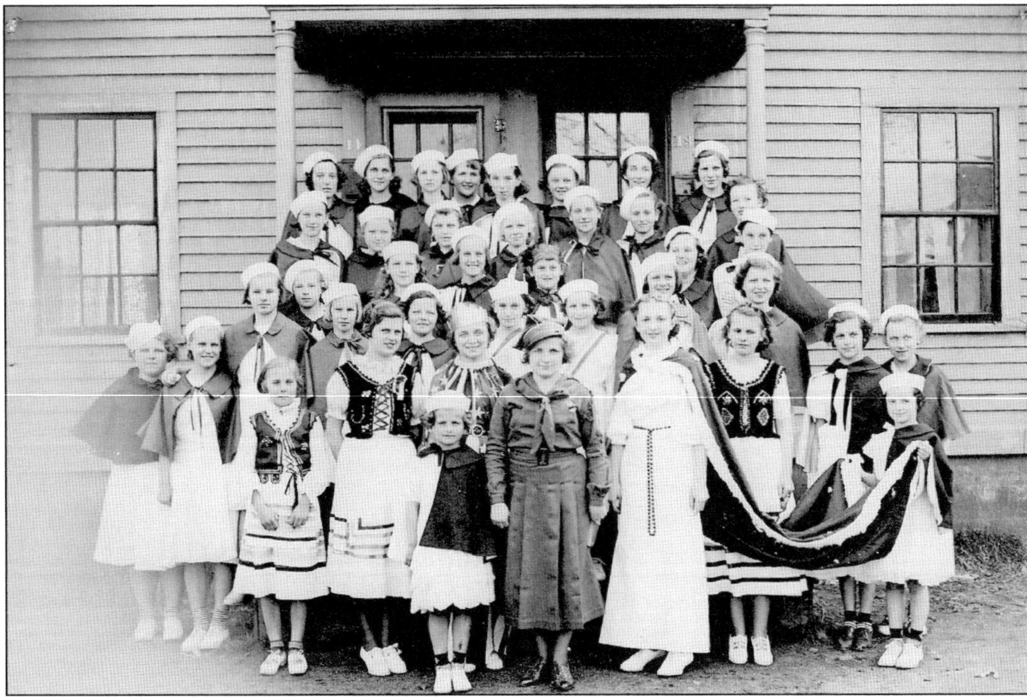

Inspired by the United States Constitution of 1787, Poland on May 3, 1791, adopted the first democratic constitution in Europe. In military dress, Antonina Grzeszczak (front center) poses with Polish American girls prepared to march in Southbridge's Polish Constitution Day Parade in May 1935. Hedwig Swiacki is identified in the back row, second from left. Swiacki and Grzeszczak collaborated on plays to entertain the Polish community.

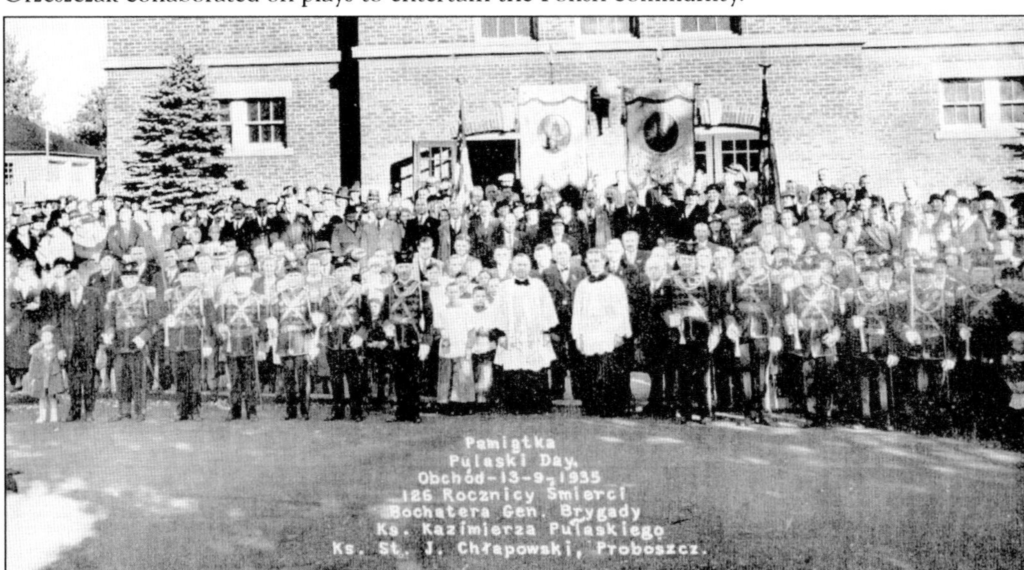

Parishioners and local dignitaries assemble outside St. Joseph's Parish, Gardner, in 1935, during an observance of the 126th anniversary of Casimir Pulaski's death. At front are Rev. Stanislaus Chlapowski (left) and his assistant, Rev. Maximilian Lewandowski. The uniformed men in the front row may be the St. Stanislaus Society Pulaski Guards, organized in the parish in 1923.

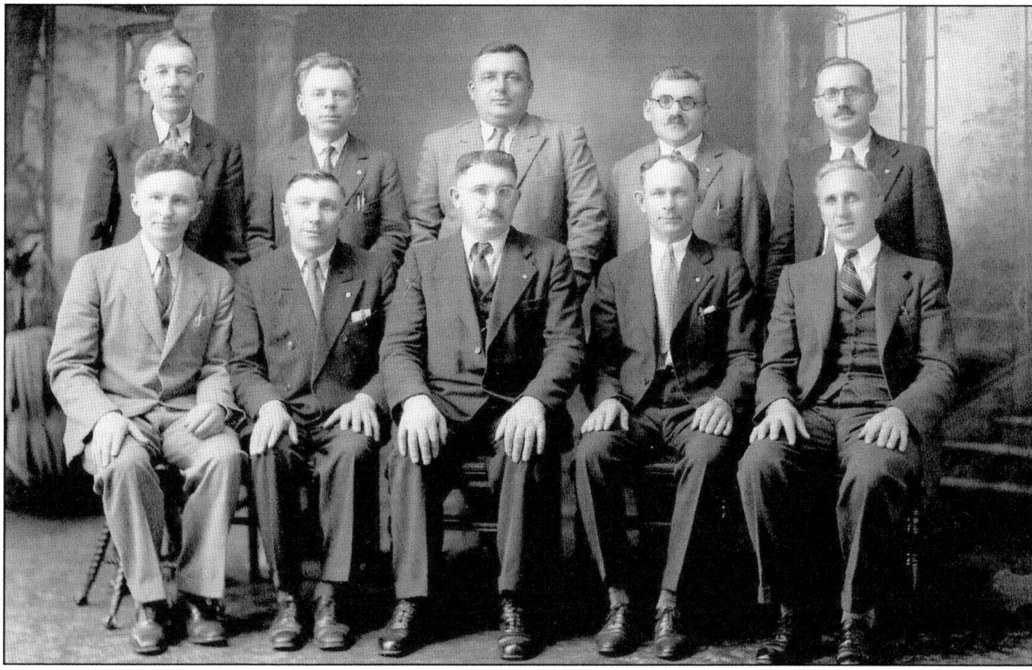

The directors of Worcester's Polish Roman Catholic Union 713, around 1935, are, from left to right, (first row) Stanley Sadowski, John Starczewski, president Wladyslaw Arasniewicz, vice president Joseph Pietrzak, and Bronislaw Skindzier; (second row) unidentified, Alexander Wolosz, ? Wolanin, Teofil Wojdyl, and financial secretary Wicenty Karbowski. The group had 400 members. Other chapters of the national fraternal benefit society were based in Clinton, Gardner, Southbridge, Webster, and West Warren.

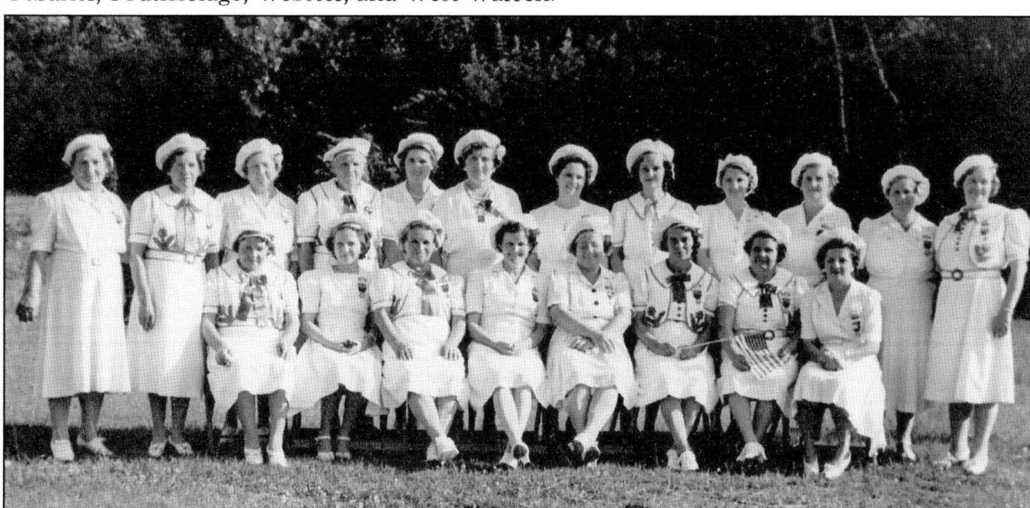

Uxbridge's Kolko Polek (Polish women's circle) was formed in 1937. Members from left to right are (first row) ? Wisniowski, Celia Niedzielski Kohut, Mary Gniadek, Genevieve Marteka, Anna Kosciak, Tekla Wisniowski, Mary Kusiak, and Jennie Niedzielski Fish; (second row) ? Gresian, ? Knapik, ? Podeski, ? Odrobina, Jadwiga Radziewicz, Mary Mucha, Josephine Galas, unidentified, Jennie Wisniowski, Bertha Kozacka, unidentified, and ? Lamanski. Kolko Polek groups were also active in Gardner and Southbridge. (Seagrave Studio.)

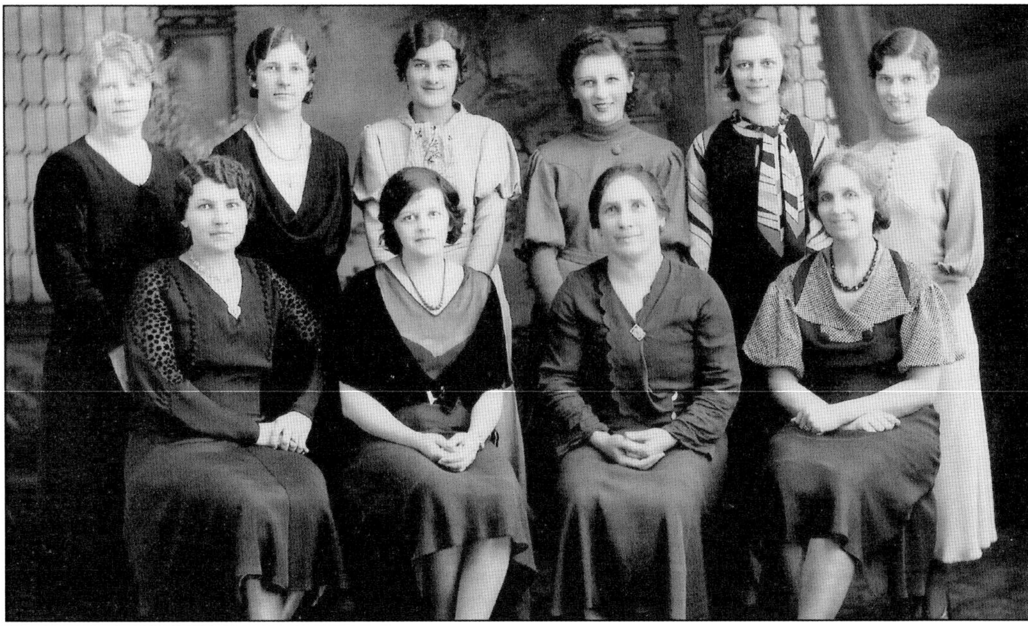

Group 716 of the Polish Women's Alliance of America (Zwiazek Polek w Ameryce) was founded in Webster by Victoria Szynal and Stefania Gorska in 1936. Within a year, it grew from 15 to 62 members. Pictured here are the officers and committee chairs. Clinton Group 718, West Warren Group 756, and Worcester Group 775 were other local chapters of the Polish Women's Alliance.

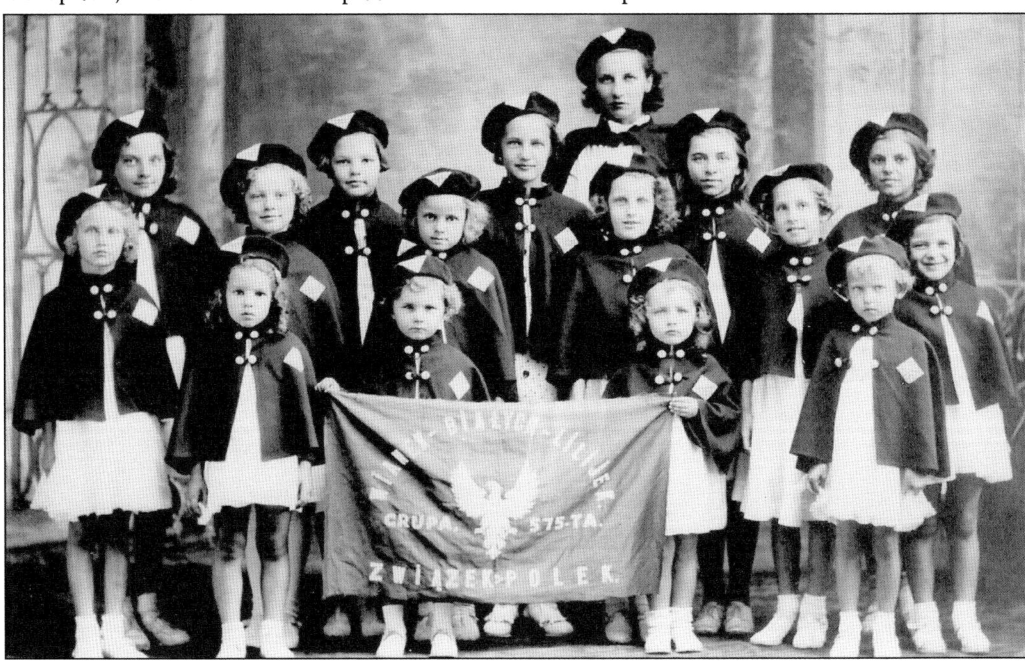

In 1937, Polish Women's Alliance Group 716 member Katarzyna Szynal organized a group for girls ages 2 to 12, the Garland of White Lilies (Wianek Bialych Lilijek 575). The original members are pictured here. Providing children's programs, activities, and events was common among the Polish Women's Alliance and other national organizations, which aimed to foster an appreciation of Polish heritage and values in the younger generation.

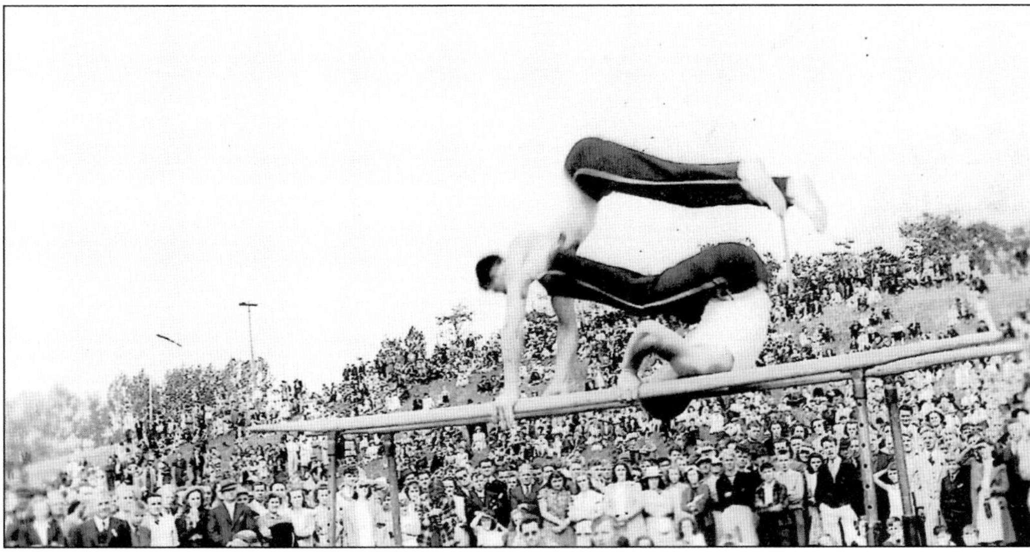

At a 1937 Polish Falcons meet in Pittsfield, Worcester Falcons Nest 250 team members Chet Baldyga (left) and Henry Wolosz somersault during the double-man parallel bar competition. Both young men were accomplished gymnasts and weight lifters. Nest 250 sponsored the 1937 Polish American Olympic Games, with events held at Worcester Academy's Gaskill Field; the guest athlete was world champion runner Stella Walsh (Walasiewicz).

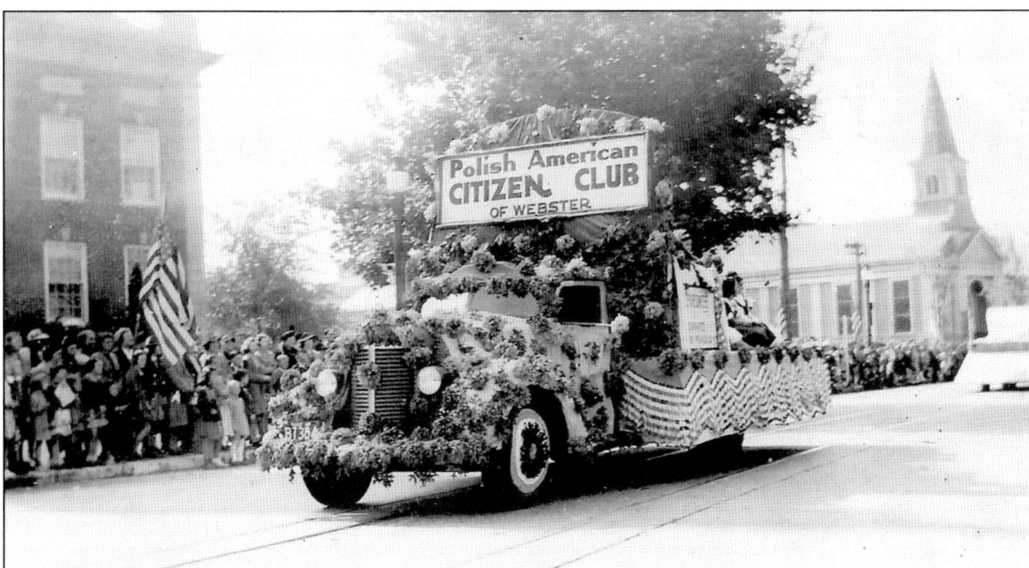

"Preparedness is a guarantee for peace," proclaims the sign on this parade float sponsored by the Polish American Citizen Club of Webster on the eve of World War II. A preparedness rally around 1940–1941 had Webster and Dudley residents lining the streets to view patriotic floats and marching units. It may have been held in conjunction with the local Yankee Division call-up.

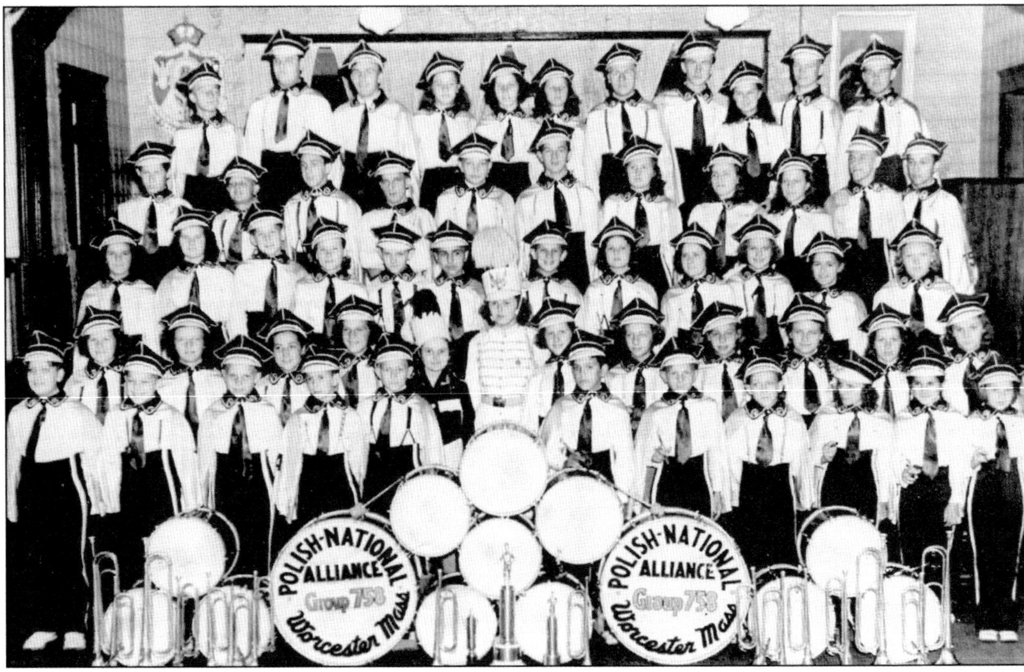

Organized in 1933, the drum and bugle corps of Polish National Alliance Lodge 758, Worcester, won trophies in several competitions in 1940. Majorette Josephine Gragowski stands behind the drums. Identified from left to right are (first row) Ted Siemaszko, second, and Irene Smiech, ninth; (second row) Marian Krenczez, second; Hedwig Sieniawski, third; and Irene Skowronska, fourth; (fourth row) Joseph Siemaszko, sixth, and Mary Jablonski, eighth; (fifth row) John Jablonski, third.

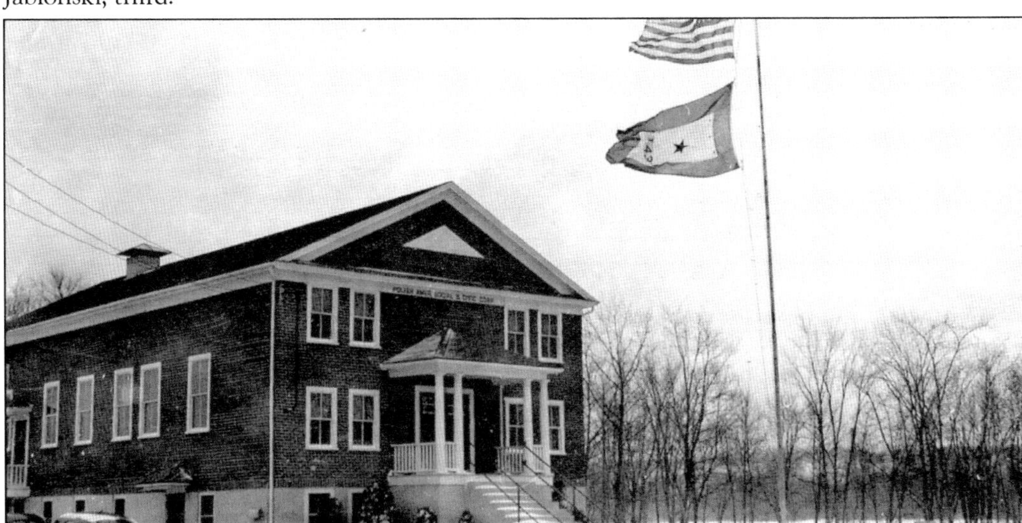

Since it was dedicated in October 1936, the Polish Home (Dom Narodowy Polskiego) at Mendon and Hecla Streets has been the hub of Polish American social, civic, cultural, and political life in Uxbridge. Although its Polish population is substantial, Uxbridge does not have a Polish parish, making a central meeting place like the home all the more important to people dedicated to preserving their heritage.

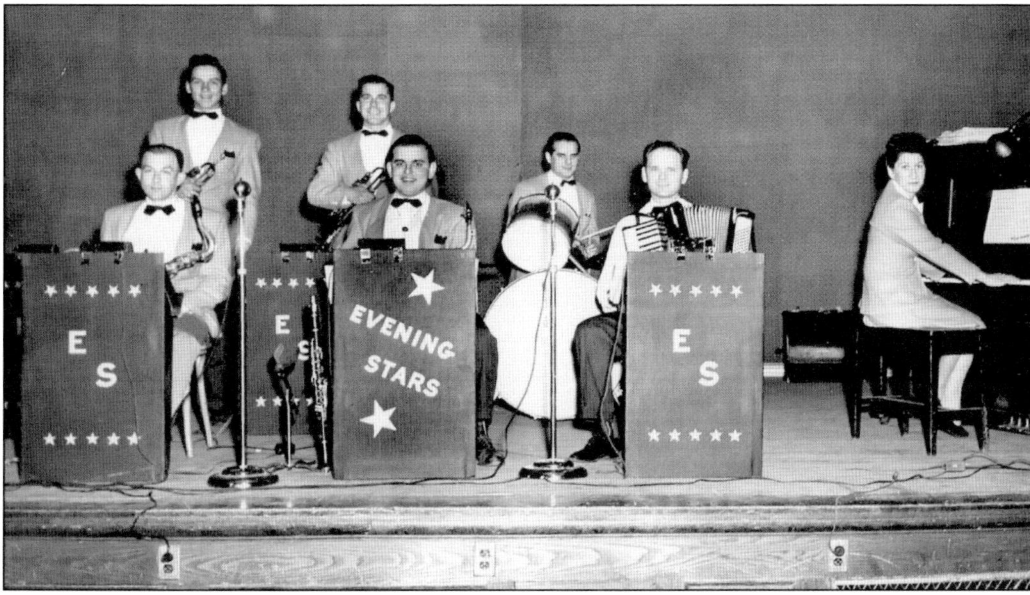

The Evening Stars perform on stage at the Pilsudski Club in Gilbertville in the 1940s or 1950s with Helen Wypych at the piano and Walter Pluta standing at left rear. Located on Joslyn Road, the facility features a large auditorium, kitchen, bar, and outdoor pavilion. It is owned by the Joseph Pilsudski Building Association, which developed in 1925 from the St. Stanislaus Association founded in 1908.

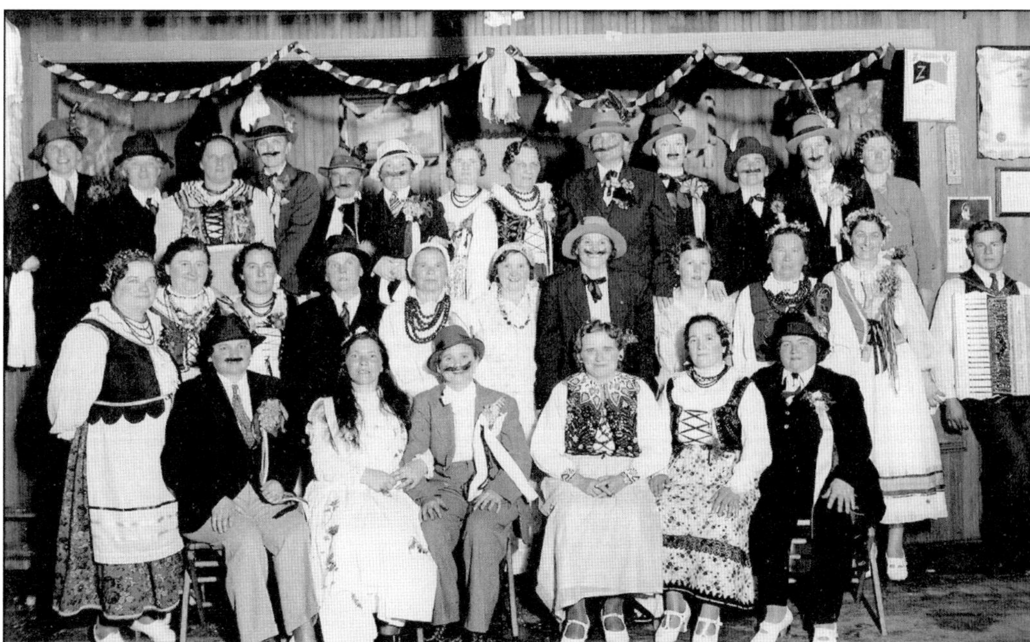

The 30 members of a predominantly female theater troupe don traditional Polish garb and some men's suits and obviously fake mustaches for a cast photograph taken at the Polish National Alliance home in Webster. Although undated, the photograph was probably taken during World War II, when male cast members were scarce. Identified in the back row (ninth from left) is Mary Piechota Sak, looking serious despite her comical attire.

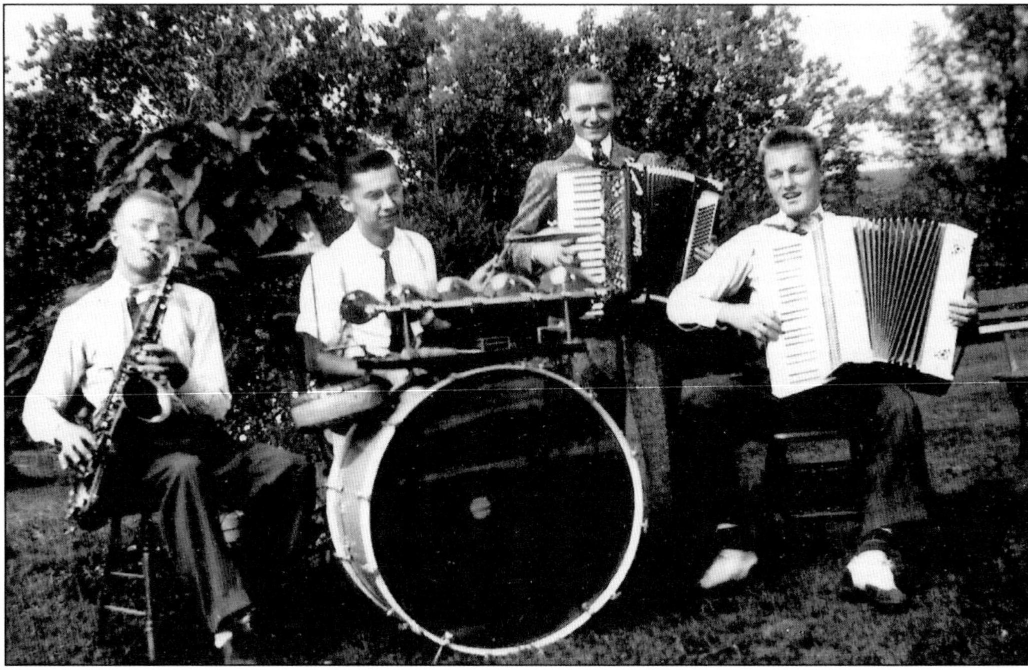

Musicians, yet unnamed, practice informally around 1939 at the Obara home on Farnum Street, South Grafton. From left to right are Ted Obara on saxophone; Frank Kuras, drums; and Stan Koziol and Vincent Obara, accordions. This group was the forerunner to the band Wisla, which grew into a nine-piece ensemble that played locally at weddings and other functions.

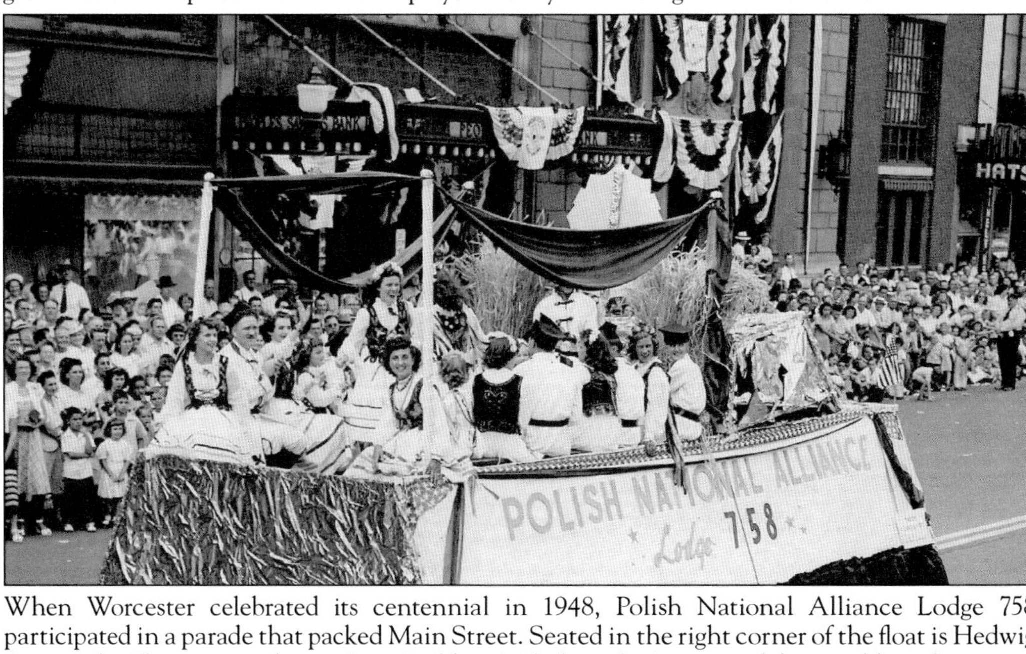

When Worcester celebrated its centennial in 1948, Polish National Alliance Lodge 758 participated in a parade that packed Main Street. Seated in the right corner of the float is Hedwig Sieniawski Chesna; standing is Jean Stoklosa Mikolajczyk. A national fraternal benefit society, the Polish National Alliance sponsored wide-ranging programs. By 1964, it had 2,500 members in Worcester County, with lodges in Blackstone, Dudley, East Douglas, Farnumsville, Gardner, Southbridge, Webster, and Worcester.

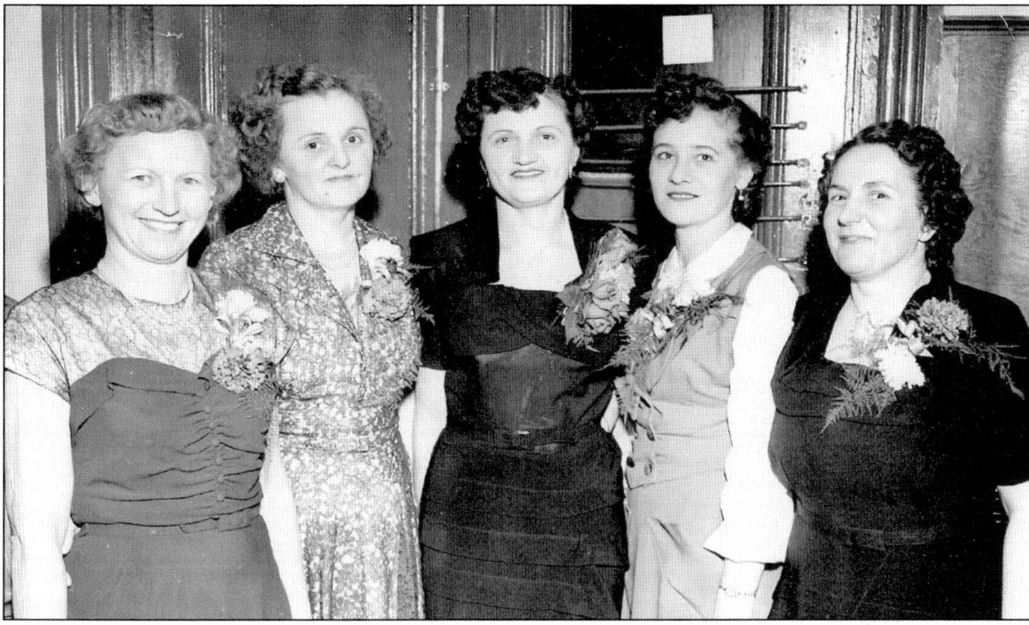

Corsages suggest a festive event for the Polish American Women's Club (Klub Niewiast) of Clinton around 1950. Genowefa Kowlzan Krysiak (center), a longtime member, served over the years as club president and treasurer. Irene Lepkowski Sieminski (second from right) moved from Clinton to Gardner after marrying Henry Kaczynski. The women's club, founded in 1934, focused on parish needs.

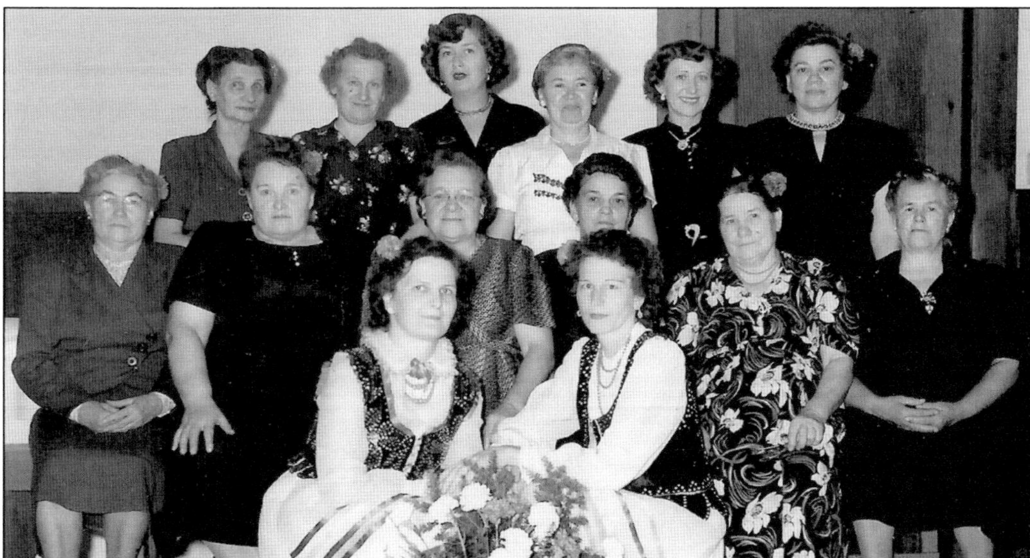

The "Pierogi Pearls," more formally known as Polish Women's Alliance Group 756 of West Warren, made pierogi and golabki for Polish picnics and performed in minstrel shows. Pictured in 1954 are *Krakowianki* Stephanie Dolina (left) and Cecilia Olearcek; from left to right (seated) Josephine Trzepacz, Caroline Fortuna, Sophie Piszarczyk, Nellie Wozniak, Maria Waskiewicz, and ? Zaleski; (standing) Carolina Ziemba, Victoria Wansick, Lillian Kasuba, Zofia Dolina, Honora Pioria, and Helen Baron.

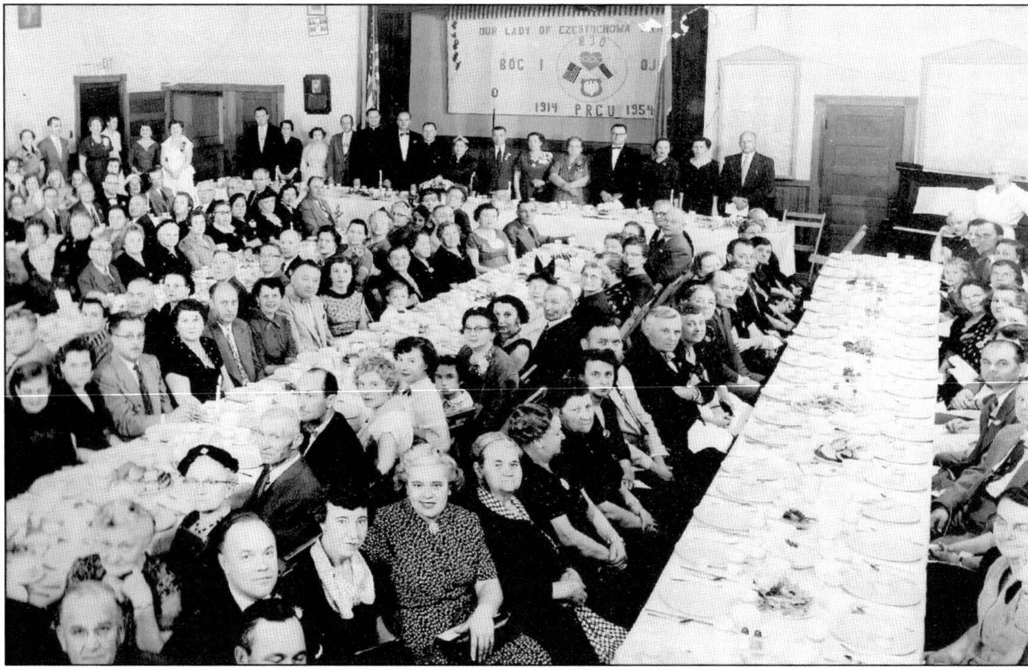

Polish Roman Catholic Union 830 of Gardner celebrated its 40th anniversary with a banquet at the Polish American Citizens Club in October 1954. Society president Antoni Cwalina gave the opening address, and Rev. Ladislaus Radzik, pastor of St. Joseph's, offered prayers. Invited guests included John and Stephanie Burzynski of Polish Roman Catholic Union Circle 72 of Worcester. Seated eighth from top at the right side of the far right table is Mary Sylwestrzak.

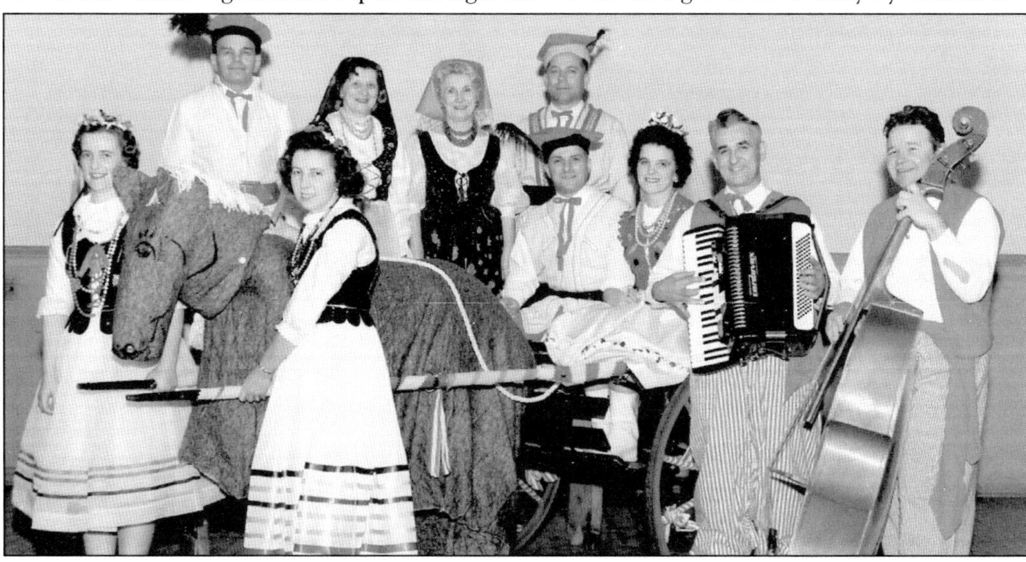

The Choraleons of Webster, formed in 1958, presented *Krakowskie Wesele* throughout New England for more than a decade. Here a horse-drawn cart led by Carolyn Madura Peck (left) and Marie Sielawa transports "bride" Anna Sielawa and "groom" Francis Aniszewski to church for their wedding. Chester Mackowiak plays accordion, and Paul Trocki plays bass fiddle. Cast members in the rear are, from left to right, Walter Nalepa, Rose Skrzypek, Lena Mackowiak, and Steven Bielawski.

On the arm of her father, Henry Wolosz, debutante Karen Wolosz of Worcester curtsies at the 11th Biennial Kosciuszko Foundation Presentation Ball held in November 1965 at the Statler Hilton Hotel, Boston. Twenty-five young Massachusetts women of Polish descent were presented that evening. Sponsored by the Massachusetts Federation of Polish Women's Clubs, the ball is a prestigious fund-raiser for the nationwide Kosciuszko Foundation.

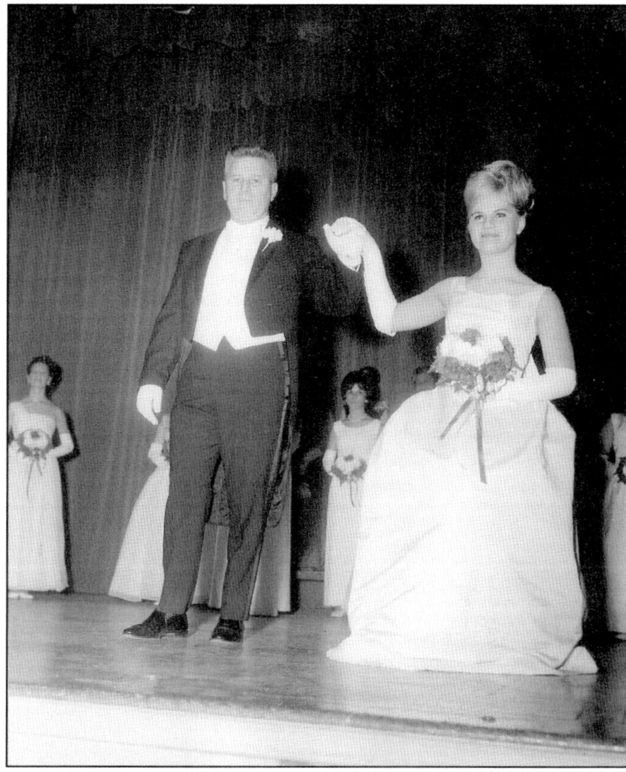

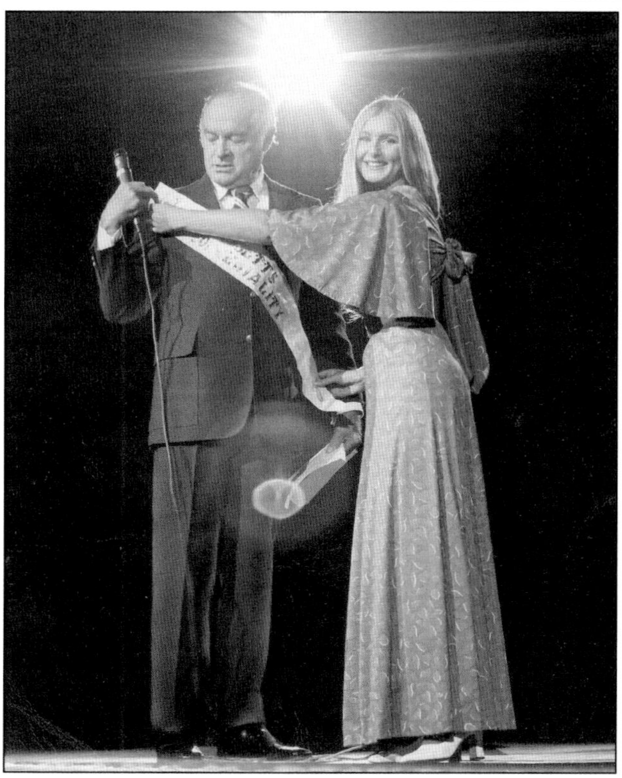

Miss Massachusetts Kathleen Sterczala shares her "Miss Congeniality" banner with comedian Bob Hope at the opening of the Providence Civic Center in 1972. After winning the Miss Worcester title as a high school student, Sterczala became Miss Massachusetts and competed in the Miss U.S.A. Pageant. She won the Miss Congeniality award as the friendliest delegate. A Webster native, she grew up on Lake Chargoggagoggmanchauggagoggchaubunagungamaugg and later became an artist.

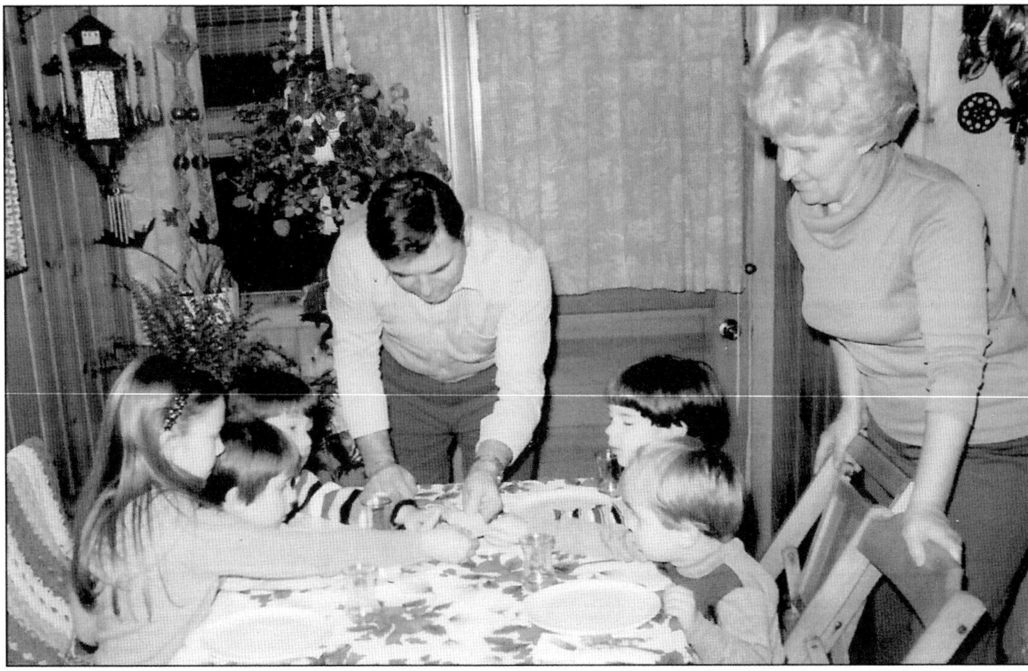

Raymond and Gertrude Zaleski of Auburn introduce their grandchildren to a Polish Christmas Eve *wigilia* tradition, the sharing of the *oplatek*, an unconsecrated wafer. Reaching out to break off a small piece of their grandfather's wafer are, from left to right, Pamela, Timothy, Craig, Brian, and Scott Zaleski. Expressing wishes for one another's good health and happiness and asking forgiveness for any possible ill feelings is part of the ceremony.

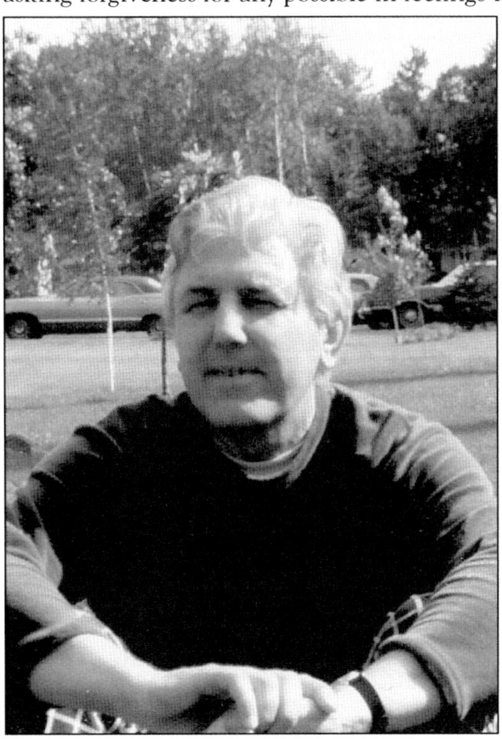

Matthew Babinski is the author of *By Raz 1937* (1978), a novel about growing up Polish on Worcester's "Island." The main character is a "Polish Huck Finn" who lives in a three-decker near the gasworks, attends St. Mary's School, and keenly observes the details of city life during Holy Week. The son of Apolinary and Michalena Targonski Babinski of Sigel Street, the author worked as a corporate patent lawyer.

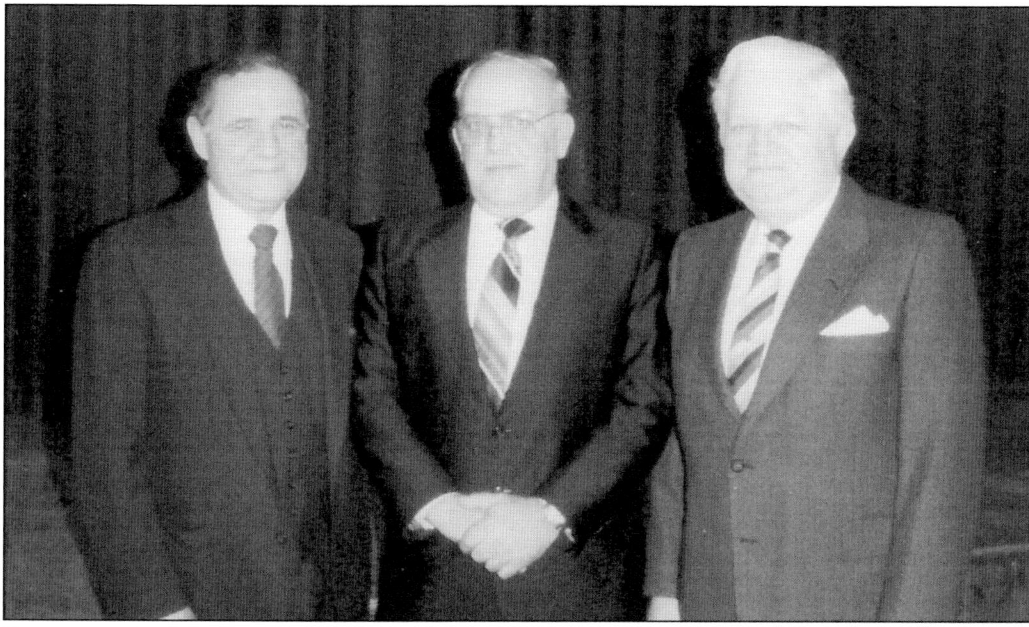

For outstanding service, Wallace Dymek (center) received the Diamond Pin award of St. Mary's Boosters Club of Worcester in 1985. He owned Dymek's Arco Kelley Square Service Station for 38 years, then served as parish school custodian for nine years. He was a member of the PAV of World War II and Vernon Hill Post American Legion. With him are Dr. Thaddeus Jankowski (left) and Joseph Stodulski.

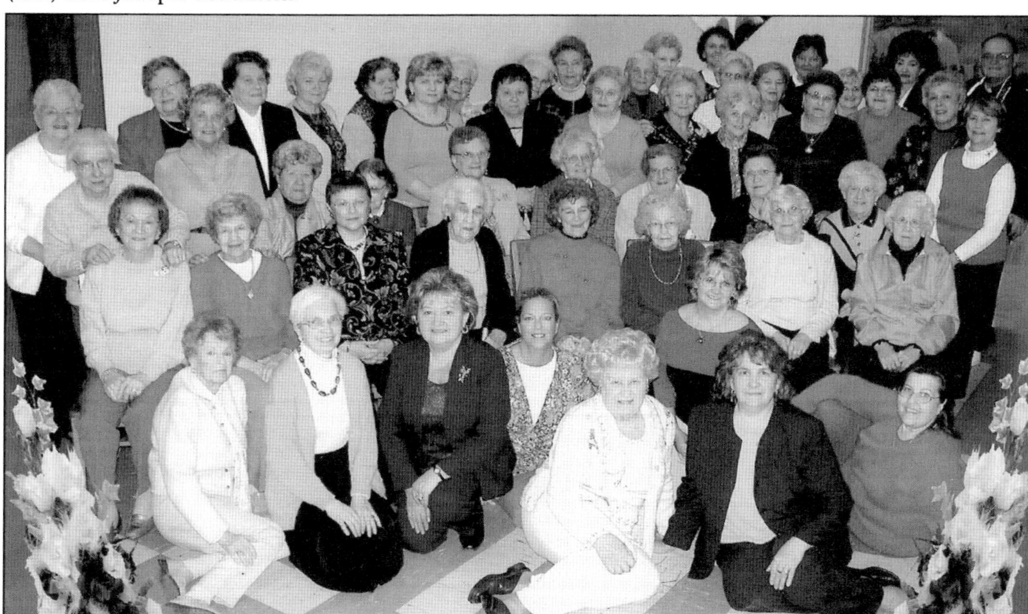

Our Lady of Czestochowa Guild of Catholic Women, Worcester, commemorates its 40th anniversary with a photograph. Founded in 1965, the guild provides financial support to the parish schools through various endeavors. Annual events are a Palm Sunday weekend bake sale, a fall festival, and a *chrusciki* sale. The guild's predecessor, the Polish Women's Club, organized in 1946, had similarly sponsored social, cultural, and fund-raising activities at the parish.